THE — BEHAVIORAL ADVANTAGE

THE BEHAVIORAL ADVANTAGE

What the Smartest, Most Successful Companies
Do Differently to Win in the B2B Arena

TERRY R. BACON

and

DAVID G. PUGH

AMACOM

AMERICAN MANAGEMENT ASSOCIATION

New York • Atlanta • Brussels • Chicago • Mexico City
San Francisco • Shanghai • Tokyo • Toronto • Washington, D.C.

This publication is designed to provide accurate and authoritative information in regard to the subject matter covered. It is sold with the understanding that the publisher is not engaged in rendering legal, accounting, or other professional service. If legal advice or other expert assistance is required, the services of a competent professional person should be sought.

Various names used by companies to distinguish their software and other products can be claimed as trademarks. AMACOM uses such names throughout this book for editorial purposes only, with no intention of trademark violation. All such software or product names are in initial capital letters or ALL CAPITAL letters. Individual companies should be contacted for complete information regarding trademarks and registration.

Library of Congress Cataloging-in-Publication Data

Bacon, Terry R.
    The behavioral advantage : what the smartest, most successful companies do differently to win in the B2B arena / Terry R. Bacon and David G. Pugh.
        p.   cm.
    Includes index.
    ISBN: 0-8144-7225-7 (hardcover)
    ISBN: 978-0-8144-1670-9 (paperback)
    1. Organizational behavior.   2. Organizational effectiveness.   3. Strategic planning.   4. Selling—Psychological aspects.   5. Customer relations.   6. Industrial management.   I. Pugh, David G. (David George), 1944–   II. Title.

HD58.7.B34228   2004
658'.001'9—dc22   2003024328

Printing number

10   9   8   7   6   5   4   3   2   1

Contents

CHAPTER 4:

Checkmate! How Business Development Is Like Chess 77

CHAPTER 5:

Opening Game: Conditioning the Market 95

CHAPTER 6:

Middle Game: Conditioning the Customer 129

Acknowledgments

Numerous people helped with this book in one way or another. We wish to thank everyone whose generous contributions, ideas, reviews, reflections, and plain hard work led to this book. First, we wish to thank the many professionals at Lore International Institute and Heidrick & Struggles who offered their expertise, shared their thoughts, assisted in our research, or were otherwise supportive through a process that would have been arduous and demanding had it not been for their encouragement and good cheer. From Lore, they include Allison Andersen, Andrea Seid, Anna Pool, Barb Singer, Becky Yeager, Bruce Spining, Chesney Frazier, Dan Osby, Darnell Place-Wise, DeNeil Peterson, Don Scott, Eric Baker, Greg Elkins, Jan Maxedon, Jana Freeburn, Jennifer Myers, Joey Maceyak, Joy Bartel, Kathy Uroda, Linda Simmons, Mark Arnold, Martin Moller, Matthew Zick, Nancy Atwood, Sean Darnall, Sharon Hubbs, Terryl Leroux, Torrey Tye, Trish Gyland, Val Evensen, and Wendy Ludgewait. From Heidrick & Struggles, they include Tom Friel, Joie Gregor, Jocelyn Dehnert, Gerry Roche, John Gardner, Andy Talkington, Richard Eidinger, Carol Emmott, Linda Heagy, Caroline Ballantine, Bonnie Gwin, Rene Fernandez, Rafael Mora, Eduardo Antunovic, Emeric Lepoutre, among our other partners and friends at Heidrick & Struggles.

We would especially like to thank the following people:

■ Jeremy Silman, an extraordinary author of many fine books on chess. He was gracious in allowing us to quote liberally from his works.

■ Ron Curry, another chess master, teacher, and author, who also allowed us to quote extensively from his writings on chess.

■ Meredith Ashby and Stephen Miles of Heidrick & Struggles. They interviewed a number of Heidrick & Struggles partners for this book and for our previous book on behavioral differentiation, *Winning Behavior: What the Smartest, Most Successful Companies Do Differently*. Among the partners they interviewed, and whom we have quoted in the book, are John Gardner, Michael Flagg, Kyung Yoon, and Emeric Lepoutre.

■ Joanne Kincer and Jeffrey Neal, who were gracious in allowing us to quote them in the book.

■ Dr. Laurie Voss and Dr. Pamela Wise, whose extensive research on companies that exemplify behavioral differentiation gave substance and validity to our ideas about companies that use behavior to differentiate themselves.

■ Karen Spear, who has always been an extraordinary thought partner, reviewer, and critic and whose help was as invaluable on this book as it was on *Winning Behavior*.

We would also like to thank the hundreds of CEOs, purchasing directors, supply chain management executives, program or project managers, and other professionals in buying or selling organizations who participated in our research on purchasing, supply chain management, and behavioral differentiation in organizations. We cite by name in the book those who could be cited. However, some executives could not be quoted by name because of their organization's policies about such matters. We are profoundly grateful to all of them for their information and insights, and we wish to acknowledge their contributions, whether or not we are allowed to mention their names.

Special thanks as well to Dr. Lisa Ellram, professor of supply chain management at Arizona State University, who gave us considerable information about her field and allowed us to quote extensively from one of her major studies in the field; Paul Krauss, a retired director of McKinsey & Company, who offered some keen insights into behavioral differentiation; John Tarpey of Centex Construction Group, who has broken new ground for leadership and differentiating behavior in his industry; Don Traywick, whose many stories about winning and losing bids have always been enlightening; Deke Lincoln, who gave us a great story about the importance of behavior in next game; DeNeil Hogan Petersen, one of the best practitioners of endgame we've ever met; and Danny Hicks, whose story about pursuing a contract was extremely helpful.

As for our previous books, the incomparable Tom Fuhrmark created the artwork. Donna Williams managed the manuscript through its creation, secured permissions, tracked down quotations, and proofread the drafts. Sheri Ligtenberg also proofread the drafts and offered numerous suggestions for improvement. These fine people were instrumental in the completion of the book.

Finally, we would like to thank our editor, Ellen Kadin, of AMACOM. Ellen has been endlessly supportive, has a wonderful sense of humor, and had the good fortune to be born on the same day as Willie Mays, Rudolph Valentino, and Sigmund Freud. She has something in common with all three of them.

Introduction

In *Winning Behavior: What the Smartest, Most Successful Companies Do Differently* (AMACOM, 2003), we introduced the concept of behavioral differentiation. In our research on successful companies, we noted that the best-in-class companies had more than great products or services, a unique business model, and a wealth of talented employees; they also *outbehaved* their rivals and created a behavioral advantage for themselves in the markets they served. By *outbehaving* their rivals, we mean that their behavior toward customers—and employees—was significantly better than the norm for their industry.

They showed more care, respect, and commitment than their rivals did. They were more responsive to customers' needs, including their unspoken and unrecognized needs. They devoted more time and attention—including senior executive time and attention—to customers. They established processes for ensuring that their customers were better treated at every touch point, and they created policies and procedures that empowered their employees to resolve problems faster, to think creatively with customers, to share ideas, and to go beyond the standard relationship building to create a level of candor, trust, and connectivity that results in *de facto* partnerships with customers.

In *Winning Behavior*, we explored why Southwest Airlines has consistently performed so much better than United Airlines, American Airlines, Continental, U.S. Airways, and the other "majors." We asked why Kmart is in Chapter 11 while Wal-Mart continues to thrive as a company. The answer wasn't merely that the superior performers had better business models, although this is nearly always true, or better leadership, or more luck, or lower prices. The answer was that the superior performers had found ways to behaviorally differentiate themselves and gain a strong competitive advantage through their behavior.

Some business writers instinctively understand behavioral differentiation (BD),* although they may not use that term. Jim Collins's bestseller *Good to Great* is a case in point. His Level 5 leaders are great examples of business leaders who exemplify behavioral differentiation. He describes them as having "a paradoxical mix of personal humility and professional will"; "ambitious first and foremost for the company, not themselves"; "infected with an incurable need to produce sustained results." And he says they "display a compelling modesty, are self-effacing and understated," and "display a workmanlike diligence—more plow horse than show horse."[1] These are leaders who give others credit, who build strong teams because they enable others to fulfill themselves, and who are caring and respectful toward employees and customers. They also ask consistently and often "What do you need from me to be successful? How can I help? What can I do?" In other words, they behave in ways that distinguish themselves and their organizations from the run-of-the-mill companies, those led by narcissistic self-aggrandizers, and those brought down through dishonesty, greed, and avarice. What Collins describes as Level 5 leadership, we would label behavioral differentiation.

However, some business writers continue to focus on the basics of business management as though getting the basics right is all it takes to prevail. As we were writing this book, an article appeared in *Harvard Business Review* entitled "What Really Works," by Nitin Nohria, William Joyce, and Bruce Roberson. The authors conducted a "groundbreaking, five-year study" that revealed the "must-have management practices that truly produce results."[2] They argue that businesses must excel at four *primary* practices: strategy, execution, a performance-oriented culture, and structure (a fast, flexible, flat organization). They add that a business should also excel at two of four *secondary* management practices: talent, innovation, leadership, and mergers and partnerships.[3] It's hard to argue with the authors' conclusions. Indeed, companies that have not mastered these management basics are unlikely to succeed and will certainly not rise to the top of their industry. Nonetheless, there are hundreds of sound companies that meet the authors' criteria—which amount to a graduate business school prescription for success—and still never rise above the norm in performance in their industry. Hundreds of them continue to struggle year after year—and CEO succession after CEO

Behavioral differentiation is a mouthful, so throughout this book we often use the abbreviation BD to signify behavioral differentiation, behavioral differentiators, and other variations of this expression.

succession—with the bewildering challenge of producing new products and services faster than their rivals can copy them feature for feature and building new business in increasingly tougher markets.

In *Winning Behavior,* we described how the smartest, most successful companies use behavior to differentiate themselves from their competitors. However, we devoted most of the book to discussing B2C (business-to-consumer) companies, like Ritz-Carlton, Volvo Cars, Southwest Airlines, Men's Wearhouse, Nordstrom, Marshall Field's, Enterprise Rent-a-Car, and Wal-Mart. In B2C companies, it's easier to see how BD might work because these companies sell to consumers and much of their BD would look like great customer service. In *Winning Behavior,* we did discuss some B2B (business-to-business) companies (EMC, Hall Kinion, Heidrick & Struggles); however, a number of readers said they wanted to know more. In particular, they wanted to know how BD applied throughout the complex business development (or sales) process that B2B companies face—a process that typically involves multiple people representing both the buyer and seller, is much longer (lasting from a few months to several years), and involves significant sums of money (often billions of dollars). So we wrote this book as a sequel to *Winning Behavior* and as a further discussion of BD in the complicated work of B2B buying and selling.

The Organization of This Book

In the first two chapters of the book, we explore how B2B buying and selling has changed in the past century and what buyers today want from suppliers. Chapter 1 offers a historical look at concepts about selling from one of the earliest books published in America on selling, William Miller's *The Art of Canvassing,* through the more recent works that offer advice on how to sell your products and services to other businesses. We called this chapter "The Death of Selling" because selling, as it has been known and practiced for the past century, is virtually dead in the contemporary world of B2B business development. Increasingly global competition, the professionalizing of purchasing, the growth of supply chain management, and other factors have radically reshaped the world of selling today.

Chapter 2, "The Changing World of Buying and Selling," presents the results of our research into B2B purchasing today. Over nearly a year, we interviewed dozens and dozens of senior executives, supply chain managers, and purchasing directors for some of the largest B2B buyers in the United States. We asked them what they look for in suppliers today, whether their expectations have changed in the past ten years, and what they have experienced from the worst and best of the suppliers they have dealt with. Their answers are illuminating, to say the least, and provide considerable substantiation that behavior is critically important today in B2B selling.

Chapter 3, "The Chemistry of Preference," discusses how customers determine which suppliers they prefer to work with and elucidates the principles of behavioral differentiation. This chapter will be familiar to any readers who have previously read *Winning Behavior*. For other readers, this chapter summarizes the concepts and is an important prelude to the rest of the book. In Chapter 4, we describe our model for the B2B business development process: It is like the game of chess and can be viewed as having an opening game, a middle game, and an endgame. This metaphor will help you identify the different challenges in B2B business development through the life cycle of marketing, building a customer relationship, pursuing a particular business opportunity, and completing the requirements and events that typically precede a contract award.

In Chapter 5, we discuss opening game in depth, including everything that smart companies do to condition the markets they serve. Opening game represents about 20 percent of your win probability, so it is crucial to get it right. A failure in opening game means that the rest of the business development process will be considerably tougher. Chapters 6 through 8 describe middle game—the part of the process where you seek to condition the customer and build preference in your favor. Middle game accounts for about 70 percent of your win probability, and we divide it into early middle game (Chapter 6), mid–middle game (Chapter 7), and late middle game (Chapter 8). Much of your opportunity for BD during business development occurs during middle game, so it's even more important to get middle game right. Chapter 9 describes endgame, which includes the proposals and presentations that are typical in B2B business buying and selling. Although endgame accounts for only about 10 percent of your win probability, there are numerous opportunities here to differentiate yourself behaviorally, and failing to do so could cost you a contract.

Chapter 10, "Creating a Behavioral Differentiation Strategy," is a serious "how-to" chapter. It describes the process we use with our clients to help them create and implement an overall BD strategy for their company. It also describes the Differentiation Needs Analysis, or DNA, tool that we recommend for creating a differentiation strategy for an opportunity pursuit. We show throughout the book that positive differentiating behavior during business development can make a significant difference in your ability to win new business.

We further contend that behavior can be managed. Business leaders have the opportunity through behavioral differentiation to substantially improve their business results—if they have the skill and the will to do so. And this brings us to our final chapter, which explores why B2B companies find it difficult sometimes to institute and sustain BD. In researching this book, we also surveyed a number of companies and asked how they did or did not use behavior to create a competitive advantage, as well as what their operating values were. The results showed us why some companies find it difficult to achieve and sustain BD.

The bottom line of our books on behavioral differentiation is this: Behavior is one of your last, best opportunities to create and sustain a competitive advantage in your markets. You can have fine products, flawless execution, and great service and still be middle of the road today because it's so easy for your rivals to copy what you do and how you sell it. However, it's difficult for rivals to copy BD because it requires a level of skill and will that many business leaders don't have. First, they fail to recognize the competitive potential of behavior, and second, they don't have the wherewithal to implement sustainable BD throughout their organization. If you are reading this book, then you are at least aware of the competitive potential of behavior, and if you have the determination and leadership strength to see it through, you can implement behavioral differentiation throughout your organization and give yourself a substantial behavioral advantage.

CHAPTER 1

The Death of Selling

> *There is no new thing under the sun.*—*Ecclesiastes 1:9*
>
> ■
>
> *It is always the latest song that an audience applauds the most.*—*Homer,* The Odyssey

Incredible breakthrough! The first wholly new sales paradigm of the twenty-first century! This unique sales system has been proven successful by the world's leading sales teams. Featuring the umpteen habits of high-performing salespeople, this method will end rejections and objections; shorten your sales cycle; guarantee that you reach the right top-level buyers; and increase your revenues by 200 percent, 500 percent, or even 1,000 percent! Using a unique questioning method, you will learn how to identify your customer's hidden needs, create breathtaking solutions, and build powerful and enduring customer relationships that make you a consultant to your customers instead of a salesperson.

Does this sound familiar? In one form or another, this language appears on the dust jackets of hundreds of sales books that have been published in the past twenty years. If you believe the hype, the past two decades have been a phenomenal period of evolution in sales technique. Breakthroughs occur with the publication of each new book on selling. If that is not remarkable progress, then nothing is. Furthermore, many of these books purport to offer *unique* sales systems, approaches, or strategies, which, upon cursory examination, are very similar to other authors' *unique* sales systems, approaches, and strategies, thus violating the physical law that prevents two objects from occupying the same space.

We wondered if *any* of the sales systems or techniques described in these books truly represented new thought, so we researched how selling has been written about and taught throughout the past century. During our study, we read scores of books on selling. The earliest was written in 1894 and the latest . . . well, they are still rolling hot off the presses. We reached several conclusions from this research.

First, the basics on selling were well established in the earliest years of the twentieth century, if not before. Although much has been written since about understanding the buyer's motives, asking good questions, listening, meeting the buyer's needs, developing sales strategies, planning for the interview, crafting a compelling argument, presenting your solution, handling objections, and so on, the overwhelming majority of later authors are mostly covering well-trodden ground, despite their claims of novelty. However, the selling environment itself has changed considerably, especially since World War II, because of the growing complexity of business organizations, the professionalizing of purchasing, and other factors. Consequently, the basics of selling—at least as described by writers in the early twentieth century—are no longer appropriate for the selling environment of the twenty-first century.

Second, at this point in history, the rudiments of selling are so well understood that people in business who don't understand them have simply not been paying attention. Everyone today knows that you have to build relationships, you have to manage your key accounts, you have to be more of a consultant to customers than a high-pressure salesperson, you have to sell solutions (not products), and you have to demonstrate your value. You have to be customer oriented, know your customer's business and industry, sell at the top, make allies of gatekeepers, listen to customers, ask good questions, yada, yada, yada.

Been there. Done that. What else you got?

It's not that these "eternal truths" are wrong; they're just used up. Legions of salespeople have learned these things and used them endlessly. Customers know them already. What's more, customers use these same approaches and techniques to sell to *their* customers. *Everyone* today does consultative selling, or tries to. *Everyone* does relationship selling. *Everyone* tries to quantify their value. If they don't, they're not even in the game. What used to be fresh and innovative is now exhausted and boring. *The sales pitch is dead.* Everyone's heard it over and over. Furthermore, today's sophisticated customers can scope you out on your Web site faster than you can put together your presentation. In this age of the Internet, reverse auctions, online catalogs, and Web-based purchasing, your Web site is now your pitch. Customers qualify you as a supplier by looking up your company and products or services on the Web, and if your Web site does not give them adequate qualifying information, you may not even make their supplier list. Today, they may not have to talk to you to know whether you can provide what they need. Many buyers prefer it that way because they want to reduce their purchasing transaction costs, and it's easier and faster for them to research you on the Web than it is for them to meet with you and sit through your PowerPoint presentation.

In our previous book, *Winning Behavior*, we argued that in this age of global competition, markets are becoming increasingly entropic, which means that they relentlessly reduce product, channel, and other traditional forms of differentiation and create a numbing sameness. It's becoming harder and harder to build a better mousetrap because competitors copy your innovations practically as fast as you can roll them out, and when capability becomes commodity, all you can do is lower your price and sing that old sad song as you watch your margins erode.

It's becoming increasingly clear, however, that *selling has also become a commodity*. In the B2B world in particular, nearly every salesperson uses the selling techniques that have been promoted over the last few decades—to the point where the selling process itself has become commoditized. Not only are your products and channels virtually the same as your competitors', your selling process is too.

The paucity of new ideas in selling is evident in a review of the recent articles published in journals related to selling and sales management. In the two-year period from November 2000 to December 2002, for instance, *Selling Power* magazine published 216 articles or short "tips" pieces on topics related to selling. Thirty-three percent of those articles focused on sales management, including articles on hiring and motivating salespeople, conducting sales meetings, running trade shows, and managing incentive and compensation systems. Another 22 percent of the articles dealt with selling skills, including articles entitled "Handling the Tire Kickers," "Overcoming Price Objections," "Presentations to Wow a Group," "Demanding Customers," "Use Your Sell Phone," and "Effortless Closing." There were fourteen articles on motivating salespeople (we can only conclude that this is highly problematic), seventeen articles on prospecting, twenty-three articles on using technology to improve sales (including thirteen on CRM—customer relationship management systems), eight articles on dealing with difficult customers, twelve articles on sales presentations, four on time management, and three on the power of positive thinking. As we will show in this chapter, these articles are fundamentally no different from the advice written to salespeople over a century ago. In reading *Selling Power* magazine, one would be forced to conclude that little has changed in the field of selling since William Miller offered fifty tips to salesmen in 1894, including this one: "Never sit in your office and do nothing because the weather is bad. [On a] stormy day men have more leisure to give you and more inclination to listen."[1] Talk about the power of positive thinking!

The Art of Canvassing

To appreciate how and why selling has become commoditized, it's useful to understand how concepts about selling evolved (or not) in the United States during the past century. Professional selling developed during the post–Civil War era with westward expansion, postwar reconstruction, and the relentless march of the Industrial Revolution. In late nineteenth-century America, armies of commercial travelers rode horses, wagons, steamboats, and rails to hawk their wares to a rapidly developing class of merchants, storekeepers, manufacturers, miners, builders, and craftsmen as they were laying the foundations for the vast middle class of consumers who have always been the backbone of the American economy. From 1865 to 1910, America was transformed from a predominantly agrarian economy to a predominantly industrial economy, and with that transformation came the development of selling as a profession. Competition was increasing, and there was a greater need for a competent and repeatable approach to persuading customers to buy one's wares.

One of the first American authors to articulate the art of selling was William Miller, whose slim, leather-bound advisory on selling life insurance is a classic on early sales thinking. Like many nineteenth-century authors, Miller takes a trait-based approach to selling: "An Agent's natural fitness for this profession," he argues, "depends chiefly upon his business qualifications, industry, persistence, alertness, and a certain tact and persuasiveness which are acquired by practice, rather than by observation and instruction. It is the art of doing and saying the right thing at the right time, in the right way, and of discreet suppression when silence is golden."[2] Miller believed that successful salesmen had the essential qualities of politeness, honesty, and industry; that they won the confidence of their customers by being earnest and direct; that they cultivated customer friendships through geniality and kindness; and that they built their business by being methodical. "Appear cheerful and happy," he advised. "Do not complain of hard times. Seem to be happy and prosperous. People will like you all the better for it. Be honest and conscientious. Try to satisfy and please your customers."[3]

In the language of the times, a salesman's *canvass* was his sales pitch or presentation. Like many early authors on the art of selling, Miller believed that it was crucial to practice your canvass until you could recite it from memory and then to present it forcefully and earnestly. Furthermore, he did not believe in giving customers alternatives: "Have no option for your patrons. By presenting different plans you induce the disposition to compare and hence to delay. This defeats you, temporarily at least. It is better to take a given point and carry your patrons to it."[4] Nor did Miller believe in responding to or anticipating objections: "Never anticipate objections," he counseled. "It is 'borrowing trouble.' Ignore them if possible. If compelled to answer them, do so very briefly, though courteously, and resume the original argument."[5]

In these kinds of statements, Miller was reflecting the origins of the hard-sell approach. Get the appointment. Make your pitch. Ignore objections and stick with your argument. All you need is the right stuff and the discipline to be systematic in your selling: "System is indispensable. It can accomplish wonders. It reduces labor to its simplest form and is essential to the rapid dispatch of business and the accomplishment of great results."[6] Although Miller's advice is aimed at insurance salesmen working in a much simpler world than today, his advice can still be found, in one form or another, in the pages of *Selling Power* magazine and in numerous recently published books on sales.

The Knack of Selling

Miller's go-getter philosophy sprang from the optimism and belief in progress that characterized early twentieth-century America. If you have gumption and pluck, you are bound to succeed. Walter Moody shared Miller's belief that determination was the most important trait of successful salespeople. In *Men Who Sell Things* (1907), he said, "Pure grit constitutes one of the most essential elements of successful salesmanship. It is the best there is in a man; it is that fine quality that whispers in our ear in moments of discouragement, 'Never lie down.' When exhausted and sinking in the mire of Despond, it calls cheerily from the banks of Hope along the shore: 'Don't give up! I'll pull you out.' "[7] Moody's book is largely a character study of successful and unsuccessful salesmen. The latter he describes as knockers, order-takers, wheelbarrows, sky-rockets, fussies, quick-tempered types, know-it-alls, and old-timers. The former, he says, are the product of positive qualities and intelligent application of principles. Moody was among the earliest twentieth-century sales authors to talk about the *science* of salesmanship: "I assert without hesitation," he said, "that the really big men, those who have made the profession worthwhile, are the ones who have employed the highest degree of science in their work."[8] He believed that buyers' motives could be understood scientifically and that salesmen could devise plans for arousing buyers' interests based on *facts* about human decision making that enabled salesmen to influence buyers in predictable ways, although his book does not classify buying motives. For that, we have to turn to The System Company.

♛   *The crowding of the field of salesmanship, and the exhaustion of old-time resources in the art of selling goods, have forced a revolution in this special branch of industry. The pressure of business has intensified; manufacturers and merchants who employ large forces of traveling salesmen are looking for a new degree of greatness in salesmanship based on scientific methods.*—*Walter D. Moody*, Men Who Sell Things *(1907)*

The Chicago-based System Company was one of the earliest American firms devoted to the art and science of business and the first to publish extensively about it. In *How to Increase Your Sales: 126 Selling Plans Used & Proven by 54 Salesmen & Salesmanagers* (1908), The System Company was among the first to lay out a sales system and describe its parts. Its book includes chapters on the steps in a sale; selling to end users; getting past the outposts; answering objections; landing the order; getting reorders; following up between calls; and, significantly, a chapter by W. F. Hypes entitled "The Salesman as the Customer's Partner." We used the word *significantly* because it is generally assumed today that this idea originated with the first book on consultative selling (published in 1970). However, the unfortunately named Mr. Hypes, a sales manager for Marshall Field & Company, argued in 1908:

> Help for the dealer, the kind which cements the business relationship and really creates a spirit of co-operation between house and retailer, is generally known to be of two kinds, that which originates with the house itself [the salesman's company] and that which the salesman himself furnishes independently from his own fund of information in his daily calls. There is no questioning the ultimate value of both kinds, but the latter capacity brings the salesman into so much closer touch with the customer that it frequently proves of far greater and more immediate concrete value to him than he would ever derive through adapting methods on his own initiative from the printed ammunition of the house. In fact, some wholesalers and manufacturers recognize this to the extent that they depend entirely upon their salesmen to aid the trade in a purely personal way.[9]

In Hypes's view, salespeople can be a clearinghouse of ideas for customers, and the more they know about their customers' business, the more effective they will be. Readers today should find this perspective familiar. It's been cited as "news" in at least thirty books on consultative, relationship, or solution selling in the past three decades.

The System Company's most famous publication on selling was the six-volume *The Knack of Selling* (1913). What is groundbreaking about this set of books is the formulaic approach to the psychology of selling: "You get an order from a prospect because of what he THINKS," the first volume argues. "Signing an order or handing over money must be a VOLUNTARY operation. The prospect must be WILLING. To be WILLING he must think certain thoughts. YOU must lead him to think those thoughts."[10] Here is selling as prescription, and while this may seem arcane today, it was an evolutionary step forward from the character studies and self-help advice offered by Miller and Moody. *The Knack of Selling* focuses on the salesman's methods instead of his character and offers a step-by-step process for persuading customers to buy. Although the book does not use the term *psychology*, it is the first book on selling to address the buyer's motives directly. "Back of every mental decision a man or woman makes lies a MOTIVE," volume one says. "Back of every decision a man or woman makes that leaves him willing to BUY something, lies one of these five particular motives: gain of money, gain of utility, satisfaction of pride, satisfaction of caution, and yielding to weakness."[11] Understanding how buyers think, therefore, makes salesmen more effective. "There is the way a Sale is made. The salesman must arouse the motive. The motive creates willingness to buy. The salesman must take advantage of this willingness and turn it into resolve—he must close. Then the way to find what thoughts your prospect must think in order to make him willing to buy your goods, is to find what motive must be aroused."[12] Much has been made since 1913 about understanding how buyers think. Neil Rackham's *SPIN Selling* (1988), for instance, has much of this flavor and is based on extensive research of sales calls. In virtually every book on selling written since 1913, authors have acknowledged that understanding buyers' motives is fundamental to selling.

> ♛ *When a prospect has granted you an interview—when he has given you his attention at his desk, or come into your store, or when a woman has opened her house door to you—that interview is YOURS and you have a right to manage it and to direct it according to your own particular plan. And you not only have a RIGHT to manage it, but it is absolutely NECESSARY for you to manage it, if you are to get in your canvass in an effective manner.—The System Company,* The Knack of Selling *(1913)*

The System Company's approach to selling would be offensive and dysfunctional to today's buyers and sellers, but it must have seemed comforting at the time. There is *one* right way to do it, it claimed, and once you discover that right way, you will succeed: "If one way of canvassing a prospect is the BEST way in the long run, then no other way is so good. And every time a salesman uses a canvass different from the one BEST canvass, he is throwing away chances." This makes the salesman's task simple: "The salesman who is willing to work out the BEST canvass for his proposition—work it out along the lines of always leading the prospect to think the thoughts that will make him willing to buy—can sell MORE goods, regardless of how good a salesman he is today."[13]

The authors advocate what we would recognize today as a very hard-sell approach. The first step is finding something the prospect is interested in and making a remark that will force the prospect to reply. Then you should hold the prospect's interest by making personal comments or being so assertive that the prospect is compelled to listen. If the prospect raises an objection, use a trick, if necessary, to interrupt and get his mind off what he was saying. "It is only the haphazard salesman who gets mixed—confused—baffled—and finally squelched. The man who knows exactly what he is driving at and has a definite plan for getting there, can be interrupted, bothered, argued with, but he always sticks to the main line and comes out of every difficulty with his face towards the straight course."[14] Wow. Today, we would call this badgering, and it would get you booted from a buyer's office faster than you could ask for the order and with enough force to achieve orbit.

The Psychology of Selling

The mechanistic approach to selling described by The System Company reflects the intellectual currents of the times. Although Albert Einstein published his special theory of relativity in 1905, the clockwork universe described by Newton still dominated scientific and popular thought in the early years of the twentieth century. People believed, in business as well as science, that if you knew the *cause* you could always predict the *effect*, that systems could be analyzed scientifically and then managed in efficient ways. In 1911, Frederick Winslow Taylor published *The Principles of Scientific Management*, perhaps the most influential management book ever written. Taylor believed that the remedy for inefficiency in manufacturing was systematic management rather than "searching for some unusual or extraordinary man," which would appear to contradict McKinsey & Company's recent argument that there is a war for talent and only by attracting the most "unusual or extraordinary people" can companies prevail.[15] Taylor argued "the best management is a true science, resting upon clearly defined laws, rules, and principles, as a foundation." Further, "the fundamental principles of scientific management are applicable to all kinds of human activities, from our simplest individual acts to the work of our great corporations."[16]

This faith in law, rules, principles, and systems also gave rise to behaviorism, which grew out of Pavlov's classic conditioning experiments with dogs (which were begun in 1889) (see Figure 1-1) as well as the philosophy of naturalism, which held that the material world is reality and everything can be explained in terms of natural laws. The first behavioral psychologists were John B. Watson, who published *Behavior: An Introduction to Comparative Psychology* in 1914 and *Psychology from the Standpoint of a Behaviorist* in 1919, and Edward L. Thorndike, who published *Educational Psychology* in 1903 and who formulated the law of effect, which states that responses to stimuli that result in satisfaction are strengthened and those that result in dissatisfaction are weakened. These psychologists are important because they had an influence on the thinking of Edward K. Strong, one of the first industrial psychologists and the author of four books on the psychology of selling, advertising, and business. Also influencing Strong were Norval A. Hawkins, director of global sales for Ford Motor Company from 1907 to 1919 (see Figure 1-2) and author of *The Selling Process* (1920), and Harold Whitehead (*Principles of Salesmanship*, 1920). These influences are important because they helped shape Edward Strong's thinking about selling, and he was perhaps the most influential thinker on selling skills from the 1920s to the 1960s.

Edward K. Strong is best known today for the *Strong Vocational Interest Blank*, which hundreds of thousands of high school and college students have taken as part of their career exploration. However, he devoted much of his professional life as an applied psychologist to the study of selling. His initial interest in the psychological effects of advertising led to his publication of *The Relative Merits of Advertisements* in 1911, but his first book on sales was *The Psychology of Selling Life Insurance*, which was published in 1922. The first academic study of selling, it brought together thinking by the behavioral psychologists as well as commercial men like Hawkins and Whitehead. Strong's psychological approach to selling consisted of a strategy with five parts. First, the salesman had to understand to whom he was selling, which meant that he had to discern the customer's interests

FIGURE 1-1. Father of the knee-jerk reaction. Pavlov's stimulus-response experiments with dogs influenced generations of psychologists and sales managers, who believed that selling was a matter of finding the right arguments for each potential buyer. (Photo of Pavlov and his staff courtesy of Bettmann/CORBIS. Copyright Bettmann/CORBIS. Used with permission.)

and personality. Next, he had to know exactly what he was selling, what his proposition was. To convince the customer to buy, the salesman then had to understand what convictions the prospect had to have before he would buy. What was necessary for the customer to believe? However, belief alone was not sufficient. It was also important to understand the buyer's impulses: "Men do not buy because of an argument (presentation of the facts), although they think they do. They buy because their emotions have been aroused in such a way that buying seems the most natural thing to do under the circumstances."[17]

Finally, the salesman had to determine what appeals would be most effective. "What ideas or incitements must I present so that the prospect will have the necessary convictions and impulses to buy?" According to Strong's behavioral approach to selling, "Convictions are developed through the presentation of ideas; impulses are aroused through the use of incitements. Consequently, the fifth step in the strategy of selling is to determine upon the ideas and incitements to use in order that the prospect will finally be possessed of and activated by certain convictions and impulses."[18] Clearly, this is a conditioned-response approach to influencing customers. If you can

FIGURE 1-2. Norval A. Hawkins. Hawkins was Henry Ford's first global sales director. He was also one of the first corporate sales directors to write a book on the selling process, and he influenced Edward K. Strong's thinking about the psychology of selling.

find the right arguments and emotional incitements for each customer, then customers will have the impulse to buy. This logic remains alive and well today in advice on the right questions to ask buyers, the right product demonstrations to give, the right way to handle objections, the right way to deal with "tire kickers," and so on.

Earlier authors had identified buying motives, but Edward Strong created a more exhaustive and psychologically based catalog of buying instincts, including securing favorable attention, following a leader, jealousy, gregariousness, and social and parental instincts. "If the salesman would be successful," he argues, "he must arouse the prospect's feelings and emotions. To do so it is necessary for him to have an understanding of what they are."[19] Strong devotes much of his book to exploring those instincts, but he also argues that the salesman must have a clear selling plan (a *canvass*, although he doesn't use the word) but be flexible and adapt to the customer's responses:

> The salesman should prepare several well-worded portions of selling talks which bring out each of the nine points given above [the buying instincts], so that he can discuss any one of them with different types of prospects. These "bits" of a sales interview should not be memorized so that, once started upon a paragraph, the salesman has to finish or lose his place, but they should be gone over sufficiently so that the phrases and sentences can be given freely and easily and without requiring full attention to them. For a salesman must be attending to three things when engaged in selling: (1) he must conduct a well-thought-out argument; (2) he must continually motivate the argument; and (3) he must continually adjust his interview to the responses the prospect is making to what has been presented.[20]

Throughout his book, Strong emphasizes the customer's view of the selling process, which is an important departure from the sales literature preceding *The Psychology of Selling Life Insurance*. He notes, in particular, how the prospect reacts to the salesman and the proposition, how the prospect invokes defenses against the proposition, and how the prospect decides whether or not to buy. In focusing so much on the customer, Strong was laying the groundwork for generations of future writers who talk about being customer oriented. Strong also argues that it is important to know your value proposition and be able to demonstrate the value to the customer. In a number of illustrative dialogues, he shows how salesmen might demonstrate the value of a life insurance policy, in both economic and emotional terms. Today's notions of value-based selling are consequently not a modern invention but were well established by 1922.

> 📖 *The human being responds to outside stimulations. Just how he responds depends upon two factors—the situation itself and the internal make-up of the individual. If we know what the situation is and what the internal organization of the individual is, we can prophesy what he will do in response to any particular situation.—Edward K. Strong,* The Psychology of Selling Life Insurance *(1922)*

Sellers as Business Consultants

The first book to explicitly discuss the distinction between the *features* of a product and its *benefits* to customers was *Tips and Pointers for Underwear Dealers and Their Salesmen*, published by the Cooper Underwear Company in 1923. "Men buying union suits are influenced by comfort, fit, durability, color and weight," it advises. "We have, in other chapters, covered the subject of stouts, slims and regulars. We have also referred to the collarette, non-ravel sleeve, the elastic cuff, left dress, and sloping shoulders of extra width. In all, there are sixteen different parts of a union suit. Each one contains a feature which might be discussed with the customer."[21] Among the benefits listed are agreeability in contact, the comfort of elasticity, the warmth, fit, long life, and effect on vital organs. If you are selling, buying, *or wearing* a union suit, this is clearly important information.

The approaches, strategies, tactics, and philosophies of selling did not change substantially from the early 1920s to the late 1950s. Perhaps the most important reason for this period of stability (or stagnation, depending on your viewpoint) was the nation's economy. As you can see in Figure 1-3, the real U.S. gross domestic product did not grow significantly from 1900 through the years just before World War II. War spending drove up the economy, but it fell again after the war and did not grow substantially again until 1960, when the postwar economic recovery was in full swing and the baby boomer generation began entering the workforce. The forty years from 1960 to 2000 were decades of unprecedented growth and prosperity, despite some minor glitches along the way. The explosive growth of the economy had numerous effects, including the rise of the modern corporation, the globalization of markets, and tremendous growth in consumer spending.

This era also saw the shift from a predominantly industrial economy to a predominantly service economy in the United States as labor costs increased and manufacturers either located offshore or succumbed to foreign competition for the production of goods. Last, and significantly, it also saw the birth of the information age and the meteoric rise and fall of the dot-coms. Perhaps the most important developments during this period, at least from a selling standpoint, were the increasing sophistication of buyers and the growing complexity of buying organizations; these transformations set the stage for the death of selling.

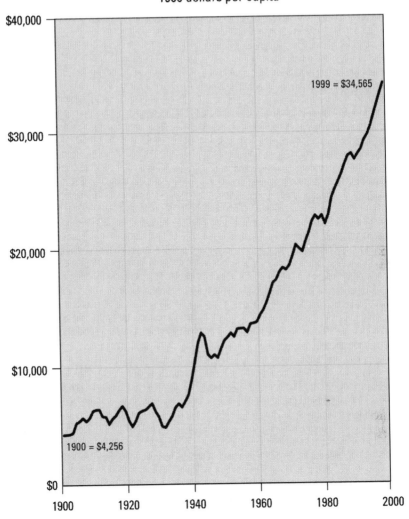

Real Gross Domestic Product
1999 dollars per capita

1999 = $34,565

1900 = $4,256

FIGURE 1-3. U.S. Real Gross Domestic Product: 1900–2000. The meteoric growth of the U.S. economy since World War II has led to significant changes in the nature of B2B selling.

Strong, who had worked as a psychologist for the U.S. Army during World War I, reported in 1922 that "psychological tests given to approximately two million men in the army showed that the average man did about as well as an average fourteen-year-old school child, and that he had not finished the seventh grade in school. On the basis of these tests—and they were so numerous as to be fairly representative—one-half of the men in the United States are thus of fourteen-year-old intelligence or less, and of an education limited by seventh-grade standards. Consequently, talking to a prospect in terms of his interests and in a way that he can understand may mean getting down pretty low in many cases."[22] In contrast, by 2001, 84 percent of all American adults ages 25 and over had completed high school and 26 percent had completed a bachelor's degree or higher.[23] B2B customers in the latter half of the twentieth century have been considerably better educated and, in many cases, know the products or services being sold nearly as well as the people selling them, which means that the seller's knowledge advantage has diminished substantially. Moreover, because they are exposed to products and services from so many competing companies, buyers often know more about the range of competing products available to them than do the people trying to sell a particular product.

Partly because of the increasing sophistication of buyers but also the increasing complexity of business organizations, Harvard University's Theodore Levitt concluded, in a 1960 essay published in *Harvard Business Review,* "It should be obvious that building an effective customer-oriented company involves far more than good intentions or promotional tricks; it involves profound matters of human organization and leadership." He also said, "The organization must learn to think of itself not as producing goods or services but as *buying customers,* as doing the things that will make people *want* to do business with it."[24] In subsequent essays, Levitt wrote about the globalization of markets, the industrialization of service, the marketing of intangible products, exploitation of the product life cycle, and innovative imitation.

Although numerous other authors have addressed these subjects, Theodore Levitt is our poster boy for modern thinking about marketing and selling. More than anyone else, he offered innovative ideas about the importance of being customer oriented and building competitive advantage through marketing. He also wrote about the role of the seller's behavior in building and sustaining customer relationships, a subject we will return to later. Levitt recognized the paradigm shift that was happening in the way business organizations operate and in how marketers and sellers need to approach them, and his writings presaged a number of later developments, particularly in selling or marketing to complex organizations.

In 1970, Mack Hanan, James Cribbin, and Herman Heiser published a slim book called *Consultative Selling,* which gave a name to an approach to selling that reflected the new reality of selling in the B2B, high-economic-growth environment (although, as we noted earlier, W. F. Hypes made the same argument about cooperating with customers in 1908). As the authors said in their introduction,

> Midway through the 1960s, the selling environment began to change. Since the end of the Second World War, few significant innovations in selling had taken place, or were really required, in what was largely a seller's market. Then, in a short period of time, many of the old assumptions became unworkable. As the cost of each sales call rose steadily, suppliers were compelled to redefine the essential characteristics of a "good customer." In turn, customers reclassified their supplier relationships and created new definitions of the "good salesman." Lists of alternate suppliers were drawn up in most major purchasing categories, and salesmen frequently found that no matter how they tried to "sell harder," they were hemmed in by an unofficial quota system that acted as a ceiling on their performance. Many companies exhorted their salesmen to "sell smarter" instead of just harder, but few salesmen could be sure of exactly what they meant.[25]

The consultative seller is not a salesperson, in the traditional sense, but a business planner, manager, and advisor. According to Hanan, "Consultative Selling replaces the traditional adversarial buyer-seller relationship with a win-win partnership in profit management."[26] So the seller's goal is to help customers improve their profits by improving their business. To do this, the seller must understand the customer's business and must have the customer's best interests in mind. "It means," Hanan says, "that you stop selling products and services and start selling the impact they can make on customer businesses."[27] Of course, to be accepted as a consultant to a customer organization, the salesperson must develop expert knowledge that customers value, must be able to take a broader business view of customers' situations, and must be creative problem solvers. Developing solutions, rather than selling products, becomes one of the principal ways the salesperson adds value and builds customer relationships and loyalty. This sometimes means that consultative salespeople must advise against purchasing something that customers don't need or is not right for them, even if the salespeople lose the commission, and this conflict-of-interest minefield is one that many salespeople don't negotiate successfully. Nonetheless, this is the concept.

Hanan argues that consultative selling enables sellers to avoid purchasing department gatekeepers: "Vendors sell price-performance benefits to purchasing agents. Consultative sales representatives sell up. They form partnerships with business function managers whose processes they improve. They also partner with line-of-business managers whose sales they improve. These are their first levels of partnership. At the second level, they partner with purchasing, forming a relationship that permits both partners to work with function managers and line managers in a triad of mutual interests."[28] As we will see in Chapter 2, however, avoiding these "gatekeepers" may be harmful rather than helpful. Partnerships that involve purchasing are increasingly essential in B2B selling today. Clients sometimes ask us how to avoid the purchasing function, and our response is that if you want long-term relationships with customers, you had better learn to partner with purchasing directors. But more on this later.

Since Hanan et al first described consultative selling, numerous others have jumped on the bandwagon. Today, a search on google.com for "consultative selling" yields over 85,000 hits. Moreover, the concept has become diffused as more followers have redefined the concept and tried to put their own stamp on it. In its original incarnation, consultative selling had these characteristics:

1. Sellers considered buyers to be *clients* rather than customers. This distinction implied a professional relationship rather than a buyer-seller or vendor relationship. It also signaled a shift from a transactional relationship to a consultative relationship.

2. Sellers provided a broad range of services in addition to products. The purpose was to increase clients' profits by improving their performance.

3. Sellers provided solutions and were more concerned with profitable client relationships than with volume or quantity of sales.

4. Sellers were businesspeople first and used business planning to maximize their own business as well as their clients' business. They thought long term rather than short term and took the broad view of their clients' needs.

5. Sellers were thought partners with their clients and strived to provide innovative answers to clients' questions, problems, and needs.

Not surprisingly, the notion of consultative selling coincided with the rise of management and professional consulting generally. Although some of the great consulting firms, such as McKinsey & Company, began much earlier than the 1960s (McKinsey was founded in 1926), in the decades following World War II the consulting profession and the number of consulting firms grew tremendously. It was inevitable that someone would "reinvent" selling as consulting, but this development also reflects the customer-oriented philosophy articulated by Theodore Levitt and others in the 1960s. It also highlights the gradual movement of selling from "pusher of products" to professional problem solver, and the selling profession is slowly adopting the ethos and practices of professional consulting (more on this in Chapter 2).

In 1985, Robert B. Miller and Stephen E. Heiman published *Strategic Selling*, which explicitly addressed what they termed the *complex sale*. Much of their book presents familiar ideas in selling: Analyze your account and do account planning, profile the ideal customer, use a sales funnel, know what results customers want to see, sell to the right people, and so on. Norval Hawkins and Edward Strong were writing about these concepts in the 1920s. However, Miller and Heiman were among the first to describe how sellers needed to approach the new, complex organizations of the late twentieth century. "A Complex Sale," they said, "is one in which several people must give their approval before the sale can take place."[29] To be effective, they argued, you have to know who will make the buying decision and how they will make it. "In the Complex Sale, there are *four* critical buying roles. We call the people who play these roles *Buying Influences*, or, more simply, *Buyers*."[30] They go on to discuss economic buyers, user buyers, technical buyers, and coaches, along with what each of these types of buying influences looks for and is most interested in. The notion of analyzing complex buying decisions in complex customer organizations was an important development in the concept of selling, perhaps one of the few since 1922.

Subsequently, few late-twentieth-century authors have contributed substantially new ideas on the practice of selling. The exception is Neil Rackham in *SPIN Selling* (1988). Like Miller and Heiman, he also focused on the "fast-moving and complex environment of today's major sale."[31] Rackham observed that sophisticated buyers react negatively to traditional closing techniques, and he advocated a questioning process designed to make buyers' needs explicit. His prescription for sales calls was to get down to business quickly, concentrate on asking questions and listening, and not talk about solutions too soon. He also felt that the traditional socializing at the beginning of a sales call was unwise: "The last thing a buyer wants is to tell the tenth seller of the day all about his last game of golf. The more senior the people you're selling to, the more they feel their time is at a premium, and the more impatience you're likely to generate if you dwell on nonbusiness areas. . . . Many buyers become suspicious of people who begin by raising areas of personal interest. They feel that the seller's motives aren't genuine and that it's an attempt to manipulate them."[32] Rackham's disdain for the vacuous socializing of some salespeople and his rejection of the traditional sales pitch made him one of the most iconoclastic advocates for a new approach to selling, especially when compared to many recent books on selling and articles in *Selling Power* magazine, among others, which show little insight into the B2B selling environment today.

The scores of books on selling published after Rackham have not really introduced anything new, although claims of breakthrough strategies abound. Ironically, the most recent advances in sales thinking have come not from the world of sales but from David H. Maister, a former Harvard Business School professor who was not writing about selling *per se* but rather about professional services firms and how they are managed. In a series of essays published between 1982 and 1993, he explored how professionals build business and manage their firms. Of particular interest is "How Clients Choose," which appeared in *The American Lawyer* in 1991. In this essay, he describes what it feels like to be a buyer and what buyers look for. Maister concludes, "Unless their skills are truly unique, unmatched by any competitor, professionals are never hired because of their technical capabilities. Excellent capabilities are essential to get you into the final set to be considered, but it is other things that get you hired."[33]

Like Rackham, Maister believes that questions are a professional's most important tool. Furthermore, recalling that William Miller, Edward K. Strong, and other early writers on selling advised salespeople to polish their canvass and push objections aside quickly, Maister's attitude sets up a very different conception of selling that applies not only to professional services firms but to B2B companies in all industries. Speaking as a client, he says:

■ "If I interrupt you, deal with my question. I want to see how you handle yourself when I ask a question, not judge how practiced you are at your standard spiel."

- "I want you to prove that you can listen, by picking up on my comments, adapting, in real time, what you say to what I've just said. Involve me. Ask what I think. I know someone's listening to me when they show the ability to depart from their prepared scripts and base their subsequent comments on what I've just said."

- "When I challenge you with an objection, hear it out, don't interrupt. Don't tell me I shouldn't be concerned about that: I've just told you I am concerned. Acknowledge what I said as a valid concern."[34]

Although Maister's ideas are focused on professionals, his perspective on working with clients challenges the traditional approach to selling. Gone are the days of preparing a canvass, giving high-pressure sales pitches, handling objections, and using "proven" closing techniques. The traditional approach to selling, still practiced by some companies and salespeople who haven't gotten the message, is dying a certain death, especially in the B2B world. Today's buyers are too sophisticated for slick sales techniques and are suspicious when they see them. However, what's causing the death of selling is not simply the greater complexity of buying organizations, the increasing sophistication of buyers, and the explosive growth of Web-based information, but something that is having a much more profound effect on how B2B purchasing is done—the rise of supply chain management and the growing professionalizing of the purchasing function. When the supply chain management revolution is finished, the Willy Lomans of the world will truly have perished (see Figure 1-4).

> Willy was a salesman. . . . He's a man way out there in the blue, riding on a smile and a shoeshine. And when they start not smiling back—that's an earthquake. And then you get yourself a couple of spots on your hat, and you're finished.— *Charley*, Death of a Salesman, *Requiem, by Arthur Miller*

CHALLENGES FOR READERS

1. We argue in this chapter that B2B selling has changed significantly since William Miller wrote *The Art of Canvassing* in 1897.

FIGURE 1-4. Arthur Miller's *Death of a Salesman*. This haunting image symbolizes the passing of an era. In today's B2B selling, a shoeshine and a smile won't get you very far. (Photo courtesy of Laurie Schendel Lane, Laurie Lane Studios. Used with permission.)

What changes have you seen in your business and industry? How has selling changed? How have your customers changed? Looking forward, what changes do you foresee in the coming years?

2. Salespeople in the last twenty years have been expected to be more consultative, ask more questions, be better listeners, and become more professional in their approach to *clients* (rather than *customers*). Have your salespeople made this transformation? Are they effective in the selling environment of the twenty-first century?

CHAPTER 2

The Changing World of Buying and Selling

> *We pick our supplier partners on the basis of who they are, not what they are. Everything becomes possible through people who clearly have customer satisfaction as their number one operating priority. In this world of commodities, the companies with the best people distinguish themselves and win our attention, our business, and ultimately, our loyalty.*—Brad Holcomb, Vice President and Chief Procurement Officer, Waste Management, Inc.
>
> ■
>
> *We and our first-tier competitors have a value proposition. We offer the right solution. We see ourselves not as sales people but as consultants to our customers. The challenge is the selling itself. Our competitors say they can do the same things we do. Thus, at the end of a very long day, many of our markets see our industry as made up of companies who are equally "normal" in how we try to win work. The behavioral advantage lies in supplier trust, integrity, focus, and delivery, and new and ever more concise differentiation.*—Jean-Pierre Jacks, Commercial Vice President, Kellogg Brown & Root

Does supplier behavior make a difference to buyers? The answer to this question seems self-evident, but we have met countless supplier executives and salespeople who would argue vehemently, "No, *all* that matters is price." We wondered how true this is, so we researched what buyers today really want from suppliers. What we discovered has profound implications for selling in this new millennium, and it illuminates just how much selling has changed since William Miller wrote *The Art of Canvassing* in 1894.

If you believe the conventional wisdom in most industries, the people responsible for building business will tell you that this is a brutal market, that all customers are looking for is unreasonably good deals, that price is king, and that they are being pummeled relentlessly in the most one-sided buyer's market they can ever remember. While there is undoubtedly some truth to this, it's a myopic view. Price is critically important *because all businesses today have to find ways to reduce their costs*, and when a significant proportion of their annual expenditures is for outside products and services, they have no choice but to find ways to reduce the amounts they spend with suppliers. However, they can't purchase fewer goods and services. The *challenge* is buying the same or more for less, and the *art* is doing it in a way that benefits the buyer without harming the seller. We said at the end of Chapter 1 that supply chain management and the professionalizing of the purchasing function are having profound effects on how B2B purchasing is done. In this chapter, we describe how these developments in the way businesses buy goods and services have affected selling and what the future holds for executives and professionals engaged in business development.

The Professionalizing of Purchasing

During the period of extraordinary economic growth following World War II, national markets became global markets, and companies were challenged by fierce competition to substantially improve the quality of their products while becoming more price competitive. In the ensuing decades, businesses have tried to meet this challenge in three principal ways: (1) by improving quality and streamlining manufacturing and other operations, (2) by reducing the cost of the raw materials and other goods and services they purchase through pressure on suppliers to reduce their prices, and (3) by using supply chain management techniques to drive costs down throughout the supply chain. One important consequence of these movements has been the professionalizing of the purchasing function. Once the backwater of organizations, populated by administrators who, in some cases, had washed out of other functional areas, purchasing in most large companies today has become a strategic business function led by highly educated specialists in supply chain management. For businesses trying to sell to this new breed of purchasing agent, the implications of this evolution are profound.

> ♜ *There are some old school people out there who have traditional thinking about how you have to go there and sell, sell, sell, and get the deal signed. That doesn't work today, but there are people out there still doing that.—Joan Selleck, Associate Director of Materials, Nikon Precision*

The quality movement, which was born in the 1950s and grew rapidly into adolescence in the 1960s, was the initial business response to increasing competition, fueled by a rapidly expanding consumer base that demanded higher-quality products. For the next three decades, businesses tried to improve both quality and the efficiency of their manufacturing operations through tools like quality circles, statistical process control, process mapping, total quality management, benchmarking, just-in-time manufacturing, continuous process improvement, and other such programs. In the late 1980s, this intense focus on quality improvement resulted in the first Malcolm Baldrige National Quality Awards. Today, these kinds of programs have evolved to Lean Six Sigma, the latest approach to using statistical methods to improve business processes, quality, and efficiency. Across the country, legions of Six Sigma Black Belts continue to measure, analyze, dissect, and scrutinize business processes, but there is only so much you can do with process improvement. Quality and efficiency gains significantly beyond Lean Six Sigma may come at too high a price.

So businesses also tried to drive costs out of their systems by beating up on their suppliers—demanding free services, expecting suppliers to assume a disproportionate share of the risk, commoditizing markets through ruthless price competitions and reverse auctions, leveling the playing field by sharing each supplier's technical innovations with other suppliers, and using the purchasing process as a way to build their knowledge (cynical sellers argue that some customers use the process to get free consulting). A few well-known companies are famous for these practices, but to some extent every company large enough to wield marketplace power has tried to drive costs down by pressuring suppliers to reduce their prices or risk losing their company's business. However, this approach, too, can gain only so much, as one survey respondent explained:

> Historically, we were a really bad partner. We had a lot of buying power and did not treat our suppliers very well. For instance, we have carriers who haul materials from point A to point B. We drove their rates down so low that the carriers had to run illegally to make a buck. We would shop volume out of our shipping stations every day. If someone could haul the material at eight cents a ton cheaper than the other guys, we would go with him. Ultimately, the carriers couldn't afford insurance or new tires, so they would try to get more out of their equipment, and that caused us numerous problems. So when I started here, I raised the rates, which caused some concerns internally. But it's a better solution. The carriers have to win for us to win. If they're running illegally, that's bad for us.[1]

Today, most companies appreciate that beating the tar out of their suppliers is ultimately as harmful to them as it is to the suppliers and can net only so much in savings before quality and reliability—and the supplier's goodwill—are degraded. However, significant cost savings are still possible in purchasing and supplier management, and the leading-edge purchasing and supply management companies, like Pepsico, McDonalds, Waste Management, and Wal-Mart, to name a few, use supply chain management to reduce their cost of goods and services and improve their relationships with partner suppliers.* According to Dr. Lisa Ellram, professor of supply chain management at Arizona State University, when companies began examining costs throughout their supply chains, they learned that some costs associated with logistics, ordering, and inventory management resulted from their own purchasing policies and that they could drive costs out of the system by being more thoughtful and efficient in how they managed purchasing. They also learned that if they worked more collaboratively with suppliers, they could jointly find ways to reduce their suppliers' costs.

---

*Companies like McDonalds and Wal-Mart are B2C companies in that they sell their products to consumers. However, they are major buyers of goods and services as well, and the companies that sell to them are B2B firms. We are discussing them in this chapter because, in this context, they are customers.

> ♛ To be a truly great company today, you have to continually drive costs out of the total supply chain, while you aggressively innovate to drive new revenue. If you don't do that, your competitors will pass you by.—*Jim Kozlowski, Director of Purchasing, Pepsico*

Finally, most concluded that they needed to work with *fewer* suppliers—to reduce transaction and relationship costs—and build better, more partner-like relationships with the suppliers who remained.[2] To achieve these gains, however, companies also learned that they had to upgrade their purchasing function and the quality of the people managing the supply chain and important supplier relationships. According to Bob Douglass, vice president of commercial production and planning for Triangle Pharmaceuticals, "Historically, the personnel rejects were sent to the purchasing departments. If a corporation had someone they didn't want to fire for some reason yet they weren't living up to the standards elsewhere, they'd send them down to work in the purchasing office. The climate has changed. Now purchasing people need to be much more business savvy rather than transactional (strategic sourcing/buying instead of clerical duties)."[3] Furthermore, the purchasing function is gaining more visibility in buying organizations. At SBC Communications, for instance, the senior purchasing executive has a "president" title and reports to the CEO. In many companies today, the senior purchasing executive reports to either the CEO or one of the CEO's direct reports and plays a critical role in strategic and business planning.

Some companies are demanding that their purchasing professionals have advanced degrees in supply chain management (one of the hot new business Ph.D.s) and/or have a Certified Purchasing Manager certification from the Institute of Supply Management.* Given the importance today of strategic sourcing and its role in helping businesses be more competitive, it's not surprising that companies are now staffing their purchasing functions with executives and professionals who are experts in supply chain management. The implication

---

*Likewise, in government circles such as the Department of Defense, procurement professionals are required to complete more than 600 hours of training to be certified, and the U.S. government is the largest buyer of goods and services on the planet.

for sellers is significant. In this selling environment, buyers are more sophisticated, knowledgeable, and demanding than ever before, and they are trying to make B2B buying and selling a far more rational, analytical, and objective process. Sellers who cannot meet them on that sophisticated playing field will soon no longer be in the game. Furthermore, in the winnowing process that's taking place as large B2B customers reduce the number of suppliers they work with, if you are not one of the preferred suppliers, you may find yourself locked out of many customer organizations and purchasing processes and, once out, face steeper entry barriers as you try to penetrate new or former buying organizations that have created a satisfactory set of preferred supplier relationships.

The Impact of Supply Chain Management

Wal-Mart gets much of the credit for inventing supply chain management. According to Ellram, in Wal-Mart's relentless drive to lower costs, it discovered that its own process for ordering goods from manufacturers like Procter & Gamble created costs and inefficiencies for P&G, which the manufacturer then had to pass on to Wal-Mart. By working as buyer-supplier partners, the two companies were able to remove a number of systemic inefficiencies and achieve cost savings that helped both companies.[4] The essence of supply chain management is to forge closer relationships up and down the supply chain— from the raw materials providers to the ultimate consumers of the goods and services created—and to discover ways to improve quality and reduce the costs of manufacturing, distribution, logistics, service, and so on. Ellram, who conducted a comprehensive study of strategic cost management, concluded that "cost management is not a passing fad; it is a way of life that will continue, and perhaps grow even more important."[5] Among her other findings were these:

■ There has been an improved understanding of supply base/market issues, and supply management is more integrated into organizations' operational processes and decisions.

■ Cost-consciousness is a way of life in today's organizations. "This philosophy is felt and lived from the chairman of the board to the administrative staff to the workers on the manufacturing floor."

■ "Cost management specialists, either from within the purchasing and supply management organization or from the finance organization are the focal point for supporting supplier cost analysis, building cost models and should-cost models, and validating results."

■ "Effective cost management is not a one-off approach that the company takes when it really needs to reduce its costs, but an ongoing expectation that is built into supplier relationships and the organization's reward and measurement system."[6]

Woven throughout her study is the notion that buying decisions are migrating from *users* to *purchasing professionals*. By "users" we mean the local department heads, superintendents, functional managers, and business unit leaders who have traditionally made or approved important buying decisions. Increasingly, says Ellram, purchasing is being centralized so companies can develop a comprehensive understanding of the purchases they are making and can leverage and properly manage supplier relationships and cost issues.[7] This is unwelcome news to the sellers who view purchasing managers as gatekeepers or blockers and do what they can to avoid them. Paul Seibold, president of Purchasing Support Services, explained that purchasing agents act impartially on behalf of their company and consequently have no *wants and needs*.* Furthermore, their performance measures are based on their ability to reduce procurement costs and directly impact the bottom line. Users, on the other hand, have *wants and needs*, and those can preempt all other considerations, including price. Naturally enough, suppliers want to sell directly to users because suppliers can sell to their needs and gain a psychological advantage. They would prefer to avoid purchasing agents, whose decisions are more objective and therefore more rational.[8]

The good news, for suppliers who understand supply chain management and today's purchasing environment, is that it presents a wealth of opportunity for suppliers willing to do what it takes to become a good supplier partner. "Suppliers and supplier relationship management will grow in importance as sources of cost savings and improvement," says Ellram. "There is a limit to the amount of year-

*The traditional advice to salespeople is to discover customers' wants and needs, which are partly psychological, and then sell to those wants and needs. Professional purchasers seek to take the psychology out of the equation, which frustrates traditional sellers—to the point where they try to avoid those purchasing professionals and sell directly to users.

over-year cost savings attainable from on-line reverse auctions. The long-term opportunities lie in working more closely with suppliers."[9] So what are the implications for sellers today? Among them are these:

■ The psychological advantages sellers have enjoyed by understanding buyers' motives, giving compelling sales presentations, skillfully handling objections, and using the right closing techniques will still work with consumers, but in B2B selling, the approach must increasingly be fact based and rational. Tony Millikin, vice president of purchasing and supply management for Sealy, reinforced this point: "Buying is not about emotion. It's about data and doing what's best for your company. Many buyers and executives allow the emotions of a situation to drive their decision. Decisions need to be based on the data, price, delivery, and quality, not emotion. Salespeople will always try to create an emotional attachment, and I tell my people to watch out for that."[10] Avoiding purchasing professionals and trying to sell directly to users is a strategy that may occasionally still be effective, but it is not a healthy long-term option and is unlikely to remain an option in the most sophisticated customer organizations.

One might conclude from the above that behavior does not matter. On the contrary, as we will see throughout the rest of this chapter, the correct conclusion is that the *right* behavior matters, and what's right has changed since purchasing became more professional. As sellers, you can still gain a psychological advantage, even with purchasing directors, but you have to do it by understanding their world, adopting a supply chain management perspective, and working with them in ways that make working with you easier and more valuable for them.

■ While relationships remain important, the nature of those relationships is changing. To develop a strong relationship with a purchasing director, you must demonstrate your willingness to be a good supply chain partner and must participate in customers' efforts to improve quality and reduce costs throughout the supply chain.

■ Understanding the buying influences in an organization remains important, but more important is understanding and aligning yourself with customers' efforts to make purchasing a critical component of its business model. This implies that your executives, sales managers, and salespeople must be versed in supply chain management. In the coming years, it won't be enough to know your own products, know your customers, know your competitors, and have good selling skills; it will be essential to be fluent and skilled in strategic sourcing throughout the supply chain in which you operate. Moreover, the admonitions you hear about "selling to the top" or "selling high" will need to focus less on the CEO, COO, and CFO and more on the CPO (chief purchasing officer).

■ Charging premium prices is likely to be more difficult than it has been in the past, particularly if you cannot prove higher value. Consequently, brand value in many industries will decline. You will need to improve your bottom line by taking costs out of your business and passing on at least some savings to your customers. In fact, most large buying organizations today expect you to *reduce* the *annual* cost of the goods and services you sell to them and enable yourself to do that by finding greater efficiencies in your own operations and reducing your own supplier costs.

Tony Millikin told us that he has suppliers who in ten years have never taken a price increase. "To account for cost of living and inflation, suppliers have to increase their efficiencies and reduce the cost of doing business. They have to become better businesses in their own right and can't focus on raising prices. Sealy is probably the nation's largest buyer of foam, and we haven't paid more than the commodity line for foam since the mid-1990s."[11] Millikin's experience may appear to contradict the story one purchasing director told about low rates driving suppliers to cut corners to earn a profit, but there is a crucial difference. The lesson learned in purchasing organizations today is that you can't beat up suppliers to the point where they have to cut corners to stay in business. Instead, you have to work with them collaboratively to find ways to jointly take costs out of the supply chain, and that's what Sealy has been able to do.

What Buyers Today Want from Suppliers

To better understand the B2B selling environment today and the impact of professional purchasing and supply chain management, we interviewed nearly fifty senior executives, including CEOs, business unit presidents, purchasing directors, and consultants in purchasing and supply management, all of whom had central roles in buying goods and services for major corporations in the United States. They represented diverse industries: electronics, aerospace, defense, energy, consumer products, engineering and construction, pharmaceuticals, foods and beverages, manufacturing, and waste management. Among the first questions we asked them were: "What do you look for in suppliers today?" "What characteristics are most important to you?" and "How has what you look for in suppliers changed in the past ten years?" Their responses were illuminating.

As we indicated above, one of the overriding themes emerging from our study is the changing importance of price in supplier selection criteria. According to Art Schick of Pepsico, "Years ago, it was much more of a bid-out business. We'd take the lowest-cost supplier and get on with life. Today, the top-quality suppliers are truly looking at customers as partners. They allow us to participate in the creation of the product, what we want it to look like, smell like, and so on. In B2B, the smarter suppliers are beginning to treat their top customers this way. They are really trying to understand what their customer's business is all about and be proactive in working with us."[12] We heard a similar message from Greg Schwartz , who is director, Smart Sourcing and senior vice president, OmniBrands, for Safeway's supply operations: "More and more today, if you want to be a world-class procurement group, you need better, stronger supplier partnerships—and that means long-term partnerships and commitments from suppliers to provide you resources, bring you ideas first, and find ways to take costs out of the system. You can no longer gain a huge competitive advantage by negotiating a price. That's what you did five years ago. Today, you focus on taking costs out of the system."[13]

> ♛ *The worst thing to do is base everything on price.—Lance Kaye, Buyer/Planner, Waste Management, Inc.*

Nearly all of the senior executives in our purchasing study agreed that today lowest price is not the primary criterion for selecting suppliers—more important is lowest total cost or total cost of ownership. "Lowest price is not the right measurement," said Bonnie Keith, now a college teacher and president of Performance Purchasing Group but formerly a vice president of supply management for Pepsico, General Electric, and ABB. "You want to find lowest total cost. You want to work with suppliers who understand the costs of your business as well as their own cost drivers, suppliers who are able to tell you where you have cost-reduction opportunities in your own business."[14] As important to many purchasing executives was a supplier's willingness to be open and transparent about costs. One purchasing director told us: "We primarily look for honesty. We want people who share their assumptions and rates. An open-book approach."[15]

"Suppliers should be very open with you about what constitutes their pricing," Paul Seibold said. "If they are up front with you about how they work out their pricing, this is beneficial. If they are tight on the pricing information, then you become suspicious and trust drops. A lot of it comes down to behaviors: honesty, openness. These are the key elements. Buyers also want to be respected. They don't want to be sold to. They want to work with salespeople who respect their knowledge."[16] Joan Selleck, associate director of materials for Nikon Precision, said that she is disappointed by suppliers "if they are not able or willing to tell us why we are spending more money than we should. If they say, 'The market is bad and we're going to have to increase your prices by X,' they should explain why. If they are not willing to share the information with us, or work with us, or help us understand what's driving the cost, then that's disappointing, and we find out what's happening by talking to their competitors."[17]

As we said earlier, *every* business today needs to drive down costs, so if you are going to satisfy your customers' current needs, you must adopt a lowest-total-cost perspective and partner with them to drive costs down throughout the supply chain. The more proactive you are about cost reduction, the more attractive you will be to existing and potential customers. Beyond these price and total-cost considerations, we learned in our study of buyers that they look for three aggregate characteristics as they search for supplier partners: total needs satisfaction, added value through partner-like relationships, and differentiating behavior.

Total Needs Satisfaction

Fundamentally, of course, you have to satisfy customers' needs. These vary by industry and the nature of the customers' business, but essentially these needs include meeting customers' product or service specifications; delivering consistently high quality; delivering on time, as promised; having the capacity to deliver what customers need, which may mean delivering multiple products to multiple geographies; and having the financial strength to be a reliable supplier. Most of the buyers we interviewed said that these fundamental need satisfactions meant *predictable supplier performance.* Anything that kept suppliers from performing predictably diminished their value and trustworthiness.

So to work with buyers today, you must be predictable and dependable, which means you must have the capacity to understand and meet their needs and an unwavering commitment to supply those needs. Buyers must trust that you will deliver on your promises and deliver high quality. Furthermore, you should think strategically and be a good fit as a business partner. These qualities will open doors for you, but they will not necessarily make you the preferred supplier. To do that, you must also add strategically significant business value.

Dave Gabriel, formerly Tenneco's senior vice president and general manager of North American Aftermarket, elaborated on this point: "Frankly, what I look for at a very high level," he said, "is a supplier's financial strength, technology position, intellectual skill set, quality, and geographic reach. Understanding these helps you get into the real elements of how a supplier operates. Intellectual capacity is one of the key drivers. You want people who look at their business the same way you do, who think strategically and translate that into business results."[18]

> Suppliers all look suspiciously like one another, and the price differentiation is not enough to decide which way to go. You have to look at other things.—*Joan Selleck, Nikon Precision*

Added Value

Since the quality movement began in the 1950s, the bar has been raised continually. Over the years, as customers adopted programs like continuous process improvement, benchmarking, total quality management, and the like, they have begun expecting their suppliers to do the same. To be acceptable today as a supplier partner, you must match the quality and business process initiatives your customers are using. To help achieve lowest total cost, you must reduce cycle time to market and seek supply chain innovations that eliminate redundancy and improve buyer-supplier integration—throughout the life cycle from product development to purchase to after-sales service.

Yet it is no longer enough simply to have a continuous improvement orientation or an internal quality program. "These concepts have been out there for a dozen years," says Bonnie Keith. "In the leading-edge companies these are now expected. We don't talk about quality improvement anymore; we talk about Six Sigma performance. Companies like GE, Allied Signal, Motorola, and others have adopted Six Sigma and are expecting their suppliers to apply Six Sigma, too."[19] Of course, you add value not simply through Six Sigma techniques (or Lean Six Sigma) but by consistently behaving in ways that drive Lean Six Sigma performance internally and throughout the supply chain (upward to your customers and downward to the suppliers). Cycle time compression is expected. High quality is expected. As Bonnie Keith says, "In today's marketplace, quality is a given. There is much, much lower tolerance for getting something that does not meet the requirements. Fifteen or twenty years ago buyers were inspecting constantly. That's shifting now because we expect suppliers to do the quality inspections. Give it to me the way it's expected, when it's expected, and don't surprise me."[20]

Another way suppliers can add value is by bringing new ideas to customers, by demonstrating a commitment to continuous innovation and idea sharing. Beyond cost-saving ideas, customers are looking for ways to improve their business processes, find improved materials, improve maintenance, make better use of technology, and discover new technologies or methods that will add value to their business. Safeway's Greg Schwartz said, "It's always nice when a supplier comes to you with something new—a new process, way of doing business, product, equipment, or technology that allows you to be the first to do something in a marketplace, which in turn enables you to gain a competitive advantage."[21] For Bob Douglass at Triangle Pharmaceuticals, the key is choosing suppliers who are willing to be part of the new product development process. Not all of them are. The ones who will partner with customers to develop new products and bring new ideas, technologies, and perspectives to the table can enhance the development process and the resulting new products. Through their differentiating behavior, they create an insider's position for themselves as partners in the supply chain.

Supply chain consciousness begins with suppliers' willingness to be transparent with buyers about their own costs. Paul Seibold tells an interesting story that illustrates this point:

> A very large company was in the market to buy services. Normally, they would put out an RFP [request for proposal], bring the suppliers together, and explain what they wanted, then allow the suppliers to bid, and so on. Instead, they decided to do what they called "target engineering." They met with each potential supplier individually and asked them a series of questions. If they felt "selling pressure" from a supplier or if a supplier was reluctant to divulge its costs, that supplier was eliminated. It came down to one supplier who was very open, who connected well culturally, and who was transparent about its pricing, and this company got the deal. The buyer wanted this relationship to last a long time, so they invested in building the relationship, and this was for a straightforward commodity service.[22]

Finally, suppliers can add value by being willing to take part in the product development process, by challenging the customers' thinking, and by anticipating their needs. Too often, suppliers just push products and deals. "We have this new piece of equipment," they might say. "Or we can get you this deal if you buy X quantity this quarter." It should be apparent that this method of selling is rapidly becoming old school. Buyers see it for what it is—the salesperson trying to make quota or the company pushing its latest product. Both are "me oriented" instead of customer oriented, and customers know the difference.

The finest suppliers today are able to anticipate what their customers need and to act as surrogates for the internal purchasing agents that buyers might otherwise have to hire. Joan Selleck from Nikon Precision told us: "I'm looking for somebody who will anticipate what we need and help us understand it before we need it. It's really coming up with solutions. Here's how to place your orders. Here's how we'll analyze your high-use items and help you determine when to buy them. So it's the suppliers who can do for us what a purchasing manager might do. They have a lot of data and can tell me what's going on in the market. We look for the availability of information that helps us make good purchasing decisions."[23]

So suppliers add value today by using state-of-the-art quality and lean concepts to help customers improve their business processes, by investing in R&D and technology to bring innovation and new ideas to customers, by being transparent about their costs and finding ways to reduce costs throughout the supply chain, by taking part in customers' product development processes, and by anticipating their customers' needs. Further, these means of adding value need to be part of "how you do business." To gain a behavioral advantage, they can't be optional extras. They have to be part and parcel of what buyers get when they purchase from you instead of from your competitors.

Differentiating Behavior

In our survey of executives responsible for making purchasing decisions, we discovered that beyond the basics (meeting the specifications, delivering on time, etc.) and adding value, buyers choose the suppliers they prefer to work with based on the suppliers' behavior. Indeed, behavior can be one of the most powerful differentiators because most suppliers today can deliver on the basics and can add some degree of value. However, suppliers differ considerably on their behavior, so this is a rich source of potential competitive advantage.

The intangibles often outweigh the tangibles, particularly when competing suppliers offer essentially the same tangible benefits. Frank Muschetto, senior vice president, worldwide supply chain management, for McDonalds, told us, "There are many things we look at when selecting suppliers: product innovation, for example, suppliers who challenge our thinking in order to achieve better business results. More importantly, we want suppliers with a passion for the business, with a demonstrated commitment to their customers and a demonstrated focus on the ultimate consumers. We want thought partners, not vendors."[24] Moreover, it's important for both buyers and suppliers to be vested in each other's growth and well-being. The director of raw materials for another large industrial company said, "We look for suppliers who are not only interested in their own growth but in ours as well."[25]

We heard that theme of partnership over and over. Francois

Gauthier, vice president of materials, supply chain management, for Coherent, told us that the old saw about finding a "win-win" really is meaningful in today's buyer-supplier relationships: "If we are looking to do business with a subcontractor who will do some level of assembly for our product, we're looking for a partner, rather than a vendor. In terms of a partnership, I am looking for somebody I'm comfortable doing business with, somebody I can count on when we represent a small amount of their volume but need their full attention. In partnerships, I'm looking for advantage to go both ways. They should be benefited by working with us, and vice versa."[26] Partnership is a two-way street, but many suppliers don't behave like partners, as Gauthier indicates: "If the supplier is selling a commodity and is acting like a used car salesman ('What would it take to put you in the driver's seat today?'), I am likely to use another supplier. Behavior matters to me. I don't need to feel pressured."[27]

A number of the executives we surveyed said that they want suppliers to designate people to serve them who understand them and their needs. These account managers or account team members should devote the time necessary to get to know the customer, and they should remain with the customer for as long as possible. Furthermore, it mattered whether and to what extent suppliers' senior executives engaged with customers. Jim Kozlowski at Pepsico said, "We look at all the companies within an industry and ask, How can we partner with them to take costs out of the supply chain where they can achieve a reasonable profit but also drive down costs? We look for the most cost-effective operations, the highest quality and service, and their willingness to invest."[28]

A number of purchasing executives also cited "ease of doing business" as a critical behavioral factor in selecting preferred suppliers. They said they wanted suppliers who were flexible and willing to work with customers the way customers wanted to be worked with. They also looked for alignment, in culture and values, between their organization and the suppliers' organizations. Lance Kaye, a buyer/planner for Waste Management summarized: "Behaviorally, we look for a willingness to bend to our rules. We have certain processes we want suppliers to follow and implement. They have to be willing to adapt to our way of working. We also want designated people who understand our needs. It gets down to a pretty personal level. They are partners in our business, and we are partners in theirs."[29]

It goes without saying that buyers want integrity and trust in their suppliers. However, as we will see later, they sometimes don't get it. Greg Schwartz of Safeway said, "There are many things we go through to find suppliers. First, we look for integrity and trust. That's fundamental. If you are going to go into a strategic partnership, you have to believe in the supplier's integrity. You have to trust them. You have to know that they will protect your proprietary processes and protect what they learn about how you do business."[30] Integrity should not be a behavioral differentiator; it should be present in all commercial relationships, but it would be naïve to assume that's always true. On the other hand, suppliers are sometimes *so* open and *so* candid and *so* transparent that they do differentiate themselves from their competitors. So while integrity is a fundamental, you can enhance the impact of it by being more open, candid, and transparent than your competitors, and you can diminish it by being more guarded, more protective, and less open with information.

Naturally, an absolute *negative* behavioral differentiator occurs when suppliers are deceitful or dishonest. Lance Kaye told us that in his previous employment he dealt with suppliers who would blatantly lie to him about their deliveries. Furthermore, some suppliers were dishonest on their invoices. Sometimes, the impression of dishonesty was created when suppliers included items on an invoice that had not been discussed. "They may have a good reason for adding something," Kaye said, "but they don't communicate it ahead of time." Finally, suppliers sometimes make promises during their sales presentations that they don't keep and probably never intended to keep. "When it's time to renegotiate, that kind of behavior is really held against them," Kaye said.[31]

How Suppliers Disappoint Buyers

It is clear that much of what buyers want from suppliers is behavioral. What can differentiate you are these kinds of behaviors:

- You are more transparent about your cost structure.

- You take a total supply chain management view and are proactive in seeking ways to reduce costs throughout the supply chain.

■ You anticipate your customers' needs and give them information to help them make the best buying decisions.

■ You are innovative and bring new technologies and solutions to customers. You act like a thought partner rather than a supplier.

■ You are easier to do business with than your competitors are. You are more flexible on how you do business, and you adapt to customers' preferences, requirements, and needs.

■ You communicate clearly and frequently, especially when there are issues or problems to resolve that could impact the customer's business.

■ You designate key people to work with customers, people who invest the time and energy to really understand their business, industry, and customers.

■ Your senior executives invest their own time in the customer relationship and demonstrate their commitment and customer focus through action, not words. Francois Gauthier said, "I judge how important we are to suppliers by the amount of time their CEO or other key people allocate to us. When I can get five or six hours of a CEO's time, that's great. It's great behavior on their part and sends a great message. The CEO's gone beyond what was expected, and this sends the right message to the rest of that supplier's organization."[32]

■ You behave like a partner, rather than a vendor, and you avoid using worn-out sales techniques and high-pressure gimmicks to close sales.

> *Don't waste my time by taking me to a ball game. That does not help me build my market or improve my business.—Bonnie Keith*

These behaviors can yield a significant competitive advantage in today's markets and with today's more sophisticated buyers. It seems like common sense, doesn't it? Surely, everyone who is responsible for sales and customer relationships knows this. Or do they? We were astonished to learn in our purchasing research that a remarkable number of suppliers have not figured this out. They still behave in ways that *negatively* differentiate them from their rivals. Bonnie Keith told us that while failing to meet contract requirements is bad enough, worse still is not telling customers about it:

> Even more of a crime is not communicating when they start to get in trouble or have a failure in their plant or a quality hiccup—and don't tell you about it! You wind up on the short end and don't get your materials when you need them. . . . They *must* give you forewarning. You may have other options, but you need to be aware of the problems as quickly as possible. Furthermore, when they disappoint me, they will find it difficult to recover. You start to build a level of distrust. You no longer find them credible. If you are forced to work with that supplier, you are always putting in safety precautions in your planning because you don't trust the supplier. That adds a cycle, and a cycle adds cost. And if you can do anything about it, you will get rid of the suppliers who create distrust.[33]

Bob Douglass of Triangle Pharmaceuticals concurred that poor communication was one of the worst supplier behaviors. "They don't keep you informed of problems in delivery, so you're surprised when a shipment doesn't arrive. Or, on an annual basis, and unbeknownst to you, they say their costs are going up, but this is the first you've heard of any problems. So if suppliers experience problems, they need to inform you throughout the process."[34] In Douglass's experience, only 20 percent of suppliers kept customers very well informed. Doug Beebe, manager of packaging purchasing for Scotts Company, also said that the typical disappointments come from the failure to deliver and the failure to communicate. "In a world of constant change, failures are inevitable. When we know about them or are told about the risk of failure, we can anticipate problems and plan for them. Some suppliers are better than others at communicating the risk of failure and the reasons why it happens when it does."[35]

Another negative supplier behavior occurs when suppliers overcommit and underdeliver. Obviously, this occurs because the salespeople representing the supplier are "optimistic" in their projections because they want to get the contract. Whether or not they intentionally deceive customers, they often create a more favorable impression than reality will allow them to deliver. Dave Gabriel of Tenneco tells the story of a rental car company that disappointed his company in such a way: "When I first came to Tenneco, [Company X] was the car rental company of choice. Then we cut a deal with [Company Y]. We reduced the price by 25 percent the first year, which was great. They offered a lot of features in their selling process, including the issue of clean cars. Afterwards, although we complained and complained, they just could not deliver clean cars. That tainted the entire experience we had with that supplier."[36]

Coherent's Francois Gauthier said that a big red flag for him occurs when suppliers start quoting the contract. "I put contracts in the drawer and hope never to look at them again. It's a big red flag when suppliers start quoting the terms of the purchase order. When they start doing this, it's because they are less interested in your business."[37] Suppliers who begin relying on contract terms have, in an important respect, stopped communicating through other means. Instead of discussing and resolving problems, they rely on contract terms to enforce agreements or understandings they've had with customers, even if the circumstances have changed.

Pepsico's Art Schick said that sometimes there is a very amicable relationship leading up to the contract award.

> Everyone's happy and friendly until the contract is signed, then the business relationship starts. I saw one situation where the supplier would do only things in the relationship that were verbatim in the contract. The supplier was manufacturing products for us, and we asked for a summary report, but if that report was not specifically laid out in the contract, they wouldn't do it. What you think would be a simple request was not fulfilled because they were sticking only to what was explicitly in the contract, and anything more they saw as avoidable expenses. They were looking at the situation outside the context of the relationship, and it hurt them.[38]

Another disappointment, especially for purchasing directors, occurs when suppliers try to go around them and deal with the people they believe are the "real buyers." In today's complex organizations, "going to the boss" may give a supplier a temporary advantage, but it creates powerful enemies, in large part because the purchasing directors can't do their jobs if suppliers are cutting side deals. Eventually, this kind of behavior will come back to haunt these suppliers because, like elephants, purchasing agents have long memories.

Two other strongly negative behaviors are worth mentioning. First are those suppliers who take every advantage of customers. When supplies are tight, they raise prices to capture as much profit as they can, despite the long-term relationship they may have with a customer and the negative impact price increases will have on the customer's business. These suppliers may also "short" deliveries to a particular customer because of increasing demand from other customers, despite the loyalty the customer may have shown toward them when times were lean. Art Schick of Pepsico refers to the suppliers who behave this way as *supplier predators*.

Second, there are the Willy Lomans; the throwbacks to the selling techniques of yesteryear. These are the glad-handing salespeople who waltz in, take you to a ball game, and expect your business but fail to deliver what they promised. One of our respondents said this was the typical approach back in the 1960s or 1970s: "The worst thing is what happened in the 60s. They would come in and buy you a hamburger and take you out to dinner. They'll send you a smoked ham during the holidays and ask about your family, but when it comes time to deliver value, they are nothing but empty suits. We know who those guys are and don't care to deal with them."[39]

In summary, suppliers disappoint buyers when they behave in ways that are unhelpful, manipulative, guarded, dishonest, or blatantly self-serving:

- When they don't live up to their commitments

- When they promise more than they can deliver

- When they raise prices year after year without justification

- When they conceal their actual cost structure

- When they don't anticipate customer needs and instead expect to sit back and take orders

- When they are reactive, do not innovate, and think in terms of products rather than solutions

■ When they are inflexible in their terms or product/service designs

■ When they fail to communicate about problems, risks, or upcoming issues

■ When they don't invest time to learn the customer's business

■ When they rely on the contract to resolve issues rather than dialogue and mutual understanding

■ When they try to go around the prescribed purchasing channels and avoid the customer's people who are responsible for supply chain management

■ When they are predatory in their customer relationships and seek every possible advantage without ever giving back

■ When they use the "tricks of the salesman's trade," such as gifts, dinners, and ball game tickets, instead of adding real value to the customer's business, as a way to build "favors"

These kinds of behaviors have a *repulsive effect* on customers. Beyond simply causing you to lose the business, these negative differentiators can lead customers to oppose you actively, not only within their own company but throughout their professional network and in their broader industry. Conversely, there are a number of behaviors that have an *attractive effect*. These behaviors delight buyers and can lead them to support you actively. Consequently, behaviors that positively differentiate you from your competitors create more customer loyalty.

How Suppliers Delight Buyers

Not surprisingly, when we asked purchasing executives what happened when suppliers delighted them, we heard stories about suppliers who were selfless, responsive, conscientious, and value adding—essentially the opposite of the behaviors that disappointed buyers. Delighting buyers is not difficult if you are committed to serving them exceptionally well, but it does require a commitment to behaving in ways that are well above the norm. Here are some of the stories we heard:

■ They provided a solution beyond what they offered to help me take advantage of opportunities in my business. They helped me improve communications, quality, or product flow essentially at no cost. Those are the kinds of things that make my job more efficient and drive cost out of my business.

■ I had a gear manufacturer, and I called and said we'd lost a bunch of gears, and this manufacturer ran their systems over the weekend and changed their manufacturing process in order to meet my needs. That was an extraordinary example of customer service. I haven't forgotten it, and this was twenty years ago.

■ Actually, we've had a supplier who lost business in order to help us. They showed us ways to use less of the product, and they recommended that we use someone else because their product wasn't really what we needed. Then they found the right supplier for us. They were looking out for our best interests—and, in the long run, theirs, too.

■ We had a supplier several hours away, and we were really having issues on inventory and scheduling between the two plants, and we sat down and worked at the floor level, traded people, exchanged people, and saved a lot of money and split that evenly with the supplier. They were easy to do business with, even on the toughest issues. They would do whatever it took and change their process to make us both better.

■ After we award business to a supplier, the start-up portion is so important, and when they plan for execution and overkill it, that is delightful. In start-ups there are always issues, and when they plan for failures and have people there to handle the exceptions and resolve the problems, we are delighted. That goes a long way toward earning our trust. Often, our biggest headaches are start-ups. When they put all hands on deck, even when it's not justified, and have more trucks there than they need, that is fantastic and we can use them as examples in other markets.

■ We have one supplier partner in Houston who offered something fantastic. There are different technologies for achieving better fuel economies and engineering how you unload a trailer. This supplier offered to sit in a meeting with our other equipment suppliers and share engineering ideas so they could reach a consensus on how best to engineer the trailers to improve the equipment and build a world-class waste management trailer. They were willing to share their knowledge and work with their competitor suppliers to help us build the finest equipment. It showed how strongly they felt about our partnership. That will help them ensure long-term business with us.

■ They were always one step ahead of me. They proactively came in with insight into what was happening or what was going to happen in the marketplace. They had a well-thought-out recommended solution and action plan.

■ This supplier had frank discussions with us about what drives cost in their business. They told us what factors they were vulnerable to and couldn't control, so we could anticipate cost changes as we watched raw materials prices fluctuate.

■ We did not have metrics in place to measure a supplier's performance, so they established the right metrics and measured their own performance. That was extremely positive behavior.

■ They were great at anticipating our needs. They often thought of something before we did, or they came up with a solution to a problem before we even knew we had the problem. That was delightful. They worked hard to stay ahead of the game.[40]

No doubt you have had some of the same experiences with suppliers or sellers. Now and then, someone does something remarkable to serve you, or he or she behaves in ways that *always* distinguish him or her from others in the same business. By calling these acts *behavioral differentiation*, we are labeling something everyone has no doubt experienced as a consumer or a buyer in a business or other organization. Furthermore, it's common sense that when you are exceptionally well served, you tend to return to that place of business; conversely, when you are treated poorly or indifferently, you tend not to return. Why would you? The mystery is not that business-people don't instinctively understand positive and negative behaviors, but that *knowing the difference and knowing the effect on customers* they nonetheless sometimes act in ways that customers find manipulative, indifferent, unhelpful, guarded, dishonest, or blatantly self-serving. Yet it happens all the time.

We asked the purchasing executives in our survey whether suppliers' positive or negative behaviors had any effect on their decision to choose particular suppliers. Almost to a person, they said, "Absolutely." Dave Gabriel elaborated: "There is no question about it. In the end, human behavior is a very key element of any relationship. Behavior drives communication and trust, and without those you rarely get to root causes or business understanding about what each of you needs to be successful."[41]

Of course, even great behavior won't overcome a shoddy product, ineffective service, or an unjustifiably high price. Behavioral differentiation is not a substitute for other forms of business excellence. You must produce superb products or services, and you must do so at a competitive price. However, when product and price are relatively equal, behavior can make the contract-award-winning difference. As one purchasing director indicated: "If all you can do is offer low price, that's not enough for us. Offering price is often the easiest thing, but there's a whole lot more you can offer customers."[42]

In the past century, there have been dramatic shifts in the approaches to and methodologies of selling, although many writers of books on selling today continue to promote outworn techniques that may have worked in simpler times but are inappropriate and ineffective in today's complex business organizations with their professional purchasing staffs and institutional uses of supply chain management. Today, the ethos and practices of selling are much closer to those of professional services firms than they are to the sales force models that were dominant in large commercial businesses in the years following World War II. To be effective today, people engaged in business development must be as smart and well educated as the supply chain management professionals they are dealing with, and in this age of commoditization, they must know how to use behavior, not price, as a primary source of differentiation.

CHALLENGES FOR READERS

1. We argue in this chapter that purchasing is becoming more professional and that supply chain management techniques are trans-

forming how buying and selling are done in the B2B business environment. This evolution will be more advanced in some industries than in others, although eventually this movement is likely to transform all B2B commerce. How is it in your industry? How have B2B buying and selling changed in the past twenty years? What are the implications for your business?

2. Who in your organization is responsible for business development? How savvy are they about supply chain management concepts, tools, and techniques? To what extent are they able to act as thought partners to your customers who have already embraced supply chain management?

3. Today, most purchasing executives want suppliers who are open with information, who are willing to discuss the cost drivers in their business, who are innovative and proactive about bringing new ideas forward, and who are candid about communicating issues and problems. To what extent does your company do this? Candidly, do you think of yourselves as supplier partners? Or are you still in the mind-set of producing and selling products?

4. In this chapter, we identified a number of positive and negative differentiating behaviors. Review those sections and do a candid self-evaluation. How often do you behave toward customers in ways that reflect the positive differentiating behaviors? And how often do you or your people behave in negative ways? Have you been known to overcommit and underdeliver? Do you do only what's stipulated in the contract and pull out the contract to resolve issues? Do you try to go around the purchasing agents and sell directly to the "C-level decision-makers"? Do you still have glad-handing salespeople taking customers to ball games but adding no other value? Or are you delighting customers by helping them take costs out of their business, sharing ideas and people, and doing whatever it takes to look out for them?

CHAPTER 3

The Chemistry of Preference

Today's market works to render the technologies and services we sell as commodities. This drives prices downward. Unfortunately, the market doesn't realize that in doing what seems best for survival, it is actually killing itself. If it rejects anything but lowest price as a differentiator, over time, the finest providers will disappear. The marketplace will then have nothing left to choose from but the lowest bidder, who in almost every sense represents the highest risk for the customer. Thus, we are constantly challenged to re-differentiate our product and ourselves and improve on the presentation of our differentiators.—Jean-Pierre Jacks, Commercial Vice President, Kellogg Brown & Root

∎

Behavior is playing a greater role in our efforts to differentiate ourselves. It is the last—and the only truly unique—standard from which our clients can differentiate us from the competition. It has become, and will be even more so in the future, the way we will win new work.—Dennis Norvet, Centex Construction Company

In the B2B business environment today, the challenge you face depends to a large extent on whether you already have a relationship with a customer and, if so, how strong that relationship is. In the best of cases, you are a partner supplier, an integral and trusted part of the customer's supply chain. You are working closely to understand the needs of the ultimate consumer of your customer's products or services, you are jointly innovating throughout the existing and future product line, and you are working together to take costs out of the supply chain and share in the savings.

In this best situation, your challenges are to delight the customer continuously through quality products delivered as promised, to respond vigorously to problems and opportunities, to be highly responsive and communicative, and to work at every level throughout your company to maintain a trusted and close relationship. In short, you have to behave exceptionally well as a partner supplier and resist the temptation to assume that you can put the relationship on autopilot, assign your best resources elsewhere, or do any of the myriad of things companies do when they start taking key customers for granted.

However, for most companies, these kinds of key customer relationships represent only a small portion of their overall customer and opportunity portfolio (although, following the Pareto principle,* they may represent a significant amount of revenue). Much of their business activity focuses on finding new opportunities, building new relationships, and developing new business. In new business development, the challenges are quite different. When you have an existing partner relationship, you have already created chemistry with the customer. You have worked through any relationship issues and have built trust, credibility, and compatibility. You can't rest on your laurels, of course, because chemistry, like everything else, loses its potency over time unless you do something to renew it. However, in building new customer relationships, the chemistry must be created, sometimes from nothing. This is why it is considerably easier, less costly, and less time-consuming to get new business with an existing customer than it is to get new business with a new customer.†

In building chemistry, we are striving to forge *connections* with customers that will cause them to *prefer* to work with us. When they have needs to fill and have choices among the suppliers who can fulfill those needs, and when our competitors offer roughly the same things we do at roughly the same price, we want customers to choose us because they *prefer* to work with us. Conventional wisdom would tell us that we need to build strong relationships with customers and that those relationships are the key to chemistry. Unfortunately, it's not that simple because our competitors are also trying to build strong relationships with the same customers. As we said in Chapter 1, *everybody* today knows about relationship selling. Relationships

---

*Applied to sales, the Pareto principle states that 80 percent of your revenue comes from 20 percent of your customers.
†According to conventional wisdom, it is four times more costly and time-consuming to get new business from new customers than it is to get new business from existing customers.

alone are not enough to build powerful preference. Today, you also have to *outbehave* your competitors throughout the business development process. An example will illustrate this point.

Outbehaving the Competition

During the summer of 2001, Danny Hicks worked for a large engineering company, Anontus Engineering Group, and was involved in Anontus's effort to win a contract with an estimated value of $40 million per year to manage and execute the small capital, supplemental maintenance, and turnaround work at four U.S. refineries owned by one of the major oil companies, which we will call Global Oil. Previously, such work had been done by a variety of different local contractors, but the president of Global's downstream North America division believed that having a master agreement with one supplier had potential for superior results. It would enable Global to create shared savings and improve operating efficiency. So, in the spring of 2000, he commissioned a study led by the maintenance management of the four sites. The study concluded that by implementing some form of multisite, single supplier alliance for field services could result in significant cost and efficiency improvements. Based on this recommendation, in December 2000, he assembled a six-man team consisting of representatives from the business units and a program manager.[1]

This selection team began by reviewing all contractors that Global Oil had worked with in the past and would consider working with in the future. Their criteria for including contractors in their initial set of potential partners were compatibility with Global Oil's core values, ability to perform the work within the cost parameters, relevant corporate experience, and people with the right skills who were located near Global's refineries. As shown in Figure 3-1, they initially identified twenty-two contractors who they felt could perform the contract satisfactorily. Then they began the winnowing process that would lead to the winner.

To narrow the field, Global's selection team released an RFI (request for information) to all twenty-two contractors. Responses to this RFI enabled the team to eliminate thirteen contractors who either did not meet the initial criteria or whose responses were considered

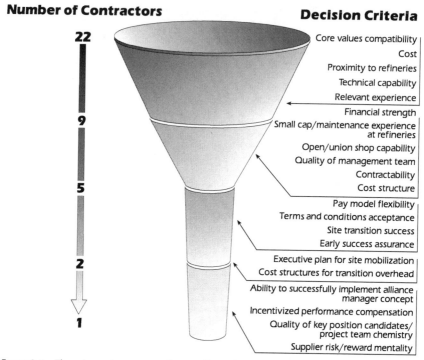

Number of Contractors   **Decision Criteria**

22 — Core values compatibility / Cost / Proximity to refineries / Technical capability / Relevant experience

9 — Financial strength / Small cap/maintenance experience at refineries / Open/union shop capability / Quality of management team / Contractability / Cost structure

5 — Pay model flexibility / Terms and conditions acceptance / Site transition success / Early success assurance

2 — Executive plan for site mobilization / Cost structures for transition overhead / Ability to successfully implement alliance manager concept / Incentivized performance compensation / Quality of key position candidates/project team chemistry / Supplier risk/reward mentality

1

FIGURE 3-1. The winnowing process in supplier selection. Most B2B supplier selection processes are like this funnel. Most potential suppliers are eliminated early for technical and cost reasons. However, the suppliers who remain at the end are evaluated primarily on their behavior.

inadequate for a number of reasons, such as failure to provide the information requested. This is a particularly egregious error in the bidding process because it suggests that those bidders really don't want the business. If that's true, one wonders why they bothered to respond at all. How potential suppliers respond to an RFI is the first evidence customers have of how those suppliers will behave if they get the contract. So it's important for suppliers to behave well (i.e., thorough, professional, responsive, compliant, committed, and enthusiastic) right from the beginning of a response to a new business opportunity. As in this case, suppliers who behave poorly at this point will probably not get a chance to redeem themselves. Other potential contractors were eliminated because of safety records that did not meet Global's standards, their inability to service all of the sites, a misalignment between their core business and Global's needs, or a mismatch between their company size and the size of the contract.

So, after the first round of RFI responses, the selection team had narrowed the field to nine contractors who would be suitable from a technical and general experience perspective and who were likely to have fees within the competitive range. Clearly, there were still too many potential providers at this point, so the team conducted a more in-depth evaluation, which required about another three months. As Figure 3-1 shows, the criteria now included the contractor's financial strength, corporate small capital project and maintenance experience at refineries, their ability to work open shop (nonunion) as well as union shop, quality of the management team, ability to reach contract terms easily, and cost structure. The last criterion was especially important because Global Oil sought to avoid "hidden margins" by finding contractors who would be open about their people costs (salaries, benefits, training, vacations, etc.) as well as overhead. Suppliers who are not open about their cost structure sometimes try to hide margin in other costs. Global Oil wanted complete transparency but was willing to pay for performance based on that open book.

In the refining business, companies subscribe to a benchmarking process from Solomon and Associates, which rates refinery performance from 1 (best in class) to 4 (worst). Global Oil's goal was to drive its refineries to 1s and 2s, and it wanted a supplier partner who was willing to put some fee at risk if that goal was not achieved. The quid pro quo was that Global would agree to process improvement changes the contractor recommended, and vice versa. Furthermore, Global sought a partner whose values would be aligned with its own. In many buyer-supplier service relationships, there is an inherent conflict of interests. Global's goal, like that of all buyers, was to reduce the number of man-hours required to perform the work while maximizing performance. Most suppliers, on the other hand, strive to maximize the number of man-hours (and hence their fee). Global wanted a partner who would share its goals, accept the Solomon benchmarking challenge, and be transparent about its cost structure so the risk-reward equation on both sides was clear. In short, what Global wanted was the kind of supply chain management relationship we described in Chapter 2.

This round of evaluations eliminated four more contenders. Some were dropped because an in-depth examination revealed discrepancies between what they claimed and what Global Oil thought it could actually deliver. To assess the remaining five contractors, Global's selection team released another RFI. This time, it probed each contractor's willingness to accept differing pay models and contract terms and conditions, their record of successful site transitions, and their procedures and processes for ensuring early success once on site. As the selection team finished this round of evaluations, it became clear that there were two serious contenders, Anontus Engineering Group and one other key competitor—one of the largest engineering and construction firms in the world, a formidable rival.

During this final round, Danny Hicks became centrally involved in the contract pursuit. Previously, someone else had been managing Anontus's pursuit team, but it was becoming more apparent that this person did not have the degree of chemistry with Global's key people that would be required to win the contract. So Danny Hicks was assigned to lead the team down the homestretch, *assuming* he could build the requisite degree of chemistry. Significantly, his title was "alliance manager" and that's how he was introduced to the customer.

Anontus views major clients with multiple business units as alliances and assigns *alliance managers* to build and maintain these relationships. The goal is to stimulate mutual continuous growth through continuous improvement with Anontus and its clients sharing the responsibility and benefits of making it happen. If an alliance manager does not have good chemistry with a key client, then that person is replaced. It's not necessarily a stigma to be replaced—everyone understands that chemistry is something of a mysterious connection between people, and you can't always predict who will have good client chemistry and who won't. We will have more to say about this in Chapter 7. For now, what is important is that Danny Hicks was the right solution for the people at Global Oil. They felt entirely comfortable with him, and vice versa.

So at this point in Anontus's pursuit of this contract, the field had been narrowed to two key contenders. As shown on Figure 3-1, Global's selection team now asked the two remaining suppliers to submit an execution plan for site mobilization. It wanted the suppliers' ideas on the order all four sites would be transitioned, how many current employees could be expected to be retained, how union issues would be resolved, what the cost structure would be for the overhead required to transition all four sites in nine months, and their capability to enact an OCIP (owner-controlled insurance program). This last point was a significant cost issue for Global. Contractors with stellar safety records would enable Global to lower its risk and insurance rates; contractors with mediocre safety records would increase risk and rates. Sometimes, even small differences in safety records can make a meaningful difference in the rates owners pay for insurance.

Although the technical content was critical at this stage, more important was Global's comfort with the supplier it chose to partner with because both of the remaining contenders were equally well qualified. In the end, the degree to which Anontus was able to successfully implement its alliance manager concept was one of the primary reasons Anontus won the contract. According to one of the Global decision-makers, the decision was based on a qualitative assessment of current active contracts, both alliance and nonalliance models of each competitor, an assessment of real results from actual safety improvement processes that seek to continuously improve site safety performance, Anontus's experience with compensation that is incentivized for performance, the quality of key position candidates, and the perceived risk and reward mentality of each potential supplier. Quantitatively, projections of cost over a theoretical year were projected and compared. Global was very uncomfortable with Anontus's initial alliance manager candidate but was delighted with Danny Hicks and the team he and Anontus assembled. In the end, the award to Anontus was based on significant study and a broad evaluation of both quantitative and qualitative criteria that were weighted and measured. We can learn a number of important lessons from this example:

- In B2B buying and selling, most large contracts come about through a process like the one described. It is common for buyers to begin by identifying a large number of potential suppliers and, through a process of RFIs, RFPs (request for proposal), or RFQs (request for qualifications), narrowing the range of suppliers to the serious contenders, which are normally no more than two or three.

- As Figure 3-1 illustrates, the criteria at the top of the funnel tend to be broad. Think of them as a coarse filter. The first pass through a large set of potential suppliers is not intended to find the best contractor; it's intended to eliminate the most unsuitable from further consideration. At each stage in this winnowing process, the filters become finer and finer.

■ Cost is an important consideration throughout, but notice how the nature of the cost issue changes. Initially, cost is used as the basis for eliminating suppliers whose costs are clearly out of line with the budget or who have not shown good cost control discipline in previous contracts. In semifinal and final evaluations, the issues shift to the degree of supplier openness about cost structure and the supplier's willingness to accept contract terms that are acceptable and beneficial to the buyer (and, ideally, the supplier, but this is not always the case).

■ Technical evaluation criteria are usually important only at the coarse level of evaluation. Once customers eliminate those suppliers who are clearly not technically qualified, they assume that the remaining contenders can do the job.

■ The most important criteria in the final stages of selection are behavioral. *If you take away nothing else from this book, you should remember this vital lesson.* In the endgame of supplier selection, *every* supplier still in contention is acceptable from both a technical and cost standpoint. The final decision is therefore based on which supplier the customer prefers, and preference is based on confidence, trust, and chemistry, which themselves are products of the supplier's *behavior.*

Throughout the pursuit, we did everything we said we would do. We never broke a promise. It was tough to put quality people in 25 positions, but we did everything possible to achieve that goal. And something like this doesn't happen overnight. It was a 2–3 year process, including identifying mistakes and correcting them. All four of the original site managers never made it past the first year, but we brought in the best available people to bring the project to completion, which they did. Global Oil had to change, too, and they did.—Danny Hicks

In this case, Anontus's superior behavior was worth an annual $40 million contract and an alliance relationship with a major oil company that could extend to other contracts and other parts of its business over time. The value of the relationship itself is hard to quantify, but if Anontus performs well on this contract, it will establish a preferred-supplier position in future opportunities with Global Oil. Finally, and this is the critical point—*there must be alignment between what the sales or business development people in a company represent to customers and what the company actually delivers.* Otherwise, as Global Oil's program manager told us, buyers will continue their process of churning through contractor after contractor. Needless to say, *walking your talk* is a crucial behavior, and many companies don't do it. Those that do give themselves a considerable behavioral advantage.

The Principles of Behavioral Differentiation

When all else is equal, how do B2B customers choose between competing suppliers? As we have shown above and in our previous book, *Winning Behavior*, when competing suppliers offer essentially the same technical skills, experience, solutions, and price, behavior becomes the most important factor in the customer's selection decision—and this is happening with greater frequency today as competing companies become more and more alike. In one of the epigrams that opened this chapter, Jean-Pierre Jacks of KBR said that today's market works to render the technologies and services his company and its rivals sell as commodities. Because competing suppliers look very much alike and offer fundamentally the same products, services, and advantages at much the same price, the customer's final selection decision will not be driven by the question, "Can you do the work?" That question has already been answered. The customer's key question now is, "Do we want to work with you?" and the answer, positive or negative, will reside in what the customer has observed in each finalist's behaviors.

Consequently, once you have passed the first hurdles in pursuit of a new business opportunity and are technically, contractually, and financially acceptable to a customer, the greatest potential you have for creating a competitive advantage and winning the work is to *outbehave* your competitors. Furthermore, as we show in the rest of this book, *you should be building that behavioral advantage throughout the entire business development process.*

This process begins before you even start contacting customers. It begins with market positioning and communication that influence how potential customers think of you, and it ends with proposal development, presentations, and contract negotiations if you win the work. Before exploring this process further, we discuss the fundamental principles of behavioral differentiation:

1. *Behavior that differentiates is, by definition, beyond what people normally experience.* We are using the term *behavior* in its broadest sense: "the manner of conducting oneself." To *behave* means "to act, function, or react in a particular way."[2] In every interaction customers have with someone in your company, they are experiencing and observing how you conduct yourself. Those interactions include face-to-face meetings, telephone calls, e-mail messages, faxes, advertisements, product installations and service, shipments and deliveries, invoices, executive lunches, sales calls, proposals, product demonstrations, maintenance, and inspections. We refer to these events as touch points.

In each of these touch points, the person representing your company makes behavioral decisions, often unconscious, including how he or she greets customers, listens to them, answers their questions, shows them options, explains something, handles a problem or complaint, addresses a need, gathers information, challenges a perspective, solves a problem, communicates, handles conflict, and tries to influence customers. The choices your people make can reflect courtesy, respect, helpfulness, and professionalism; indifference, apathy, and benign neglect; or disdain, rudeness, and outright hostility.

As a buyer of goods and services, you have no doubt experienced each of these behaviors from time to time. Most of our experiences with sellers are undifferentiated, which means that they behave the way sellers normally behave. Sometimes, however, sellers behave in ways that are noticeably better or worse than what we normally experience. These memorable behaviors can differentiate sellers and lead us to conclude that these sellers are either better to work with or worse. The key point here is that behavior does not differentiate sellers unless it is beyond what we, as buyers, *normally* experience. Some people and some companies (like Edward Jones, Marshall Field's, Nordstrom, Ritz-Carlton, Adobe Systems, Harley-Davidson, Volvo Cars, and EMC) have been able to *outbehave* their competitors so consistently that they have created behavioral differentiation in their markets.

2. Behavior can differentiate both positively and negatively. As Figure 3-2 illustrates, behavior that negatively differentiates (the left wing of the bell curve) has a *repulsive* effect on customers. When sellers behave so badly that customers take notice, customers will prefer not to buy from that seller again and will choose other suppliers if they can. Moreover, customers who are treated badly sometimes strike back at sellers by advising other customers not to buy from that seller and even actively campaigning against the seller. Conversely, behavior that positively differentiates (the right wing on Figure 3-2) has an *attractive* effect on customers. It causes customers to prefer to buy from that seller again, so it builds customer loyalty, referrals, and repeat business. In *Winning Behavior*, we offered numerous examples of positively and negatively differentiated behaviors in a range of industries.

3. Behavioral differentiation applies to employees as well as customers. Companies that excel at external behavioral differentiation are generally also excellent at internal BD. They treat their employees exceptionally well. It stands to reason that employees who are well treated will be more motivated to treat customers well, and this commonsense assumption is reflected in the fact that so many of the companies that excel at behavioral differentiation appear in *Fortune's* annual lists of Most Admired Companies and Best Companies to Work For.

Behavioral differentiation is not a customer service gimmick. It

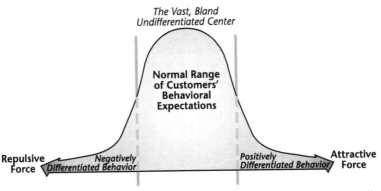

FIGURE 3-2. Behavioral differentiation bell curve. The behaviors customers normally experience from sellers fall into the middle hump of the curve and do not differentiate. Behaviors at each extreme, however, are one or more standard deviations from the norm and will have a differentiated impact on customers, either positively or negatively.

arises from shared values about the importance of people, shared attitudes about how people should be treated, and behaviors throughout the organization that reflect these beliefs. Southwest Airlines has been able to sustain its behavioral differentiation for three decades because the company's leadership is deeply committed to its people as well as its customers. In contrast, Enron collapsed in part because its leaders created a cutthroat culture that devalued people, treating employees and customers as objects to be used rather than assets to be respected and nurtured.

4. *You are onstage with your employees and customers all the time.*
This is a critical lesson. There are no time-outs. *Everything* you do or say creates a behavioral impression that the stakeholders in your business, including your customers, use to compare you to your competitors and other organizations they have worked with or been part of. Imagine that your company's business model is complicated and customers are not sure who to call to resolve an issue. A customer named Joe calls your company, is put on hold, and is then transferred to the wrong person. At this touch point, you have just created a negative behavioral impression. Imagine that Joe now calls your key competitor, which has a simpler, easily understandable business model and an excellent process for handling customer inquiries. Joe is sent to the right person, gets the information he needs very quickly, and later receives a follow-up call from the person he spoke to, as well as an invitation to a free seminar the competitor is sponsoring on the matter in question. In this example, your competitor has behaviorally differentiated itself from you and put you at a competitive disadvantage with this particular customer, no matter whom Joe works for in the future—because Joe will take his biases and impressions with him.

Now add the behavioral impressions you create at hundreds or thousands of other customer touch points every day. The plain fact is that your business fortunes will rise or fall based on how your employees behave toward your customers *every* day and in *every* interaction. Individual behaviors may not have much overall impact on your business, although sometimes a single negative act can cost you not only a particular contract but the entire business relationship. However, the cumulative impact of your employees' behavior toward customers will always be reflected in your top- and bottom-line performance. That's why it's important to manage how your people behave and to consider behavior an important strategic business asset (or liability, if your employees routinely behave badly or indifferently toward customers).

> ♛ Goodwill is the only asset that competition cannot undersell or destroy. —*Marshall Field*

5. *Your behavior is the truest expression of your attitudes and beliefs. You are how you behave, and you behave how you are.* Many companies claim that customers come first, that they are relationship oriented, that they value people, and so on, but their behavior often does not reflect those ideals. No matter what you say, your behavior communicates what you actually believe. If you say that you'll stand by your customers, then when they lose a critical shipment of gear assemblies, you will open your plant on an emergency basis and drive through the night to get the parts to customers when they need them. If your senior managers claim that they value customers, then they will spend more of their time with customers than they do in their offices. However, we have known senior managers who made that claim but rarely left their offices. And we've seen suppliers who claim they are easy to work with but won't itemize their invoices or provide information in the form that is easiest for customers to use.

It's common for people and companies to express lofty ideals, especially during the selling process. After all, everyone wants to make a good impression. But your behavior communicates what you really think of customers, what you consider important, and whether you really want their business. Moreover, the difference between your espoused values and your values in action will almost always be evident to your employees and customers. You may fool *all* the people *some* of the time, as Abraham Lincoln said in his debates with rival Stephen A. Douglas, you can even fool *some* of the people *all* the time, but you can't fool *all* of the people *all* the time. Invariably, the truth about your attitudes toward customers will be reflected in your behavior, no matter what you claim.

6. *To customers, your person currently interacting with them* is *your company.* Some customers may make the distinction between the organization and its representatives, but most won't. They will consider the treatment they are currently receiving from a company's employee to be emblematic of how that company treats customers. As they interact with more employees of the same company, they will develop more individualized impressions (as in "Ellen is more responsive and better to work with than John"), and then their cumulative impression of employee behavior will create their institutional impression. The bottom line is that every employee is a symbol of his or her company's attitudes toward customers, so if you are going to behaviorally differentiate your company, you must find ways to help each employee differentiate himself or herself while interacting with customers.

7. Your behavior is the strongest component in customers' percep- tions of you. As we researched customers' perceptions of suppliers, we learned that more than 90 percent of these perceptions are based not only on the quality or features of the product or service they buy but on the supplier's behavior toward them. Common sense would suggest that this applies more in the B2C (business-to-consumer) world than in B2B, but it's not true. Remember that nearly all of the purchasing executives we surveyed said that supplier behavior absolutely makes a difference in which suppliers they choose to partner with.

8. You can manage behavioral differentiation. A final important lesson about BD is that it can be managed. In fact, if you don't manage it carefully, it's not likely to occur. Most people, most of the time, will behave within the vast, bland, undifferentiated middle hump of the bell curve shown in Figure 3-2. To differentiate yourself positively, you must ensure that the people in your company consistently treat customers in ways that are significantly better than the way your competitors treat them. In *Winning Behavior*, we argued that there are three drivers of BD: leadership, culture, and process.

To create and sustain behavioral differentiation, you need leaders who understand the value and importance of positive BD, a culture that supports and encourages superior behaviors, and processes that both permit and reinforce superior behaviors throughout your day-to-day interactions with customers. The important lesson here is that BD is not the result of serendipity; it is the result of vigorous and sustained leadership of the kind that Horst Schulze brought to Ritz-Carlton, that George Zimmer brought to Men's Wearhouse, and Herb Kelleher brought to Southwest Airlines.

The Four Types of Behavioral Differentiation

There are four ways in which companies can differentiate themselves behaviorally: operational, interpersonal, exceptional, and symbolic. The workhorse of these types is *operational*, which occurs when companies implement policies, procedures, or processes that result in superior customer behavior as part of their normal, ongoing operations. When companies create standard practices that result in positively differentiating behavior, they set a new standard, as Disney has with Disneyland and its other theme parks. The company has gone to extraordinary lengths to hire the right people as park employees (called "cast members") and train them to provide a magical experience for all park guests.[3] Disney's customer service procedures raised the bar on service throughout the entertainment and hospitality industry. Similarly, Anontus Engineering Group's alliance manager concept, which it uses for all key, multinational clients, has raised the bar on customer relationship management throughout the engineering and construction industry.

One of the most powerful and lasting ways to compete is not to just go head-to-head with your competitors. When you have powerful, competent competitors, that's a tough way to win. Instead, compete by raising your customer's and the market's expectations. When you behave in ways that they—customers and markets—value, they will expect *all* companies in your industry to behave the same way. When your rivals don't, you have raised the bar and differentiated yourself successfully by outbehaving the competition.

Interpersonal BD is based on individual employees' emotional intelligence and relational skills with others. Some people are naturally outgoing and empathetic and are disposed to treat others warmly and respectfully. These people often distinguish themselves with customers because their personal interactions are so warm and engaging. Other people are naturally sour, disengaged, unempathetic, and inclined to be discourteous. They generally create a negative behavioral impression and are the types of employees you either don't want in your company or don't want in positions with significant customer contact. Despite people's personalities and predispositions, everyone can learn to behave in ways that are more interpersonally engaging, and the smartest companies therefore teach people how to interact with customers and manage those interactions carefully. Clearly, the best of both worlds is to hire people who are already inclined to be friendly and helpful, who have a service mind-set and disposition, and then to establish operational norms and training that result in positive behaviors with customers, and this is what the smartest companies do. Southwest Airlines, Ritz-Carlton, Nordstrom, Hall Kinion, and other companies that excel at BD hire people for their attitudes and inherent interpersonal skill and then train them in the other skills they need for their jobs.

Exceptional BD occurs when employees "break the rules" and do something for customers that is clearly beyond what customers would normally expect and beyond what the company normally does for customers. Companies promote this kind of behavior by encouraging employees to "break the rules." In other words, they reward exceptional treatment of customers by "relaxing" the rules that normally govern the kind of service customers receive and by giving employees the latitude and responsibility to decide for themselves when the rules should be broken. Jane, for example, might spend $1,800 and fly halfway across the country to hand deliver a product sample a customer needs for a meeting the next day. Her company would probably not encourage her to do this as a rule but would forgive her doing it (indeed, *expect* her to do it) on those occasions when an extraordinary gesture is the right thing to do. The cliché about "going the extra mile" applies to exceptional BD, and customers recognize when someone has clearly gone out of his or her way to do something special. The return on your investment when you do something exceptional for customers is incalculable in terms of customer loyalty, repeat business, and positive word of mouth as customers tell other potential customers or other people in their company what you did for them.

Finally, *symbolic* BD occurs when companies behave in ways that reflect either their own value proposition and product/service image or those of their customers. Harley-Davidson claims to be in the *experience* business, for instance, and the company supports the Harley Owners Group (H.O.G.) as a way of expressing and reinforcing that experience. It also sponsors numerous bike rallies and other events that capitalize on the image and spirit of one of America's best-known brands. More than half of Harley-Davidson employees own a Harley motorcycle, and many of them, including the executives, show up at Harley rallies wearing their black "leathers." The company's designers, marketers, executives, and other employees understand that their product is not a motorcycle but a lifestyle, and their behavior as a corporation reflects that lifestyle.

The four types of BD often work together to produce a cumulative effect that delights customers. Ritz-Carlton, for example, has numerous procedures and guidelines for making guests' experiences delightful, and this is operational BD. It also hires people who are likely to have good interpersonal skills and be outgoing and accommodating by nature. Consequently, in its hiring and training programs, it is creating the likelihood that Ritz-Carlton employees will behave in ways that differentiate them interpersonally from employees of other hotels. The company also empowers employees to "break the rules" whenever guests have problems or need help, which encourages employees to behave in exceptional ways. Finally, the hotel is very self-conscious about the image it conveys. Everything in a Ritz-Carlton hotel is intended to convey elegance, good taste, and refined breeding, including the Ritz-Carlton motto: "We are ladies and gentlemen serving ladies and gentlemen."[4]

Creating Preference

One of the best ways to create preference is to perform exceptionally well for a current customer. The operative word in this sentence is *exceptionally* because if you merely do a *good* job you risk being replaced by competitors whose promises are more compelling than your performance. It's the difference between customer *satisfaction* and customer *delight*. The former is expected and tends to elicit a rational response from customers when asked the question, "Did Supplier X satisfy you?"

"Yes, they did what we asked," one can imagine a customer saying. "They met our needs. We are satisfied with their performance." Customers determine satisfaction by comparing their requirements with your results. This is a logical process, and the results will be measured, documented, and reported. Executives will be briefed. While it is gratifying on the one hand to satisfy the customer, there is, on the other hand, something cold and clinical about it.

However, when you *delight* customers, you evoke an emotional response. The expression *customer delight* may be overused today, but it does signify an important difference between delight and mere *satisfaction.* Delight means "a high degree of gratification" or "something that gives great pleasure." There's nothing cold and clinical about this. Delighted clients spread the word, and they do it with conviction and enthusiasm. Delight is a powerful feeling, one that customers want to experience again, so they are reluctant to part with a supplier that delights them. How do you do it?

■ By delivering exceptional quality consistently and perhaps earlier than they expected

■ By anticipating problems and preventing them before they occur

■ By owning the problems that do occur and resolving them quickly and at little cost to the customer

■ By being consistently responsive, available, and communicative

■ By caring about customers, not just their business

■ By adding value without adding cost

> ♛ *The thing that gets to me quickest is when suppliers make commitments and then don't fulfill them, when they say they will meet with us at 2:00 and then don't show up. That alone will be a reason for changing suppliers. It's inconceivable. It sends the message that we are not important. It's time wasted for us. We have limited resources and have to make the best use of our time.—Joan Selleck, Associate Director of Materials, Nikon Precision*

In short, you do the types of things our purchasing survey respondents noted when they talked about what happened when suppliers did an exceptional job for them. It would be naïve to assume that if you perform well on existing contracts, a pathway to a pot of gold will magically open up before you, but excellence in execution is a strong confidence builder. If you are already working with a customer, nothing builds preference more than performing exceptionally well on your current contracts. Conversely, nothing will destroy your position faster than performing poorly. So performing well is good for incumbents. In fact, research Lore conducted for two large companies showed that incumbents who were performing well on existing contracts were more than four times more likely to win follow-on contracts than their nonincumbent competitors.

What if you aren't currently working for customers and have no history with them? What if you are an unknown? Then you need excellent references from sources they trust and respect. But even that will not entirely eliminate the risk they assume in awarding contracts to unknown and untested suppliers. Your credentials and experience still amount to a promise of future benefits, and customers will always be somewhat wary until you have proved yourself in their company. You can make up a lot of ground, however, by differentiating yourself through your behavior. If you are not the incumbent, then in some ways you have an advantage, especially if the incumbent has become lazy and has started taking the customer for granted. Then, even if you are less known than the incumbent, you can become the greener grass on the other side of the fence, and if you can differentiate yourself behaviorally, you can often make a compelling case for switching from the incumbent to you. We've seen it happen hundreds of times.

Everyone tries to create preference. Getting others to prefer you is so ingrained in human behavior that it would be difficult to imagine life without it. We learn it as children, experience it in every aspect of our lives, and understand it as one of the most operational aspects of competition. It's the entire purpose of dating and courtship. We want to find that magical connection—that chemistry—that binds us together. Among all possible suitors for the partner we want, we try to create a bias in our favor. In competitive bidding, as in dating, creating preference comes down to four things: building the right relationships, performing well, telling a compelling story, and behaving in ways that differentiate us from our competitors. Throughout the remainder of this book, we explore how successful businesses do these four things.

In Chapter 1, we noted that Edward K. Strong's *The Psychology of Selling Life Insurance* (1922) was the first academic study of the selling process. He was the first author to apply behavioral psychology to the selling process. In that book, Strong also made the interesting observation that selling is like playing chess. "The salesman has the white pieces and makes the first move," Strong argues. "Thereafter there is an alternation of moves between him and the prospect. If the salesman *keeps the lead* (the attack), he is likely to win. But, if he loses the attack, the chances are against his being able to recover his former advantage and to secure the coveted signature."[5] Furthermore, having a strategy and planning many moves in advance is essential: "The chess player who plans merely move by move may play a good game, but he will lose nearly every time to the player who *sees several plays ahead.*"[6]

Strong was writing about selling long before today's complex organizations, with their purchasing professionals, supply chain managers, Web-based reverse auctions, and other advances that have changed the world of selling dramatically, but he was correct in equating the selling process with chess. As we see in Chapter 4, no matter how complicated selling has become or how much it has changed since Strong's day, it is still very much like playing a game of chess.

CHALLENGES FOR READERS

1. Danny Hicks and Anontus Engineering Group were able to *outbehave* their key competitor and win a close $40 million competition. Think about your own opportunity pursuits. Why have you won or lost? To what extent is behavior a factor?

2. Anontus Engineering Group distinguishes itself by assigning "alliance managers" to manage large opportunity pursuits and key client relationships. In this era of supply chain management, this is a clever idea. However, Anontus can do it only because it genuinely reflects several of its core values. What do you do that is similar? What could you do?

3. You are onstage all the time with your customers. There are no time-outs. Moreover, to your customers, your employee who is currently interacting with them *is* your company. What are you doing to ensure that your employees behave exceptionally well in every customer interaction?

4. There are four types of behavioral differentiation: operational, interpersonal, exceptional, and symbolic. Do people in your company embody all four types of BD? Consistently? Do you have standard procedures that result in BD? Do you hire and train employees who are likely to be interpersonally excellent? Do you enable employees to "break the rules" and do exceptional things for customers now and then? Do your behaviors reflect your messages? In short, do you set a new standard, show that you care, break the rules, and walk the talk? Where are your biggest opportunities for improvement?

5. How effective are people in your company at building preference? Think about some customer relationships that have gone extremely well and some that have gone poorly. To what extent was good or bad chemistry a factor in those outcomes? What could you do to ensure that your people have good chemistry with their counterparts in customer organizations?

CHAPTER 4

Checkmate! How Business Development Is Like Chess

> *A well-known Grandmaster once said, "If I lose a game, my opponents have to beat me three times: they have to beat me in the opening, then they have to beat me in the middlegame, and finally they have to play a perfect endgame."—Jeremy Silman,* Complete Book of Chess Strategy
>
> ■
>
> *Like Sun Tzu's Age of the Warring States, today's business world is one of continual conflict between companies as they strive for survival and success across the globe. Faced with scarce and expensive resources and an ever-changing environment, competitors seek even the slightest advantage.—Mark R. McNeilly,* Sun Tzu and the Art of Business: Six Strategic Principles for Managers

In war and business, opponents compete for supremacy in a defined space using rules everyone understands, disguising their own intentions while striving to discern their opponent's, maneuvering their forces to gain advantage, and acting decisively when presented with an opportunity. Numerous authors have drawn parallels between war and business. In the last decade alone, more than a dozen books have been published that examine how Sun Tzu's 2,500-year-old principles in *The Art of War* can be applied to modern business strategies and tactics. As Donald G. Krause notes in *The Art of War for Executives*, "Warfare is one of the more common events in the history of man. Because of its importance to survival, warfare has been studied carefully. The factors that contribute to success in war are fairly well understood. Fundamentally, success in war, as well as in business, is based on leadership."[1] Moreover, as we said earlier, leadership drives the values and processes that individuals in an organization use to accomplish their aims. In its own way, this is also true of chess.

In its earliest incarnations, chess was a game of warfare, invented, some historians believe, to teach the principles of warfare to rulers. Though its precise origins are lost in the fog of time, chess was apparently invented in northern India in the sixth century A.D. Its precursor was a game called Chaturanga, which featured four players, each controlling one army. Pairs of players worked together to defeat the opposing alliance, and victory or defeat depended on protecting the rajah and capturing the opposing armies' combatants. The other pieces in each army consisted of infantry, cavalry, elephants, chariots, and a counselor. Chaturanga used dice to determine which pieces were moved in each turn, so success depended as much on luck as skill. By around 600 A.D., however, Hindu law forbade gambling, so the dice were eliminated, the allied armies were combined, and a two-player form of the game emerged.

The game's migration—first to Persia, Greece, and Egypt; then east to China, Korea, and Japan; then west to Iberia and the rest of Europe—followed the paths of traders and the conquests of armies. As chess spread throughout medieval Europe, some pieces changed: The rajah became a king; elephants became bishops (symbolizing the church); chariots became castles (rooks); and the counselor, which had limited power, became the queen, which was imbued with the greatest mobility and power of all the pieces. Today, chess remains humankind's most venerable and challenging game of war. The thousands of varieties of chess pieces still symbolize opposing armies with their foot soldiers, cavalry, battlements, ministers, and heads of state (see Figure 4-1).

In chess and war, as well as in business, success derives from the astute application of both strategy and tactics. As Russian grand master Eugene A. Znosko-Borovsky said, "Chess is not played move by move, but in well-considered series of moves, which should meet all requirements, namely, freedom for the player, constraint for the adversary; proper timing of each individual move; use of the maximum power of each piece at all times."[2] That should sound familiar to strategic account managers who have ever spent months (or years) pursuing major contracts with important customers, marshalling their company's resources, and directing teams in the development of proposals and presentations.

FIGURE 4-1. Chess pieces. Chess piece design often symbolizes the game's origins in war.

B2B Business Development

In the B2B world,* purchasing of products, services, and supplies is generally accomplished through competitive bids and proposals, but there are numerous variations on this theme, including partnering arrangements; sole-source awards; online auctions; and a host of purchasing laws, regulations, requirements, or practices within buying companies that dictate how purchasing will be managed, how bids are solicited and evaluated, and who makes the buying decision. The *ideal* circumstance for most buyers is an efficient decision-making process where they can evaluate qualified providers objectively and make rational buying decisions. In the *real* world, these decisions are almost never as rational as buyers believe they are, nor as they present to the outside world, despite supply chain managers' attempts to make buying totally logical and fact based. As objective as buyers strive to be, they are invariably influenced by such factors as:

---

*For the sake of simplicity, we are focusing on B2B commerce and will not elaborate on B2G (business-to-government). We acknowledge that many businesses sell their products and services to local, state, federal, and foreign governments, which are among the largest customers in the world. However, the business development process we describe applies equally well to both B2B and B2G forms of commerce. Governments typically have much more formal purchasing requirements and regulations, but opening, middle, and endgame are characteristic of the business development process whether you sell to another business or to a government agency. You should try to use behavioral differentiation regardless of the type of customer you are serving.

EXCERPT FROM "THE MORALS OF CHESS"

Benjamin Franklin

The Game of Chess is not merely an idle amusement. Several very valuable qualities of the mind, useful in the course of human life, are to be acquired or strengthened by it, so as to become habits, ready on all occasions. For Life is a kind of Chess, in which we have often points to gain, and competitors or adversaries to contend with, and in which there is a vast variety of good and ill events, that are, in some degree, the effects of prudence or the want of it. By playing at chess, then, we may learn,

I. **Foresight,** *which looks a little into futurity, and considers the consequences that may attend an action; for it is continually occurring to the player, "If I move this piece, what will be the advantages of my new situation? What use can my adversary make of it to annoy me? What other moves can I make to support it, and to defend myself from his attacks?"*

II. **Circumspection,** *which surveys the whole chess-board, or scene of action, the relations of the several pieces and situations, the dangers they are respectively exposed to, the several possibilities of their aiding each other, the probabilities that the adversary may make this or that move, and attack this or the other piece; and what different means can be used to avoid his stroke, or turn its consequences against him.*

III. **Caution,** *not to make our moves too hastily. This habit is best acquired by observing strictly the laws of the game, such as, "If you touch a piece, you must move it somewhere; if you set it down, you must let it stand:" and it is therefore best that these rules should be observed, as the game thereby becomes more the image of human life, and particularly of war; in which, if you have incautiously put yourself into a bad and dangerous position, you cannot obtain your enemy's leave to withdraw your troops, and place them more securely, but you must abide all the consequences of your rashness.*

And, lastly, we learn by chess the habit of not being discouraged by present bad appearances in the state of our affairs, *the habit of* hoping for a favorable change, *and that of* persevering in the search of resources. *The game is so full of events, there is such a variety of turns in it, the fortune of it is so subject to sudden vicissitudes, and one so frequently, after contemplation, discovers the means of extricating one's self from a supposed insurmountable difficulty, that one is encouraged to continue the contest to the last, in hopes of victory by our own skill, or, at least, of giving a stale mate, by the negligence of our adversary.*

- Their subconscious biases formed by their exposure to the bidding companies' products, services, industry reputation, and advertising

- Their history with the bidding companies and their preconceptions about what they are likely to propose

- Their relationships (or lack thereof) with individuals in the bidding companies

- Their reactions to the bidding companies' initial efforts to respond to the buyer's needs

- Their strategic sourcing goals and priorities and their perception of suppliers' alignment with those goals

- Their impressions, perhaps subconscious, about what solution their management, other executives, users, or their team prefers

> *Formerly when great fortunes were only made in war, war was a business; but now when great fortunes are only made in business, business is war.—Christian Bovee*

It should be obvious from this list of buyer influence factors that the business development process in B2B companies does not begin with sales visits to potential customers or with requests for proposals. On the contrary, business development begins in a company's strategic and business planning phase, where executives are asking the most fundamental of questions:

- What business are we in? What value do we create?

- Who are our customers? Which segments of the market should we target?

- What are our objectives?

- What are our priorities? How should we be organized? How can we most efficiently create our products or services and bring them to the market?

■ How can we attract buyers? How can we best communicate our value? What are our core themes and messages to the marketplace?

■ How can we create competitive advantage? What are our competitors doing and how can we differentiate ourselves from them? How can we position ourselves in the markets we serve to generate and sustain an advantage?

The answers to these questions drive many decisions: which products and services the company will focus on; where in the value chain it will seek to create differentiation; how it will focus its market communications; and, ultimately, which specific customers it will target and how it will attempt to get those customers. In business, as well as in war and chess, strategy always drives tactics, and those early, big-picture decisions provide the direction and energy behind how the company tries to position itself with potential customers. Positioning is crucial, as any advertising agency executive will tell you, because it forms those predispositions and biases that subtly influence buyers, no matter how objective they try to be. If positioning weren't so crucial, then brand would have no asset value, but it does.

Indirect positioning occurs through advertising, trade shows, and other forms of marketing that reach the marketplace as a whole. Direct positioning occurs when sellers contact potential buyers, make sales calls, learn more about the buying company, build relationships with key people, and introduce their products and services. This positioning can occur before there are any specific sales opportunities. Once opportunities do arise, momentum builds rapidly—or should. Account managers begin a more focused pursuit—learning more about the customer's needs, meeting with others in the customer's organization, helping them think about how to solve their problems, and preselling the company's solutions. Sales managers track the opportunities, solicit top management's support, and bring in other company resources to help in the pursuit.

As we said earlier, in B2B business development the purchasing decisions are usually made through a bid and proposal process. At some point in the course of most opportunities, customers specify what they want and need and identify the companies that can supply it. They may or may not have worked with these companies previously. In some cases, they ask these companies to submit their qualifications, and they may narrow the field of possible suppliers following a review of each supplier's qualifications (or "quals," as they are often called). Later, customers write and release an RFP or some similar bid request document, which typically includes product or service specifications, criteria for evaluating suppliers, contract requirements, and guidance on how to prepare proposals. Once this RFP is released, suppliers generally have a response period ranging from a few days to a few months to prepare and submit their proposals.

After they evaluate the proposals, customers eliminate the suppliers they deem unacceptable—for technical, price, or other reasons—and create a shortlist of the suppliers who remain in contention. These suppliers are usually asked to present their proposal to a customer team, including the decision-maker and other advisors or members of the evaluation team. Customers already know what the short-listed suppliers are offering, so these presentations have little substantive purpose. They are primarily a chemistry test. In the customers' minds are these questions:

- Are you responsive? Are you answering our questions in ways that make us feel confident? Do you "get it" (including any elements of "it" not specifically discussed or specified in the RFP)?

- Can we trust you? Now that we're face-to-face with your team, do we like what we see?

- Do we want to work with you?

In the best of circumstances, suppliers pass the chemistry test and are awarded the contract. Then the cycle begins anew as they try to develop more business. At any one time in most major B2B companies, account managers and salespeople are at various points in the cycle with dozens and perhaps hundreds of prospective buyers. When they manage the process well, they can win more than their fair share of work. Managing the process well means understanding that the business development cycle has distinct phases, as does the game of chess.

The Three Phases of a Chess Game

Chess masters often speak of the game as having three phases: opening game, middle game, and endgame. Opening game consists of the moves on both sides that enable the players to develop their pieces. In a normal chess game, this might mean moving pawns forward to try to control the center of the board; moving the knights and bishops into position; and castling, which protects the king and unites the rooks. Of course, there are thousands of opening game strategies that include different priorities and piece movement, but the outcome of every opening game is the same: to clear the way for back rank pieces; to move crucial pieces into position on the board; and to try to gain an advantage by controlling the center, creating an open file through a pawn capture, or establishing a material advantage by capturing an opponent's knight or bishop. Opening game generally ends when the opposing forces attack on each other's sides of the board.

♜ *Never develop your pieces in the opening with the intention of looking for a plan later. When "later" comes, you are usually on your way down.—Jeremy Silman,* The Amateur's Mind: Turning Chess Misconceptions into Chess Mastery

---

Middle game occurs when the battle is fully enjoined. It features a sometimes-dazzling combination of feints, attacks, sacrifices, pins, skewers, captures, and assaults on the king's position. Whereas opening game reveals the aspirations of both opponents, middle game is the triumph or ruin of their plans. Here, strategies can be dashed by a single blunder, and the craftiness of the opponents is revealed in how they search for weaknesses, exploit opportunities, and lay traps for the other to stumble into. The art of chess is nowhere more evident than in middle game.

Endgame arrives when there are few pieces remaining for either side. The battleground has been laid nearly bare. The kings take refuge behind the remaining defensive pawns, perhaps guarded by a single bishop or knight. The queens, if they have survived, are usually on the attack. Endgames are sometimes almost mechanical in their calculated piece movements. They rely far less on cunning and insight than they do on deliberation and precision, and when one admires chess players for their endgame play, it is usually because they are masters of economy and efficiency.

Business development is like chess. It also has a clear opening, middle, and ending. It demands a thorough knowledge of the rules of the game and of the opponents. To win, you have to understand the situation as it changes from one move to the next, and you must develop and execute an effective strategy that develops dynamically as positioning leads to opportunities and opportunities become contracts. Austrian international grand master Rudolph Spielmann once advised chess players to play opening game like a book, middle game like a magician, and endgame like a machine. He could have been talking about business development as well.

Playing Opening Game Like a Book

In the 1,500-year history of chess, players have attempted countless openings. Among the classic first set of moves is 1. e4, e5, which means that white moves the pawn in front of his king two spaces forward to assert control of the center, and black makes a similar move to deny white's sole control. The two pawns block each other in the center of the board but exert control over the two squares immediately in front of and adjacent to their positions. If white next moves his knight to f3, which threatens black's e5 pawn, black may respond by moving her knight to c6, which thus protects the e5 pawn and also threatens square d4. If white's next move is the bishop to b5, the black player may recognize that white is playing the Ruy Lopez or Spanish opening (see Figure 4-2), and that may dictate how black responds. Experienced chess players often recognize from their opponent's initial moves what standard opening is being attempted and already know how to respond. In the history of chess, various openings have been attempted numerous times, and the success or failure of countermoves has been studied so thoroughly that openings seem almost choreographed.

Most of the standard openings are named for the chess master who first popularized the opening or for the city or country where the opening originated: Sicilian, Caro-Kann, Panov-Botvinnik, Danish Gambit, Giuoco Piano, and the Vienna Game. Other standard openings are named for the primary pieces in play or the area of the board attacked: four knight's game, center game, queen's gambit, queen's gambit accepted, king's bishop gambit, and so on. Collectively, these and hundreds of variations form what is known as the *opening book*. When Spielmann speaks of playing the opening like a book, he means

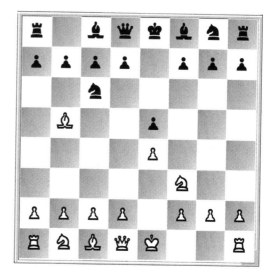

FIGURE 4-2. Ruy Lopez opening. Standard opening game movements, like the Ruy Lopez, signal each side's early intentions and strategy.

that players should have a repertoire of openings, know what's happening as opponents make their opening moves, and respond with moves that not only reflect strong chess principles but have also proven their merit in the laboratory of chess history. We should note that the book isn't everything, and modern chess teachers advise their students to avoid memorizing extensive opening repertoires. Nonetheless, when you can recognize patterns in your opponents' play and know which countermoves are likely to defeat their strategy, you will be a better player.

> *The real purpose of the opening is to create a difference (or a series of differences) in the respective positions and then develop your army around these facts.*
> —*Jeremy Silman,* The Complete Book of Chess Strategy

During a business trip to Vancouver years ago, one of this book's authors learned what can happen when players don't know the book and don't play soundly during opening game. While walking down a sidewalk in the city's central business district one autumn evening, he observed a young man who had set up a long table along the wall of one building. On the table were five chessboards and a small sign displaying his grand master rating and the number of consecutive games he had won (587)—a figure that kept growing as more people challenged him, which they could do for five dollars. When David arrived, four of the boards were in play. Shortly thereafter, a married couple walked up and the man sat down, paid his five dollars, and waited for the chess master to open the game. The master, meanwhile, was going from board to board, responding to his opponents' latest moves.

He commented to each of his challengers as he played—explaining how their moves and his countermoves had changed the situation, analyzing what was happening as the game advanced, observing where they were getting into difficulty, and suggesting how they could improve their play. He didn't speak to his latest challenger—the man who'd started playing after David arrived—until the seventh move. Then he said, "Very interesting, but you've got a potential problem in center. Let me show you what you might have done instead of what you just did." From that point on, until the man conceded, the master coached him on playing better chess. Though the man knew he was losing, he kept trying hard to counter the master's moves. Afterward, as they were leaving, David overheard the man's wife ask him how it went. He replied, "Fantastic. I've never learned so much about chess."

During a lull, after the chess master changed the number on his sign to 594, David asked him if he got much repeat business.

"You bet. I've played some people thirty to forty times. They just keep coming back."

"When do you know that you're going to beat them?"

"Usually by their fourth or fifth move," he said. "By then I know what they're doing, and I just wait for them to make a mistake."

"Is that when you start giving them advice?"

"Yeah. I've already won, so then it's just fun to help them out."

The lesson here is that experienced, capable players know from the earliest moments how skilled their opponents are, what direction their opponents appear to be taking, and what counterstrategies and tactics have succeeded in the past. Opening game sets in motion events that sometimes predetermine the outcome. Even when it's not predetermined, opening game begins to shape the outcome, limiting some possibilities while making others more probable. Chess players can't expect to be careless and thoughtless in opening and middle game and then stumble into victory during endgame. Sorry, but that's not how the game is played.

This is often true in business development as well. On numerous occasions, we've seen companies receive an RFP they had no idea was coming and decide to bid on the opportunity, fantasizing that they might win. This is the Wayne Gretzky school of bidding (he said, "You miss every shot you don't take."). However, by the time these gamblers open their mail, their smarter competitors have already positioned themselves for the win. They have known about the opportunity, often for months, and have been working the customer's hallways—meeting the right people, discussing their needs, exploring possible technologies or solutions, building stronger relationships, informing the customer about their capabilities and experience, and perhaps helping the customer write the RFP (middle game). *That* is behavioral differentiation. It's not that these opening and middle game tactics are secret; it's that many companies don't do them, though they know they should.

Chess teacher Ron Curry says that in the opening of a game, the pieces and pawns should be mobilized for attack and defense. He believes that the four primary opening goals are to control the center, develop all pieces, safeguard the king, and hinder your opponent.[3] Metaphorically, this applies to business development as well. There, opening game consists primarily of those planning, marketing, and account management activities that help you *condition the market* (Figure 4-3). As in chess, you are attempting to create differences between yourself and your competitors that the market recognizes and values. Your goal is to create competitive advantage through your

FIGURE 4-3. Opening game. In opening game, you try to set the conditions that will give you an advantage later in the game. Developing strategy and building position are the keys to victory in chess and business development.

branding, advertising, product and service development, and positioning in the marketplace, regardless of which customers you might later serve. In conditioning the market, you are trying to create bias toward yourself in the minds of all the potential buyers of your types of products and services in the market segments you choose to serve. Opening game in business development ends—and middle game begins—when you identify a specific opportunity with a customer.

Playing Middle Game Like a Magician

In his book *Win at Chess!* Ron Curry says, "After the opening, the challenging, complex, and often critical middlegame begins. It is characterized by the three elements: *strategy, positional play,* and *tactics. Strategy* is the formulation of plans to exert maximum offensive and defensive force. *Positional play* is the positioning of pieces and pawns to control important squares for optimum activity and flexibility. *Tactics,* the most powerful factor in chess, are direct threats to win material or checkmate."[4] In middle game, players develop their positions further, press for advantage, strive for material imbalances, and execute their strategies. Generally, pieces are taken or exchanged as the players attack to create a tactical advantage or defend to prevent an opponent from achieving a favorable position.

Middle games can feature subtle strategic positioning that improves the odds of a successful outcome or brilliant coups d'état that abruptly defeat the opponent (see Figure 4-4). The latter happens in business development, too, when one competitor is so persuasive that the customer awards a sole-source contract and closes down the competition. As Jeremy Silman notes, "Many games don't get past the middlegame. A checkmate ends matters in no uncertain terms, huge material losses convince experienced players to resign the contest in disgust, and the specter of a lost endgame can also lead a player to tip his King over in a gesture of defeat."[5] Because of the complexities of middle game play, it demands the most of players—strategy, skill, foresight, perseverance, and finesse. That's why it must be played like a magician.

In business development, middle game begins once you make contact with a customer and start building a relationship. It does *not* begin when you first become aware of an opportunity. This is an important point because your failure to know whether an opportu-

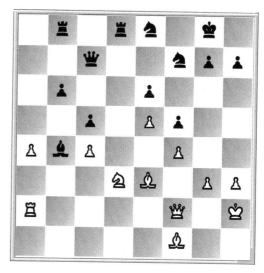

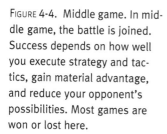

Figure 4-4. Middle game. In middle game, the battle is joined. Success depends on how well you execute strategy and tactics, gain material advantage, and reduce your opponent's possibilities. Most games are won or lost here.

nity exists is no prohibition to your competitors. The clock is ticking the moment an opportunity surfaces. From that point, a variety of activities become possible that we describe as *opportunity pursuit*, including making the pursuit (or bid/no-bid) decision, which should be revisited frequently during middle game; making sales calls; analyzing the opportunity and the customer's needs; meeting with key people and building relationships; giving product or service demonstrations; helping customers specify their needs; and introducing your core teams. These and other middle game tactics are intended to *condition customers,* to position yourself in their mind as the leading supplier (if not the sole supplier), to manage their impressions, to help them find the right solutions, and to bias them in your favor by ethical means. If you are proactive enough in middle game, you can often preempt the competition and create for yourself a virtually unassailable position from which to win the contract. Middle game ends when the customer releases the RFP. From that point on, you are in endgame, and—as in chess—if you aren't well positioned by this point, you are in serious trouble.

Playing Endgame Like a Machine

By endgame, most pieces have been won or lost and the opponents are striving to put themselves in the most advantageous position from which to bring the contest to a close. What remains can be an intricate cat-and-mouse game where individual moves will mean the difference between a win, a loss, or a draw. By endgame, the drama has largely been played out, especially if one player has a decided imbalance in material or position, though it is still possible to lose in endgame even when players have a strong position coming into it. The same is true in business development, where well-positioned bidders sometimes lose because of the poor quality of their proposals or presentations.

It is conceivable, but unlikely, for players who enter endgame in a disadvantageous position to pull off a miraculous victory. Miracles do occur, but as Damon Runyon once argued, the race may not always be to the swift, nor the battle to the strong, but that's the way to bet. Most chess games are *not* won in endgame; they are won much earlier—in the positioning during opening game and in the strategic flow and tactical achievements of middle game. As national chess master James Eade argues, "Just as middlegame planning flows logically from the opening, the *endgame* logically develops from the middlegame. In many cases, you can even anticipate the endgame as early as in the opening, where one side plays for an advantage in pawn structure that the player can truly exploit only in the endgame."[6]

In business development, endgame begins when the customer releases the RFP or similar bid request document. In opening game, you tried to condition the market; in middle game, you tried to condition the customer. In endgame, you are trying to *condition the deal.* The proposals are due on a specific date. Many of the key people in the customer's organization may no longer be available to meet with you (so you can't influence them further—at least not in person). There are formal procedures to follow, and the customer will evaluate the proposals and narrow the field to the suppliers he or she will seriously consider. The customer may then ask the short-listed suppliers to present their offers.

Business development endgame tactics are well known, which is why you should play endgame like a machine. Endgame (see Figure 4-5) is about flawless and consistent execution; however, in the real world, endgames are often very poorly played. In our experience, only a few companies execute their proposals and presentations with consistently high quality. Although the stakes are high, there is often a large gap between what companies know they should do and what they actually do. The companies that can close the gap are differentiating themselves behaviorally.

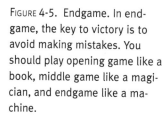

FIGURE 4-5. Endgame. In endgame, the key to victory is to avoid making mistakes. You should play opening game like a book, middle game like a magician, and endgame like a machine.

It should come as no surprise that the game is largely won before endgame begins. In fact, in our experience the three phases of the game contribute much differently to the outcome—in chess as in business development. Opening game is important because it can position a company favorably in its marketplace and create a favorable bias in customers' minds. Our research shows that it contributes about *20 percent* to the win. Roughly one-fifth of your energy in business development should be devoted to opening game strategies. Middle game is where the action is. What occurs there contributes to about 70 percent of a company's probability of winning. Clearly, this is a provocative statement, and we will have much more to say about it through the rest of the book. Endgame contributes only about 10 percent to the win, but it's an important 10 percent. By the time endgame arrives, most of the battle has been fought and won, but it is still possible to lose in endgame if you play poorly.

In 710 A.D., Omayyad caliph Walid I ibn Abdalmalik is said to have killed a chess player who deliberately played badly against him so the caliph would win. Sales managers today probably won't have to kill any of their adversaries for being too unsportsmanlike and allowing them to win contracts too easily. The stakes are too high and the opportunities too few for anything other than all-out, hell-bent-for-leather competition. Every year thousands of B2B companies compete for trillions of dollars in contract awards from other businesses or from local, state, or federal agencies. Except for such tangible and easily specifiable commodities as pencils, coffee mugs, and motor oil, most of these contracts are awarded based on competitive bids and proposals. Indeed, the proposal has become so ubiquitous in business life as to warrant a special place in the way most B2B companies organize and staff their business development operations. The large sophisticated aerospace and defense contractors have centers staffed by proposal managers, writers, editors, coordinators, graphic artists, and production specialists. Even smaller companies often have proposal specialists in departments that support the salespeople during endgame. Companies also spend millions of dollars annually to educate their salespeople on how to write proposals and millions more hiring consultants to help them craft their "must-win" bids. For endgame to be played like a machine, people must have the skill, the will, the resources, and the time to execute flawlessly.

What often makes the difference in winning or losing is the extent to which companies can behaviorally differentiate themselves during the crucial parts of the business development process—in opening game, middle game, and endgame. In this chapter, we introduced the chess metaphor as a way to think about the phases of business development. In the chapters that follow, we explore how to use behavioral differentiation in each of these phases.

CHALLENGES FOR READERS

1. If you are in a B2B company, what is your business development cycle? In your experience, does it have the kinds of phases we've described? If not, what is your business development cycle like? Map it out.

2. How effective is your company at opening game? How well positioned in the market are you? Do you do a good job of creating bias in your favor? If not, what more could you be doing?

3. In our experience, most competitions are won or lost *before* the RFP is released. This crucial period is called middle game, and it accounts for about 70 percent of a company's win potential. How capable is your company at middle game? Specifically, do you always get started as soon as you learn of an opportunity?

Do you actively and thoughtfully pursue opportunities as early as possible? By the time middle game ends, are you usually well positioned to win?

4. Endgame begins when the RFP is released. Most of endgame centers on your proposals and presentations. How capable is your company at these? Do you flawlessly execute your proposals and presentations? Do you typically gain points or lose them during this phase?

5. Think about the breadth of your business development activities—from planning and marketing through selling and opportunity management and finally to proposal management, presentations, and negotiations. Where are your strong and weak points? What can you do to overcome your weaknesses? Further, what can you do during each phase to behaviorally differentiate yourself from your competitors?

CHAPTER 5

Opening Game:
Conditioning the Market

> *The opening is the first stage of the game. Here, both sides develop their forces and create plans that will influence the proceedings throughout the contest.—Jeremy Silman,* The Complete Book of Chess Strategy
>
> ∎
>
> *The outcome of the opening determines or influences your strategic alternatives and tactical opportunities for many subsequent moves.* —*Ron Curry,* Win at Chess!

People have been making maps for eons, but the golden age of cartography began after Columbus's first voyage to the New World in 1492. Not quite eighty years later, Dutch mapmaker Abraham Ortelius published the first world atlas, the *Theatrum Orbis Terrarum* (Theatre of the World). His 1570 Latin edition consisted of seventy maps of regions of the world, including a global map based on earlier world maps by Jacobo Gastaldi (1561) and Gerardus Mercator (1569). Sixteenth-century scholars praised the *Theatrum* for its accuracy and authoritative rendering of world geography as it was known at the time. It may be difficult for twenty-first century readers to imagine the excitement Europeans must have felt four hundred years ago as the latest seafaring expeditions brought new discoveries and clarified the outlines and contours of the world. But in the sixteenth century, the latest editions of maps were prized possessions, and the *Theatrum* made Ortelius a renowned and wealthy man.

When the *Theatrum* was first published, John Speed, an eighteen-year-old lad from Cheshire, had just been admitted to the Merchant Tailor's Company in London, where he worked as a tailor for the next twenty-eight years (in the process raising twelve sons and six daughters). In the few spare moments he had, Speed developed his real talent, cartography, and in 1598 was rewarded with a position in the Custom House, where he devoted his time to preparing county maps of England and Wales. These he later compiled into a highly regarded *Theatre of the Empire of Great Britain*, but greater fame lay in the creation of world maps, and Speed completed his grand map of the world in 1627. Knowing how contemporary readers valued accuracy, he named it *A New and Accurat Map Of The World* and wrote, in florid script across the top of the map, *Drawne according to the truest descriptions, latest discoveries, and best observations that have beene made by English or Strangers*. In naming his map, Speed was conditioning the market—positioning his map as the latest and greatest, the most accurate yet created (modern marketers would no doubt have used the expression "state of the art"). He was trying to bias map purchasers to buy his map rather than older, less accurate maps or maps created by rival cartographers who lacked the "*truest* descriptions, *latest* discoveries, and *best* observations," and gain market share from his Dutch rivals, who were among the foremost cartographers of the day.

Had Speed been a chess player, he would have been playing opening game, that first stage of chess where, as Jeremy Silman explains, "both sides develop their forces and create plans that will influence the proceedings throughout the contest."[1] Of course in chess the opponents are engaged once the opening move is made, but the analogy with business development is still apt. In both cases, the opening designs are intended to create imbalances or predispositions that favor the player. Silman, an international chess master and author of more than thirty books on chess, argues, "The real purpose of the opening is to create imbalances that develop your army in such a way that your pieces, working together, can take advantage of them."[2] This is true in business development as well. The aims of early positioning are to create imbalances or biases toward you among potential customers in your target markets that you can exploit when actual opportunities arise later.

In business development, opening game occurs before contact with a particular customer. Consequently, the positioning is largely indirect—done through product invention or selection, design, development, and differentiation; packaging and labeling; advertising and other forms of market communication; market segmentation, identification of target customers, and strategic account planning; and networking in the political and social environment of the markets you are targeting. Clearly, you can be in opening game with some prospective customers (whom you have not yet contacted) while in middle game or endgame with existing customers. In business development, opening game represents everything you do to position yourself in your markets and to prepare for customer contacts. These are ongoing activities, whatever your progress may be with particular customers. Opening game never ends. You are continually positioning or repositioning yourself in the markets you serve to achieve four goals:

1. Determine or reconfirm the business purpose and means that reflect your core values and beliefs, and build or maintain the resources and skills needed to accomplish that purpose.

2. Create or re-create a unique value proposition and the leadership, culture, and processes to deliver it.

3. Position yourself in the market in a way that conditions customers to think favorably of you and your products or services—and stimulate demand by informing potential customers of what's possible.

4. Communicate your product and behavioral differentiation to the market so that you predispose customers to select you when they have a need you can fulfill.

In chess, the goals of opening game are accomplished by developing your pieces, controlling the center of the board, safeguarding your king, and hindering your opponent. In business, as we will describe next, the four goals are accomplished by ensuring that your leadership and management practices are aligned with your values, by building the resources and skills necessary to achieve your business purpose, by developing differentiated products and services that meet the needs of the customers in your target market segments, by branding and positioning yourself in the market, by advertising and otherwise communicating to your markets, by assessing and countering your competitors' actions, by building political and financial capital, and by doing strategic account planning. As this list suggests, opening game involves a complex interplay of activities intended to position you favorably in your markets. Throughout all of these activities, you can create sustainable BD. We would argue, in fact, that if you don't have BD in mind as you build market position, then it will be difficult for you to create such differentiation down the line. Behavioral differentiation isn't a program you can overlay onto your operations later; it is rooted in the core of your business and grows out of solid behavioral foundations, principally in how you think of the stakeholders of your business—your customers, employees, suppliers, and shareholders.

Gaining Alignment Internally

Behavioral differentiation has its origin in your company's fundamental values and beliefs. If your values include treating customers exceptionally well and if they are sufficiently compelling, well articulated, and aligned with your employees' personal values, then sustainable BD can follow. Part of what has made Men's Wearhouse so successful over such a long period is that its differentiating behaviors derive from founder George Zimmer's fundamental beliefs about people. As he said in an interview for *Fast Company*, "Our business is based on faith in the value of human potential."[3]

Aligning Your Values and Behaviors

Behavioral differentiation derives from within. It begins with leaders' attitudes toward customers, employees, and the nature and purpose of the enterprise. If the leaders' views are mechanical, pessimistic, cynical, or coldly utilitarian, then the company's leadership practices and policies are likely to be controlling, distrustful, and even punitive. A rotten apple is rotten to the core. Jack Welch understood this when he divided GE's leaders into a four-box matrix according to whether they lived the values and whether they got results. Those who do both are the stars, of course, and you reward and promote them. Those who do neither are gone. Those who live the values but don't get results should be encouraged and educated, Welch felt, but must ultimately be held accountable for doing the job. The toughest group, he said, are those managers who get the results but do not live the values. Though he hated to lose high-performing managers, Welch concluded that they, too, must go because keeping them sends a woefully mixed message and reforming them at the level of core values is next to impossible.

The road to sustained behavioral differentiation begins with an examination of your core values and beliefs. Do they include treating customers exceptionally? Do they reflect the values and beliefs of your people? Do they express a compelling reason for being in business (beyond making money, which may be enticing for owners and investors but generally isn't for other stakeholders)? The best-in-class companies we describe in this book and in *Winning Behavior* exist for reasons other than making money, although making money is obviously critical. But the heart and soul of the companies that are best-in-class in BD operate on a philosophy that appeals to employees and customers alike because it satisfies them at levels deeper than the pocketbook. For Harley-Davidson, it's not a motorcycle—it's a way of life. That's why Harley-Davidson defines itself as being in the *experience* business.

An important first step in BD, then, is to ensure that your core values and beliefs promote the kinds of behaviors that would differentiate you with customers. You also need to examine your leadership team, as Jack Welch did. Do your leaders have the right values? Are their values aligned with those of your employees and the institution? Do they embody those values—not only in words but also in deeds? Do they walk the talk? Do they genuinely believe in the ideals of the institution and its mission, or do they wear a game face for customers and employees that masks an underlying cynicism? If there is a gap between what your leaders say and what they do, your employees will eventually become cynical themselves, and this will erode customers' experiences of your company, no matter how lofty your espoused principles of customer service might be. Though it sounds corny to say it, BD begins with the heart and the soul, and there are scores of technically competent but uninspired and uninspiring managers leading average, undistinguished companies to prove the point.

> ♕ *The beginnings of all things are weak and tender. We must therefore be clear-sighted in the beginnings, for, as in their budding we discern not the danger, so in their full growth we perceive not the remedy.—Michel de Montaigne*

Aligning Your Policies and Practices

Behavioral differentiation will also fail if there are gaps between your core values and beliefs and your management policies and practices— if, as Harvard's Chris Argyris argues, there are gaps between your espoused theories and your theories-in-use.[4] It's easy for senior management to embrace lofty ideals about being customer centric, but it can be challenging to translate those lofty ideals into day-to-day behaviors if the people on the front line with customers didn't participate in setting the company's vision, don't understand what it means to be customer centric (How does one do that, exactly?), or feel a strong mixed message from management, which can occur when middle managers—pressured from above to control costs and hit their numbers—don't permit employees to do the things customers would experience as differentiating behaviors.

The gap between what managers *believe* (or claim to believe) and how they *behave*—which we might call the Believing-Behaving Gap—can be a serious impediment to achieving sustainable BD. Your managers must believe the values and live them. They must promote policies that reflect the values and encourage the right behaviors. And they must behave in ways that reflect their espoused beliefs. Figure 5-1 illustrates the alignment necessary to build sustainable BD, both internally with employees and externally with customers. There must be alignment between the core values and beliefs of the institution, the values of the stakeholders (especially customers and employees), management and customer service policies, management and employee practices, and the behaviors customers experience at every touch point. Misalignments at any point can create an incongruent environment that prevents you from achieving sustainable behavioral differences.

Defining the Business

Alignment with core values and beliefs is the foundation, and a company's mission and purpose are the façade. This is what customers and other stakeholders see as the emblems of underlying value. Though in our experience it's rarely done, it *is* possible to differenti-

FIGURE 5-1. Behavioral differentiation alignment. To sustain behavioral differentiation, your behaviors must be aligned with your practices, policies, and values. Misalignments can cause everything to topple.

ate yourself behaviorally while defining your business purpose or mission. Beyond including customer focus and centricity in your mission statement, you could involve customers in your business definition process. You might publish your evolving mission statement, for instance, and invite suggestions or questions from current and prospective customers in the marketplace. You could also form customer advisory boards or panels to review your statement of purpose, mission statement, and business scope. The point is to make your purpose and mission highly visible to prospective customers and to engage them in the process of determining what you do and what you aim to accomplish. You could also print your mission on your business cards (which many companies have done), print it on your product packaging or on other documents customers receive, or make it prominent in your ads. Then walk the talk. Under John Tarpey's leadership, Centex Construction Company's Mid-Atlantic Division posts a large, professionally printed sign stating its mission and core values, not just in its office lobby, but at the entrance to every job site. His people are reminded to *walk the talk* as they literally walk through the gate each day. These are behavioral differentiators because the vast majority of companies do little with their mission statements except post them on the walls in their foyers or elevators, and most customers have very little real connection with the mission statements of the providers who serve them.

> ♟ *Develop all your pieces in the opening; do not try to wage a chess war with half your forces sitting idly on their original squares. Seek effective, strong squares which allow your pieces the most scope, mobility, and aggressive prospects.—Ron Curry*

Building Resources and Capabilities

In strategic planning, which also occurs during opening game, companies generally consider what resources and capabilities they need to accomplish their purpose. Called *core competencies* by recent business writers, and *staff* and *skills* in McKinsey's 7-S model, these elements of planning also lend themselves to BD. Nordstrom, Southwest Airlines, and Men's Wearhouse—three exemplars of behavioral differentiation—hire for a person's character and personality rather than specific skill sets, which can be learned. When you establish your recruiting policies and define the characteristics of the people you wish to recruit, you determine whether such factors as emotional intelligence, interpersonal skill, service orientation, and relationship-building experience are part of your employee profile. In your case, are they? You get what you look for, so if you intend to differentiate yourself behaviorally, you need to hire people whose temperament, attitude, and operating style lend themselves to that. Beyond recruiting, there are a number of ways to promote BD through your human resource policies and practices:

■ Assign employees with the best interpersonal skills to positions with the greatest customer contact.

■ Educate employees in behavioral differentiation. Ensure that everyone understands BD and the value it brings to your customers and the company.

■ Set high behavioral expectations for employees. Build those expectations into your standard operating procedures (which can result in operational BDs).

■ Give employees the latitude and resources necessary to serve customers in ways that behaviorally differentiate your company (in other words, create the conditions that lead to exceptional BD).

■ Hold brainstorming sessions to identify behaviors that embody your company's values, operating principles, marketing themes, and slogan (i.e., behaviors that create symbolic BD) as well as sessions on how, when, and where to exhibit those behaviors.

■ Recognize and reward employees who behave in ways that differentiate you with your customers. Beyond normal customer service awards, create awards for outstanding BD. Feature these award winners in your internal newsletter. Make heroes of them in your culture.

■ Ensure that your performance measures incorporate aspects of BD. What gets measured, gets done; so establish BD as an element of everyone's normal evaluation.

Cumulatively, these kinds of actions create a culture of behavioral differentiation. They raise employees' awareness of the need for it and help them operationalize the concept. Moreover, they raise the "behavioral bar" for everyone in the company and can create an environment where differentiating behavior toward customers is the norm. When that occurs, you are also raising the bar on your competitors—a bar they will have great difficulty seeing, let alone clearing—by raising your markets' and customers' behavioral expectations. Since most companies don't do this systematically and consistently, being self-conscious about incorporating BD into your human resources policies and practices is itself a behavioral differentiator.

Marketing

Marketing is largely an opening game activity. Although it occurs continuously, the principal function of marketing is opening game positioning, and that can occur as you analyze and segment the market, differentiate your products, develop your brand, analyze competitor activity, and communicate in various forms to the market.

Analyzing the Market

Perhaps the most fundamental of marketing functions is to analyze the customer base in your potential markets and determine what customers need, how they use and define the value of your types of products and services, and what they expect from providers. Understanding the market is often viewed as an intellectual exercise best outsourced to marketing research firms, but we believe this is usually a mistake. Market analysis is in fact a rich opportunity for BD.

A few years ago, one of the world's premier professional services firms conducted a worldwide market survey that included clients it was currently working with, clients it had formerly been working with but had lost, and prospective clients with whom it had no relationship. Beyond developing a gold mine of information on how clients perceived both it and its rivals and what clients valued in its types of services, the firm also uncovered a significant number of opportunities for more business. Instead of sending written questionnaires to its clients and prospects or using a market research firm to interview clients, this firm sent its own professionals to do the interviewing. That fact alone impressed a number of the clients the firm interviewed. The firm's behavior communicated that it cared what its clients thought and were committed to improving its client services and relationships. The firm's willingness to invest the time and energy into analyzing its clients' needs differentiated it from competitors who had not made this investment, and it uncovered a remarkable number of new opportunities in the process. However, the ultimate value of the exercise was not in the opportunities the firm uncovered but in its enhanced position in the market vis-à-vis its competitors. Companies have also done the following to differentiate themselves behaviorally while analyzing their markets:

■ Use focus groups of customers and prospects to explore their needs and their perceptions of providers in the market. Focus groups are now almost passé in some industries, but in others they remain a little-used tool and would still be a behavioral differentiator. Behavior that differentiates you from your competitors doesn't have to be original—it just has to be unused by or unknown to your competitors. Other industries are often a good source of ideas for behavioral differentiators.

■ Have your senior executives meet with customers or prospects to explore their needs. What is rare and differentiating is having a CEO travel to customers' sites to explore their needs. Most CEOs delegate this to others, so it can be a powerful differentiator if your CEO makes a point of meeting with prospects to understand and explore their needs.

■ Create product advisory boards that include key customers. Give those boards real clout in influencing the direction your product development takes. *That's* differentiating.

■ Create a Web site where customers can experiment with your products or services by adding, modifying, or deleting features and by assigning values to various options. Give them discounts or something else of value in return and follow up their online experiments with telephone calls.

■ Conduct regular tours of customers' sites with your senior people to explore how customers use the product, what issues or challenges they face, and how you could improve your products or alter them to meet their needs better. Certainly, many companies already do this, but it's not a universal practice, especially not with senior people making the trip. Also, this tends to be a more common practice in large, well-established, customer-oriented companies like Procter & Gamble and IBM. It's far less common in smaller companies and has been virtually nonexistent in Silicon Valley–type start-ups, where founders often mistakenly assume that their technology alone will be sufficient to attract and retain customers.

■ Perform a value-chain analysis with customers to analyze the value your products add and where there are opportunities to add greater value. Again, some companies do this but it's still not a common practice, so it differentiates behaviorally.

The bottom line of these practices is to demonstrate a conscious and ongoing interest in understanding the dynamic and evolving needs of the customer base in your markets, to uncover what customers value about your types of products and services and what they expect from any provider who serves their needs, to learn what they think about you and your products (and how your products could be improved), and to gain insight into what would exceed their expectations and delight them. There are ample opportunities during market analysis to differentiate yourself behaviorally from your competitors and, consequently, to improve customers' perceptions of you.

Segmenting the Market

Chess expert Ron Curry said, "Controlling the center allows you to post active, mobile pieces on strong central squares while denying your opponent similar desirable development."[5] His advice about segmenting the board and controlling those segments is a good analogy for what you seek to accomplish in market segmentation—superior influence or bias in the segments most favorable to you. In deciding which market segments to target, you should consider not only the needs, price sensitivities, and buying habits of the customers in each segment but also their behavioral expectations and the norms of their behavioral experiences, which amount to the same thing. What provider behaviors are they accustomed to? What do they expect when they purchase from any provider serving their needs? The answers to these questions should offer insight into the behavioral differences that are possible within each market segment.

For example, until only a few years ago in the healthcare construction industry, every contractor suffered from the perception among healthcare providers that construction companies would cut corners, hide costs, slip schedules, and promise one thing but deliver another. A few forward-thinking healthcare constructors began in the 1990s to move away from what they called the "hard bid" image to become client-focused, relationship-based, open-book, integrity-driven organizations. In short, they based their futures on their ability to create trust where it had never existed before in their industry and markets. Essentially, these companies assessed how their markets perceived their industry; saw a golden opportunity to raise the behavioral bar; and then developed and implemented plans to grow market share by behaving very differently from the industry norm, both in acquiring the work and in performing it. In 1999 and 2000, these companies filled the top ten of *Fortune* magazine's list of Most Admired Construction Companies. That's conditioning the market.

To differentiate yourself behaviorally, you first have to understand the behavioral norms your customers have experienced, what Theodore Levitt would call the *expected product*.* Those norms may differ from one market segment to the next, so one goal of market segmentation should be to develop an understanding of the provider behaviors to which customers in each segment are accustomed and therefore expect as their *normal* experience. Next, you need to explore the two extremes of customers' experiences—those notably unpleasant experiences that cause negative BD and those exceptionally delightful experiences that form positive differentiators. In shaping the behavioral expectations of your company, you want to establish safeguards against the occurrences of those negative behaviors and find ways to encourage or standardize the positive behaviors. But that may not be possible with all market segments. Some segments may include customers whose behavioral expectations exceed what you can affordably provide. So the challenge in market segmentation is to choose segments with customers whose behavioral expectations you *can* exceed. In short, there should be alignment between your target market segments and your capacity to deliver positive behavioral differentiation.

Differentiating Your Products

In the perpetual opening game we've been describing, companies also strive to design or redesign products and services that are differentiated from their competitors. The challenges companies typically face in product differentiation can be profound:

■ How can we create products and services that are different from our competitors' products and services and that are uniquely beneficial to our customers? In short, how can we create a higher value proposition in the minds of our customers?

---

*For an explanation of Levitt's model, see Theodore Levitt, *The Marketing Imagination* (New York: The Free Press, 1986) or chapter 2 of Terry R. Bacon and David G. Pugh, *Winning Behavior: What the Smartest, Most Successful Companies Do Differently* (New York: AMACOM, 2003).

■ How can we package or deliver this value proposition in a uniquely beneficial way?

■ In choosing providers, what is most important to our customers, and how much impact do our differentiators have on their buying decisions?

■ How can we create enough added value in our products or services to justify a higher price, if that is our goal, or how can we achieve a unique value proposition at a lower price that attracts more customers and builds our market share?

■ How sustainable are our product differentiators? How rapidly are new product features commoditized? What is the cycle of *innovation and imitation* in our industry? How rapidly do we have to reinvent our products to sustain differences customers will value?

■ Do we have any significant weaknesses in product differentiation— areas where our competitors' products are differentiated from ours in ways customers value? If so, do our weaknesses constitute fatal flaws that will cost us business if not corrected?

■ Finally, what product differentiators are possible but haven't been thought of yet? How can we evolve our products and services in ways that create more differentiated value? In Levitt's terms, what is the *potential* product?

When marketing and product development teams meet to discuss the invention of new products or reinvention of existing ones, it's clear that these kinds of questions weigh on their minds. It's not clear, however, that they reflect on the behavioral corollaries of these questions:

■ What unique product features could we invent that would enable us to create or exploit BD? In other words, how could our unique value proposition integrate both product and behavioral differentiators?

■ How could we deliver our products or services in ways that behaviorally differentiate us?

■ Do we have any significant weaknesses in our behaviors toward customers at any touch point? If so, do those behaviors negatively differentiate us and cost us business?

And so on. We suspect that most companies don't consciously reflect on their behaviors with customers except to consider traditional customer service practices. However, behavior is a rich source of potential differentiation, and it should be a key consideration as marketing and product development teams think about re-creating their value proposition.

Probably the ultimate form of BD through product design is mass customization (assuming your competitors don't do it and you do). In their excellent book, *The One to One Future*, Don Peppers and Martha Rogers argue that "the mass-customization of a product, if it's done right, represents an almost air-tight guarantee of a satisfied loyal, long-term customer. When you go to a bike shop to design your own mountain bike, you are collaborating with the manufacturer. You are also, in essence, 'subscribing' to a product, and the odds go up that the bike shop will get a greater share of your business."[6] Peppers and Rogers contend that mass customization is inevitable. As customers experience the value of purchasing products that are tailor-made for them, they will come to expect it from all suppliers except those discounters who compete on low price. Why would a customer buy a prepackaged music CD, for instance, that has some songs she likes and others she doesn't when she has the option to select only the songs she likes, arrange them in her preferred order, and have her own customized CD created in the store?

In the B2B world, mass customization has long been more the rule than the exception because companies and government entities that are buying products and services have the purchasing clout to specify precisely what they want, and suppliers have little choice but to bid to the spec. Nonetheless, even in the B2B world, there remain some businesses that create and sell standard products or uniform services, and they will likely find, in the years to come, that customers will demand customization or even lower prices. As Peppers and Rogers note, "Mass-customization is the ultimate form of customer differentiation. It is nothing more, essentially, than using individualized product design to capture the greatest possible share of every single individual customer's business. It is what tomorrow's business successes will be built on."[7] Because mass-customized products build customer loyalty, mass customization is one area of marketing that offers a significant first-mover advantage. If your competitors are not already finding ways to mass customize their products and services, you have a once-in-a-lifetime opportunity to move first and behaviorally differentiate yourself from them.

Branding

Branding is an opening game activity with a high potential for BD. Strong brands exert an often-subconscious but potent influence on customers' buying decisions. A company's brand becomes an emblem of all the company stands for, and it makes an implied promise of benefits to customers. The Sargent & Lundy advertisement shown in Figure 5-2 is a good example of the brand positioning a company can do through advertising. This full-page ad, which appeared in *Engineering News Record*, has an elegant simplicity to it, a single focus

FIGURE 5-2. Sargent & Lundy's bright idea. Its advertisement is a good example of opening game market communication. This simple message conveys Sargent & Lundy's business focus, target market segment, and competitive advantage.

conveying the firm's central message: that it is dedicated exclusively to serving one market segment and has been doing so for over a century. The presumed benefit to customers is a degree of expertise and experience that may be unavailable from Sargent & Lundy's multipurpose competitors. Ads like these condition the market by biasing potential customers' perceptions of the firm. When you combine a strong brand (like Nordstrom or Marshall Field's) with superior behavior toward customers, you can create considerable customer loyalty and attract new customers. The purpose of branding is to create a unique identity in the minds of customers, an identity that can include differentiating behaviors. In *Winning Behavior* we described how organizations as diverse as Ritz-Carlton, Men's Wearhouse, Hall Kinion, Southwest Airlines, Volvo, and Heidrick & Struggles accomplished this. In their branding efforts, they have found ways to create and communicate images of themselves that symbolize their behavioral differentiators.

In both B2C and B2B businesses, branding is not merely a matter of the image created through advertising and other forms of market communication; it is also largely a function of successful execution. In fact, successfully completing a construction project like the telephone system for a state system of higher education carries far more weight with potential buyers of the telephone company's services than a flurry of ads, brochures, and promises. Excellence in execution is the strongest way for professional and other B2B service firms to position themselves with prospective customers. It breeds repeat business, strong word of mouth throughout the industry, and referrals. Client lists are also a form of branding and positioning that carries weight, especially if your list includes prestigious clients. So are awards and other forms of professional recognition, which is why Academy Award–winning actors are generally in greater demand and studios publicize those actors' awards when their films feature them. However, as our research on BDs in various professions illustrates, being a capable executor is not always sufficient to establish a favorable position. Referrals and positive buzz in the market are the consequence of excellent execution *and* positive behavior.

Your brand symbolizes who you are and what customers can expect from you, so it is the mirror customers hold up to you when they ask, "Do you walk the talk?" In other words, your brand and the associated messages about your identity are the core of what symbolic BDs symbolize. So if you do indeed walk the talk, your behaviors must be aligned with the image your brand conveys.

Analyzing Competitors

Finally, under the rubric of market analysis, we should discuss the role competitor analysis plays in BD. Your competitors' behaviors form the benchmark against which you measure your own behaviors and determine whether you are behaviorally differentiated, positively or negatively. So the key in competitor analysis is to discern competitors' behaviors. You can involve customers in this process by asking your sponsors in customers' organizations how your competitors behave. What do they do exceptionally well or poorly? What impresses other people in the organization, favorably or unfavorably? What is notable about how your competitors have tried to build relationships, position themselves, respond to opportunities, or otherwise serve the customer? Beyond knowing what your competitors have to offer, you should know how they behave toward customers and what impact those behaviors have on the customer's perceptions of them. As national chess master James Eade reminds us, "Don't get so caught up in your plans that you forget about your opponent's moves."[8]

If a move weakens your opponent's position without harming yours, and prevents or hinders your opponent from realizing his opening objectives, the move is probably a sound idea and will gain a relative advantage.—Ron Curry

---

Communicating to the Market

Within the markets themselves, the most visible elements of your company's opening game positioning are your advertising, trade show appearances, exhibitions, promotions, publications, and other forms of market communication. This is your most direct means of communicating your BDs and establishing them in the minds of prospective customers, so in all of the market communication tools you use, you should convey how customers' experiences of you are different and better than their experiences with your competitors. Beyond merely conveying the message, however, the tools you use can also behaviorally differentiate your company. Figure 5-3 shows the range of market communication tools and their potential for BD.

The mass communication tools shown on the left side of this figure generally have lower potential for BD because most companies use them in one form or another—so there is nothing particularly unique about them in their normal use—and because these tools typically focus more on the company and its products and services than on customers. Virtually every market is saturated with sellers' Web sites, brochures, press releases, advertising, promotions, print or e-mail campaigns, and newsletters. These forms of market communication are so ubiquitous that many customers don't consciously reg-

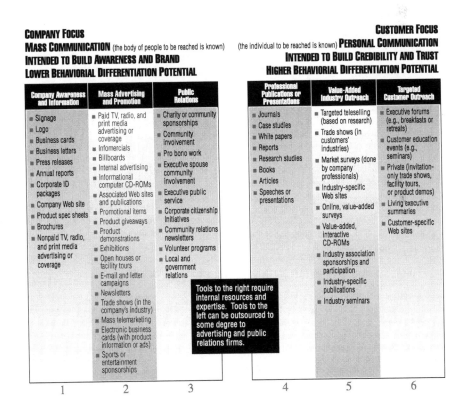

FIGURE 5-3. Market communication tools. Among the tools available for opening game market communication, those with greater industry and customer focus have more potential for creating behavioral differentiation.

ister them when new brochures, ads, exhibits, and promotions appear unless there is something extraordinary or unusual about them. The principal purposes of these tools of mass communication are to raise customers' awareness of the company and its products, to form positive impressions in customers' minds, and to build the brand. This kind of market positioning is usually critical, but it doesn't allow for BD unless you use these common tools in uncommon ways. Imagine designing a billboard, for instance, not to advertise a product to a mass market but instead to reach an individual decision-maker in a target company. Or creating a brochure for a single prospect, arranging an invitation-only facility tour for a small group of selected prospects, or conducting a private trade show at a prospect's location. Doing the unexpected with a tool that's become commonplace in mass market use is often innovative enough to grab people's attention. If your competitors aren't using the tools as creatively as you are, you will differentiate yourself behaviorally.

But even the most creative uses of these tools will eventually grow stale. The general psychological principle influencing customers' perceptions is that *the impact of any effect diminishes with repetition.* This is true in television programming, where the recent spate of "reality" programs like *Survivor* has diminished the impact and popularity of all programs in this genre. It's true in advertising as well. Even the finest, most creative ad grows stale after repeated viewing—to the point where some ads start having a negative effect on viewers because they've seen it and heard it too much. The first use of a billboard to send a message to a particular decision-maker is intriguing, attention getting, and unusual enough to have an impact. But the effect would pale quickly with overuse. So the challenge is to continually reinvent the uses of mass communication marketing tools in order to remain fresh and behaviorally differentiated.

The community and public relations tools shown in column 3 of Figure 5-3 are intended to form indirect associations between the entity being sponsored and the company, so they are less internally focused than advertising and are excellent tools for communicating a company's core values and beliefs and helping shape its image in the marketplace. For instance, Harley-Davidson and members of the Harley Owners Group (H.O.G.) have long been leading national sponsors of the Muscular Dystrophy Association (MDA). Along with financial support, H.O.G. members support MDA's dozens of summer camps for children who have muscular dystrophy. Every summer on Harley Day at the camps, H.O.G. members parade their bikes through the campgrounds; give sidecar rides; apply temporary Harley tattoos on young arms; and let the kids put on leather jackets, bandanas, and other Harley paraphernalia for picture taking. Harley also sponsors fund-raising rides, auctions, rallies, and other events that raise millions each year for MDA. This kind of charity sponsorship communicates that Harley-Davidson is not just a motorcycle company, and the owners of its products are not just bikers—they are decent, caring people who support a worthy cause and love kids. In short, their sponsorship of MDA humanizes Harley-Davidson and extends their concept of quality beyond the machines they make to the people who make and ride them. Given the outlaw image Harley riders once had, this form of market communication has been invaluable in transforming Harley's image, especially with the yuppies and professional class of motorcycle buyers Harley needed to solidify its market-dominant position.

Like charity sponsorships, community outreach or involvement can be a behavioral differentiator, especially if targeted customers know about, support, or are otherwise part of the community program you are involved with. However, community involvement *per se* is generally not differentiating because it's become an expected part of good corporate citizenship. We can't say with certainty that every Fortune 1000 corporation has some form of community involvement, but it seems highly likely. What's more important than having community involvement is having the *right* community involvement, and this is a function of the market you are serving and the values and community interests of your potential customers. It could be that having the right connections is more critical in emerging markets, especially those with high government involvement in supplier selection decisions, but being involved in the right community events and programs is critical in any market. If your community outreach includes executive spouses or executive public service, so much the better because their involvement is frequently unique and publicly noticed. Clearly, if you have the right connections and your competitors don't, you will differentiate yourself behaviorally.

Figure 5-3 shows a space between the market communication tools left of center and those to the right, beginning with professional publications and presentations. The mass communication and public relations tools to the left build awareness of the company and its products and help shape the market's impression of the company, its values, and its public image. To some extent, these tools can be outsourced to advertising agencies, public relations firms, and other image builders and marketers. However, it is more difficult to outsource professional publications; presentations; and the other, more unique tools shown in columns 4 through 6. For the most part, journal articles, case studies, white papers, research reports, and other types of professional publications must be written by professionals within the company because they require special expertise, and the company's credibility depends on the quality of these publications. Customers know this and therefore place higher value on these kinds of publications if they are relevant to the customer's business. Consequently, professional publications and presentations are more differentiating because the intellectual content is unique.

The *McKinsey Quarterly* is an excellent example. Written entirely by consultants in McKinsey & Company or others closely affiliated with the firm, this business journal is content rich and has high production values, both of which reflect the quality and professionalism McKinsey wishes to project to a worldwide business community that includes clients or potential clients of the firm. The articles in the *McKinsey Quarterly* demonstrate the firm's breadth of knowledge and perspectives about current business issues and challenges. McKinsey's investment in publishing this quarterly demonstrates its commitment to advancing the state of the art in management thinking, to sharing knowledge, and to educating business leaders in ways that appear selfless because the journal is freely available online (www.mckinseyquarterly.com). In contrast, competitor Booz-Allen & Hamilton publishes *strategy + business*, a quarterly that is available by subscription only (although teaser articles are available online), is filled with display ads, and includes articles written by people other than Booz-Allen & Hamilton consultants. McKinsey's approach to publication is more effective at building credibility because the thinking in it derives almost exclusively from McKinsey's own knowledge and experience, its availability online shows a stronger commitment to sharing knowledge, and the absence of display ads and subscription fees makes it less commercial. In these ways, McKinsey is behaviorally differentiated from its competitor.

Professional publications and presentations offer far more BD potential than mass advertising and company awareness-building initiatives, in part because they are a source of potential value to customers and in part because they are unique. Even if your competitors also publish a journal or a book or give a presentation at a major industry conference, there are differences in the amount you publish or present, the relevance and utility of the information to customers, and the quality of your professional contributions. Professional services firms like McKinsey & Company and Heidrick & Struggles (the world's leading executive search firm) often publish as a way to build credibility and customer confidence, but publications and presentations are less common in other industries. In them, the opportunity to establish behavioral differentiation through professional publications is high.

Farther to the right in Figure 5-3 are forms of market communication that have a very high potential for BD—largely because few companies do them regularly. Value-added industry positioning would include targeted teleselling—calling prospects based on industry- or company-specific research and having value-added conversations with key people around the challenges, problems, or opportunities they are facing or new solutions or technologies they may find helpful. What can differentiate this kind of cold call is the depth of research you do before making the call and the targeted way you address issues they may be facing. A more sophisticated version of this is to invite key people from a prospective customer to lunch or dinner to discuss ideas you've generated for improving their business or helping them exploit new opportunities. Clearly, this requires an uncommon level of investment in preparing for the call or meeting, and you must add considerable value once you're in contact. However, since this is so rarely done, it can be a powerful behavioral differentiator.

> ♜ *Every aspect of your communications should reflect your difference. Your advertising. Your brochures. Your Web site. Your sales presentations.—Jack Trout,* Differentiate or Die

Earlier, we mentioned a worldwide market survey one of our clients conducted. This, too, is a strong behavioral differentiator because most companies either don't invest in such surveys or outsource them to market research firms. Our client's professional staff conducted the survey themselves, which had multiple benefits. It emphasized to its customers how committed the firm was to learning more about its customers' needs, it put the firm's staff in front of many customers, it uncovered some real and immediate opportunities for more business, and it was an invaluable source of information that helped share the firm's strategy. Industry surveys are also done online, and if they add value to the customers who complete them, they can build credibility and help position the company in the market. Surveys, along with the other tools shown in column 5 of Figure 5-3, are uncommon enough to help the companies using them behaviorally differentiate themselves from their competitors. These tools are focused on the customer's industries and provide value-added information for any customer or prospect in that industry. Even greater behavioral differentiation potential exists when you find ways to add value to a particular customer or prospect.

In column 6 of Figure 5-3 are examples of the most focused market communication tools you can use—those intended for particular customers. Executive forums, retreats, educational seminars, private trade shows, facility tours, and other such special events are intended to educate, inform, and engage an invited list of key executives in target customer or prospect organizations. These types of market communication tools have high potential for BD, partly because they are less common but also because competitors generally cannot duplicate their intellectual content. Of course, these are higher-risk events. You don't want to invite the top executives in the companies you most want to work with to attend an executive forum and have the less-polite ones leave halfway through the event because they have better things to do. The quality of thought that goes into these kinds of events and the quality of their execution must be very high. Further, they cannot appear overtly commercial. The executives invited to attend will have serious demands on their time, so they must feel that the event is relevant to their business, is valuable to them, and is personally satisfying. That said, you cannot behaviorally differentiate yourself better in opening game than with tools like these.

The two nonevent tools we've seen that also have high potential for BD are living executive summaries and customer-specific Web sites. Living executive summaries are marketing tools you can use not only in opening game but throughout the business development cycle, as described in Table 5-1. Essentially, a living executive summary is an evolving story you tell, first to the market as a whole, later

Business Development Phase	Focus	Purposes
Opening Game	A problem, opportunity, or challenge for a segment of the industry; the key issues all or most companies constituting a market or market segment typically address whenever they need to procure what you are selling	Position you as a viable thought partner; get a seat at the table where the problems are discussed; initiate a dialogue with prospective customers
Early Middle Game	In addition to the opening game market focus, the key issues this customer (a qualified prospect from opening game) needs to address whenever they would buy what you sell even though they are not buying at the moment	Position you as a trusted advisor and solution provider; build relationships with key people; initiate a dialogue on opportunities; build preference for you as a supplier
Mid-middle Game	The key issues, concerns, challenges, and alternatives for a specific opportunity with the customer	Position you as the preferred thought partner for this opportunity; influence the customer's thinking about the solution; demonstrate your commitment to the work; presell your solution; if possible, preempt the competition and get the contract. If not possible, then favorably influence the specifications, requirements, and criteria of the RFP
Endgame (Proposal)	The customers goals and key issues, the features and benefits of your offer, and proof that you can achieve the benefits; whenever the procurement is driven by an RFP, the evaluation/selection criteria constitute the customer's final and formal definition of their key issues in selecting a provider	Position you as the winner; present the essence of your offer and your key selling messages to key decision makers; make it easy for evaluators to recommend you and justify the decision
Endgame (Presentation)	The same as above but focused on the key themes and benefits delivered during your presentation	Same as above for proposals; also, confirm their selection of you as the winner; leave a lasting impression of quality and the right chemistry

TABLE 5-1. The living executive summary. Initiated in opening game to condition the market, the living executive summary extends through middle and endgame to condition the customer and the deal. This approach to competing through differentiation raises the bar on the competition by raising the market's and then each customer's expectations of how providers should behave.

to customers with whom you are developing a relationship, and even later to the customers' representatives who will make a particular purchasing decision. It's the evolving nature of this tool, and its continuity in theme and use over time, that makes it a living document.

In opening game, you create an executive summary that addresses the key issues or challenges facing most potential customers in a target market segment. Your goals are to establish yourself as a credible thought partner for them, to stimulate interest in solutions you can offer, and to enjoin a dialogue that leads to further contact and discussion, which, by our definition, is early middle game. Once you begin a dialogue with a particular prospect and are building the relationship, you use the next iteration of your living executive summary to focus on the prospect's situation and needs. This enables you to broaden your network in the prospect's organization, to deepen the dialogue with key people, and to search for opportunities to identify their needs. When a particular opportunity emerges, you are in mid–middle game, and you use the next iteration of your living executive summary to influence the customer's thinking about the solution; to advance alternatives that favor your approach; and, if possible, to preempt the competition. Finally, in endgame, you use the remaining iterations of the living executive summary to persuade the decision-makers during the proposal evaluation and bidder presentations to prefer you and your solution. In our experience, very few companies have the skill and will to create first-class executive summaries throughout the business development cycle, so this tool can be a powerful behavioral differentiator.

The remaining tool in column 6 of Figure 5-3 is a customer-specific Web site. To understand the BD potential of this tool, consider the behavior manifest in the way most companies (except online retailers) use the Internet. First, they create a single Web site for promoting themselves. In this site, they typically express their key themes or marketing messages, provide the history and organization of their company, showcase their products and services, perhaps offer case studies of how they have served some customers, and indicate how the user can locate or contact them. There are numerous variations on this theme, but the essence of most companies' Web sites is a uniform self-focus. This is not entirely true with Men's Wearhouse. Its more creative Web site includes a "Connected Threads" section that showcases its philosophy; provides readings on topics like servant leadership and finding fulfillment through service; and has links to other social, philosophical, environmental, and business sites that are aligned with the core values and beliefs of Men's Wearhouse. This is not just about selling suits; it's about sharing a philosophy of life and business, and that's a strong behavioral differentiator for many customers.

Even more powerful is creating customer-specific Web sites. Clearly, this is impossible when you have millions of potential customers, as Men's Wearhouse does, but it is reasonable in the B2B world for companies with a limited set of customers or strategic accounts. Customer-specific sites, which some companies are now creating, permit a variety of behaviors that were inconceivable before the advent of the wired world, including customized product specs, solutions, price lists, inventories, proposals, surveys, project plans, schedules, and progress reports, on the one hand, and chat rooms, discussion boards, document repositories, and private e-mail on the other. Proposals, executive summaries, and animated PowerPoint slide shows can now be posted on restricted-access Web sites for the eyes of only one customer. Those proposals could include animated and interactive features that show customers what the proposed solution would look like, how it would work, and what it will take to get there. Customer users can play with options; explore alternative solutions; and discover the impact of various decisions on pricing, scheduling, and functionality. The Internet permits customization to an extent previously unimaginable, and although customer-specific sites are still rare, the gap between those who create them and those who don't is sure to narrow as the technology for creating Web sites becomes even simpler than it is today.

During opening game, every company is obliged to build market awareness of the company's products and services, stimulate demand, and build credibility and trust. These brand-building efforts are largely carried out with the mass communication tools shown on the left side of Figure 5-3, but these tools are too common to be strong BDs unless companies use them in unique, unexpected, and creative ways. The tools on the right side of Figure 5-3 have far greater potential for BD because they require an investment many companies are not prepared to make and because they require a level of skill that some companies don't possess or aren't even aware of. Generally speaking, the mass market tools generate more leads than the tools on the right, but the leads resulting from mass marketing efforts are usually of poorer quality. Moreover, extensive use of all these tools is expensive, so most companies face a conundrum. Do we invest our marketing dollars in the mass market tools and generate more leads of poorer quality? Or do we invest in targeted, value-added tools that generate fewer leads of higher quality? In our experience, the vast majority of B2B companies choose the former, which is one reason the value-added tools on the right have so much more BD potential.

> ♛ *Whoever starts the middle game with an advance in development and with the command of the center, has every reason to hope for ultimate success. Success will come to him whose endgame represents the realization of what has been achieved in the middle game.—Eugene A. Znosko-Borovsky*

Building Political Position

In opening game you plant the seeds of crops you intend to harvest later. If you are wise, you plant the right kinds of seeds, in the right numbers, in the right locations; then, to carry this metaphor to its logical conclusion, you tend your well-appointed garden so your plants flourish. Our point is that building market position is a lengthy process requiring a great deal of forethought and careful tending throughout. The political and social landscapes of your chosen markets are the areas you need to cultivate, and you can't do this as an afterthought when particular opportunities arise. You must develop your political position well in advance of middle game.

Building political position means analyzing the social, cultural, and political environment in your target markets and developing political strategies aimed at knowing the right people, having the right network, joining the right clubs or other organizations, and making the right investments in the communities of the markets you wish to serve so you are well positioned before attractive opportunities arise. It's imperative to understand and navigate the political landscape well ahead of time because these kinds of relationships and connections take time to develop. If you try to establish them overnight in response to a particular opportunity, your connections will be too superficial and too recent for you to have built much trust and credibility. Also, it often takes time to discern the right people to know and the right connections to make. If the customers in your target markets give special access to suppliers only through agents, then you need to know who the agents are and which ones have the greatest access to your potential customers. If the project you are bidding requires local suppliers or subcontractors, you need to know which local suppliers your prospects favor. Depending on your industry and your potential customers, you may need to forge networks that include local authorities or government officials, lobbyists, regulators, bankers, lawyers, special interest groups, trade unions, the media, local consulting firms, local labor or parts suppliers, and agents. You may also need to join the right clubs, contribute to the right groups, and attend the right conventions or meetings. Your presence in the market should generate leads, but the most important outcome of your opening game investment is having established political and social connections once you start pursuing particular opportunities. Assuming that you work completely within ethical and legal boundaries, being connected can mean the following:

■ Being able to introduce customers to bankers or investors they hadn't known

■ Being able to secure a better line of credit than your competitors can or being better able to help customers secure financing

■ Knowing which officials can ease a regulatory process or grant local permits

■ Having lobbyists in place who can help the customer with passage of a special bill that facilitates a key project

■ Having the support of an influential local charity that gives you and the customer favorable press—or connections with key customer executives or their families who also support the charity

■ Being able to bring a customer and a labor union together and helping to do some problem solving that results in greater support for the project

■ Being able to introduce customers to key people in the market or the community

Failing to build political position in the markets you serve during opening game will limit your options later. It can minimize your potential influence during opportunity pursuits and curtail your ability to help customers achieve their goals. Having the right political position, on the other hand, is frequently cited as a key behavioral differentiator.

Strategic Account Planning

An important opening game activity is analyzing your key targets and beginning to develop strategic account plans for them. In the strategic account-planning process, you would typically analyze the market, identify the major players, develop criteria indicating which prospects would be your ideal customers, and then analyze those prospects and develop a plan for capturing their business. As you venture closer to initial contact with these customers, you begin the transition to early middle game. In fact, in developing your strategic account plan, you might initiate contact with the target company, begin developing relationships, start diagnosing its business model and the company needs, and use what you learn from the company to complete your analysis and determine your strategic options. What can differentiate you behaviorally here is that most companies lack the discipline or the skill to do thorough strategic account planning as part of market penetration. When prospective customers see you doing it, see you engaging them as part of the process, and experience your commitment to thoroughly understanding their business and serving their needs, you are likely to behaviorally differentiate yourself from the hordes of competing companies who don't take the time, don't have the discipline, and don't have the commitment to do the same.

Engaging Senior Leadership

A final BD can occur during opening game if your senior executives play an active role in positioning the company, are visible in the markets, and actively pursue contacts with their counterparts in prospective customer organizations. Your senior executives should be self-conscious about their role as your company's ambassadors. They should promulgate the values and beliefs of your company, be available to the media, give speeches and presentations, present public awards, and participate fully in building political and social capital in the markets you wish to serve.

Although this may seem self-evident, the fact is that many C-level and vice-presidential-level executives are not as visible as they should be and don't play an active role in conditioning the market. Too many of these executives lack the skill or will to play a public role. Or they define their roles internally, become consumed with the mechanics of running the day-to-day business, and try to delegate the role to others. The unfortunate fact, for many ambitious executives, is that the higher they climb in an organization, the more public the role becomes and the less tied it is to the internal strengths and responsibilities that led to their promotions up the ladder. Of course, there are CEOs who spend most of the time in their offices, but these aren't the ones who behaviorally differentiate themselves or lead their organizations to strong BD.

Senior executives must lead the way to BD. It starts with them. They have to be visible to customers and prospects, visible to employees, and visible in the markets they wish to serve. Those who historically have been most visible—Sam Walton, Herb Kelleher, George Zimmer, Jack Welch—are leaders who instinctively understand BD and walk the talk, day in and day out. Their consistent visibility in the markets, their clear articulation of their values and beliefs, and their single-minded purpose are key factors in how successfully their organizations position themselves in the marketplace.

Opening game is about conditioning the market—positioning yourself with prospective customers, building brand awareness, stimulating interest in and demand for your products and services, and building trust and credibility. As we have said throughout this chapter, there are numerous ways to condition the market, and in each of these you can differentiate yourself behaviorally. By the time you contact particular customers and start building relationships with them, you should already have won opening game by entering into those new relationships in a preferred or biased position in the customers' minds. They should already be predisposed to favor working with you, to respect and value your products and services, and to welcome your representatives. As Russian chess master Eugene A. Znosko-Borovsky said, "Our primary object is to enter upon the middle game, which is the very life of chess, without lagging behind our opponent. If we drift into a middle game without having developed the whole of our forces, our game will be dominated by the adversary and in consequence our pieces will be weaker than his, and their freedom of action will be restricted."[9]

CHALLENGES FOR READERS

1. BD derives from within. Do your company's core values and beliefs enable you to behaviorally differentiate yourself? Do your senior executives and managers walk the talk? Do your management and HR practices enable and encourage the kinds of employee behaviors that behaviorally differentiate you from your competitors? If not, what can you do about it? Consider raising these questions at roundtables with your employees and managers.

2. Do you have a culture of BD? Is it a concept deeply embedded in your policies and procedures, in your training and development programs, in your hiring and selection criteria, in your performance reviews and appraisals? What gets measured gets done. What are you measuring? What are you not measuring?

3. Do you have strategies for BD as well as strategies for product differentiation? If not, analyze your customers' behavioral expectations and develop a market strategy for differentiating yourself behaviorally.

4. How are you branding yourself and communicating to the market? Do you tend to use mostly the mass market communication tools shown in the left columns of Figure 5-3? Have you used any of the tools shown in the three columns on the right (columns 4 through 6)? What market communication tools could you use more (or more effectively) to behaviorally differentiate the way you communicate to the markets?

5. How well are you positioned politically in the markets you serve or the target markets you wish to serve? Do you invest enough time and energy during opening game to build your political position? If not, what could you do about that?

6. How active are your senior executives during opening game market conditioning? Are they strong and visible ambassadors to the market? If not, how are they using their time? What should they be doing differently?

7. Finally, rate yourself on a scale of 1 (worst) to 10 (best) on your opening game effectiveness. Rate your key competitors using this same scale. If you're not at 10 and if any of your competitors are higher on the scale than you, what can you do about that? If you ignore opening game or play it poorly, you will have to invest more later to try to catch up—and you may not be able to do so. Some competitors' leads cannot be overcome. Are you losing some prime opportunities now because you weren't well positioned going into middle game? If so, take a hard look at where and how you are investing in your business development process. Chances are you're trying to play catch-up instead of starting earlier and building a dominant position before you enter head-to-head competition.

CHAPTER 6

Middle Game:
Conditioning the Customer

> Middlegame . . . is the phase of the game where beautiful kingside attacks are created, subtle strategic plans are put into motion and preparations for the endgame are quietly (sometimes secretly) begun.—*Jeremy Silman,* The Complete Book of Chess Strategy
>
> ■
>
> After the opening, the challenging, complex, and often critical middlegame begins. It is characterized by the three elements: strategy, positional play, and tactics. Strategy is the formulation of plans to exert maximum offensive and defensive force. Positional play is the positioning of pieces and pawns to control important squares for optimum activity and flexibility. Tactics, the most powerful factor in chess, are direct threats to win material or checkmate.—*Ron Curry,* Win at Chess!

Most contracts are won or lost during middle game. Though it is impossible to be exact about win probabilities (there are too many variables), in our studies of competitive bidding in a variety of industries during the past twenty years, we have concluded that about 70 percent of your win probability comes from what you do or don't do during the crucial period between initial customer contact and release of the RFP. In our estimate, opening game accounts for about 20 percent of win probability, and endgame for about 10. This is not surprising, because most customer interactions occur during middle game, but we have observed numerous business development efforts—usually begun very late in middle game—in which companies imagine they can snatch victory from the jaws of defeat with a brilliant endgame proposal. When they lose, customers usually explain that their price was too high, and they are inclined to accept this rationale—though it is seldom the real reason they lost—because it confirms their belief that they're in a tough market and their competitors are willing to "buy" contracts by lowering their price. In fact, they probably lost because they played a very poor middle game or had no middle game at all.

Middle game in business development begins when you initiate contact with a prospective customer and start the long and intricate journey necessary to build relationships; credibility; trust; and, ultimately, preference. You enter middle game with one overriding objective: Position your company as the preferred provider when endgame begins with the call for proposals or, in the best case, create such an overwhelmingly obvious choice for the customer during middle game that endgame never happens. If you can avoid endgame, the RFP never hits the streets; you lower your cost of sales, which increases your margin; and the customer wins with an earlier launch of whatever is being bought plus lower procurement overhead. The competition loses before it even begins to compete in earnest. For a variety of reasons including either law (government customers in particular) or policy (companies that shop till they drop), keeping the RFP off the street is difficult in many cases and impossible in some. Still, the dominant objective for middle game is building the preference that will help you to win when endgame commences.

This part of the business development process includes the disciplines typically associated with face-to-face selling: getting meetings with prospects, making sales calls, building relationships, discovering customers' needs, introducing your products, and so on. Middle game is generally a lengthy process. Indeed, it can go on for years before a viable opportunity surfaces. Furthermore, middle game is complicated; there are no infallible strategies for success. It generally involves scores of players in a shifting landscape of power relationships, budgeting priorities, and the ebb and flow of needs as customers respond to exigencies in their business environment. As chess master Ron Curry observes, "The transition from opening to middlegame often causes intermediate chess players considerable difficulty, for they are departing the known with its fixed plan (control the center, develop all pieces, safeguard the King) and venturing into the unknown with no clear idea of how to proceed."[1]

To help us master middle game—and discover opportunities for behavioral differentiation—it's useful to view middle game itself as having three phases, as shown in Figure 6-1. *Early middle game* ex-

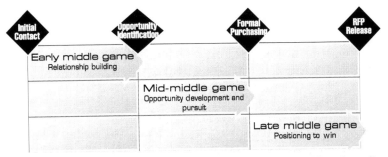

FIGURE 6-1. Middle game in business development. Middle game has three distinct phases: early relationship building, opportunity development, and formal purchasing. Most wins and losses occur during middle game, so it's critical to start early and respond in force to opportunities once they arise.

tends from the initial contacts with a prospective customer through the identification of a particular opportunity. This is the relationship-building phase, when you are extending your network of contacts in the customer organization, building relationships, and positioning yourself for consideration when appropriate opportunities arise. Once an opportunity surfaces, you are in *mid–middle game,* where the focus shifts to the opportunity and your goal is to develop preference for your products and solutions. The final phase, *late middle game,* begins when the customer initiates formal procurement. By this point, the customer is finalizing his or her selection process, has appointed the process gatekeepers, and is preparing to release his or her bid request document. If you are not well positioned to win by this point, you are way behind the power curve, as Figure 6-2 illustrates. Your ability to influence the outcome of a competition declines dramatically as middle game progresses, as the customer's perceptions and opinions become fixed, and as his or her early exploration of alternatives gives way to formal specifications and selection criteria. Your influence is highest in early middle game, which we will discuss in this chapter. It is highest here, among other reasons, because this is your best—and perhaps only—opportunity to get to the customer ahead of your competitors. Once an opportunity materializes, they will scramble, like firefighters when the alarm rings, to get to the customer. You want to be there already when that happens. In the next two chapters, we will describe the business development activities of mid and late middle game—and the opportunities for behavioral differentiation in each.

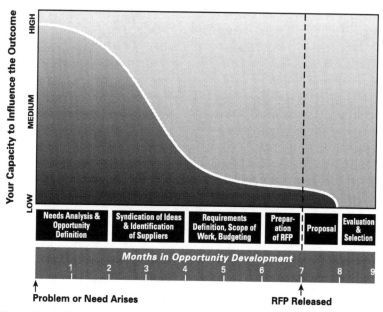

FIGURE 6-2. Influence in middle game. Your capacity to influence the opportunity wanes as middle game progresses. Starting late virtually guarantees that you will be reactive instead of proactive and will have little chance to presell your solution.

Force, Space, and Time

Russian grand master Eugene A. Znosko-Borovsky is among the many chess figures who have argued that the game of chess has three elements—force, space, and time—and that advantages in one or more of these elements decide the outcome of the game.[2] The pieces on a chessboard have different point values depending on their mobility and the threat they pose to an opponent. Queens are worth 9 points; rooks, 5; knights and bishops, 3; and pawns, 1. *Force* refers to the number and value of pieces at your disposal at any point in the game. Both sides begin with equal force, but imbalances soon appear as pieces are captured. Lev Alburt and Larry Parr, authors of *Secrets of the Russian Chess Masters*, explain the strategy of using force: "If you have a Queen (9 points), two Rooks (10 points) and a Bishop (3 points), then measured in point value, you have 22 points of force. If you see a possibility to leave the opponent with only 17 points, then your strategy is directed toward gaining the equivalent of a Rook

(5 points)."[3] Clearly, having superior force is advantageous in chess because you can apply more pressure, launch more attacks on the enemy king, and sacrifice pieces when their loss weakens your opponent's position.

Space refers to the number of board squares a player's pieces occupy or influence and the location of those squares. A player with a significant space advantage limits an opponent's mobility and constricts his pieces. Owning the center of the board is always advantageous because it reduces the opponent's options while giving the player more degrees of freedom to launch attacks in any direction. Finally, *time* refers to movement advantages players gain through the efficiency and timing of their moves. A player who advances a piece and then later retracts it to a square it formerly occupied is normally said to have lost time. A player who positions the right piece on a critical square and thus forces the opponent to make several moves in response is said to have gained time.

In the chess metaphor we've been using to describe business development, the concept of force, space, and time is insightful. *In business development, force is the amount of strength you can apply when contacting prospective customers and building your relationship with them.* Strength includes the power of your brand, the quality of your products and services, the quality of your people, your reputation in the industry, and the degree to which you are positively differentiated—in short, strength refers first to the degree of opening game positioning you have been able to establish. We think it also refers to the breadth and scope of the resources you can bring to bear in early middle game, when you are trying to win the hearts and minds of the key people in the customer's organization. If your senior leaders, experienced project managers, and key technical experts are willing to invest their time building relationships with new customers—and you have strength in brand, quality, and reputation—then you are applying substantial force to your business development effort. But this does not always happen. Frequently, the account manager who makes contact with a new prospective customer is on his or her own, perhaps with help from a sales manager but little else. Most companies don't invest enough senior resource time during early middle game. They wait until specific business opportunities arise. Even then, the CEO may not meet with prospective customers' CEOs unless the potential deals are large enough to warrant the CEO's interest. The bottom line is that few companies invest enough during early middle game, so the opportunities for behavioral differentiation abound.

Metaphorically, space in business development could apply to the degree to which you penetrate a prospective customer's organization and build strong, zippered networks. Typically, companies begin with a single point of contact in the customer's organization and find it difficult to extend their reach much further—into higher levels of the organization, for instance, or into other buying units or regions—at least in the short term. However, if you can build your network through all levels of the organization, across business units and regions, and establish relationships with the senior or key people who will make or influence the customer's buying decisions, then you will have gained a space advantage over your competitors with limited access. You will also have more information about what's going on in the customer's organization and better access to the right people when opportunities arise. Space is about access, depth of knowledge, and breadth of influence.

Time might refer to how well positioned you are to create or respond to opportunities. Clearly, you gain an advantage if you know about opportunities before they become public, if you can meet with the right people as they are discussing their problems or needs and formulating their plans to resolve them, and if you are engaged in trust-based discussions with key customers before your competitors are aware that an opportunity is about to surface. Applying the concepts of force, space, and time to business development is not a groundbreaking idea, but it is revolutionary in the sense that most companies do a very poor job of applying force when they establish contact with new prospective customers; most do not build networks of sufficient breadth, and most are not well ahead of their competitors as new business opportunities form and bubble to the surface. Why this is true is a mystery. As Jeffrey Pfeffer and Robert I. Sutton note in their book *The Knowing-Doing Gap,* smart companies do turn knowledge into action, but many, many companies do not. Though they know what should be done, they don't do it.

Companies should build force during opening game. That's when they create the kind of market position that will give them a *force* advantage once they make initial contact with prospective customers. In early middle game, they continue to build strength as they apply *space* and *time.* Moreover, they start the long process, through behavioral differentiation, of creating preference for themselves when business opportunities do surface.

Early Middle Game Goals

In early middle game, you have four goals: (1) to position yourself as a viable supplier to the customer; (2) to build close relationships with key people in the customer's organization, including purchasing and supply chain directors; (3) to establish an ongoing dialogue with those key people; and (4) to gain alignment on their needs and your value to them. This relationship-building phase is like a dance between two partners who have just met each other. The first moves are tentative and awkward as you get to know each other and become aware of the other person's movements and rhythm. If your customer has been dancing with others, and you dance the same old dance everyone else has, then your customer will recognize the dance and fall into an easy pattern, but you will be no different from the other fourteen partners your customer has been dancing with. Howard Schatz, who has specialized in photographing dancers, once observed that what made a dance unique was the dancers' willingness to venture beyond formula: "I told each dancer that when it was easy, it had probably been done before, probably many times. I explained that only when it was so hard that it was nearly impossible were we perhaps close to getting something unique and extraordinary."[4] Less-gifted dancers merely execute the moves they've learned. Their dances are predictable, uninspired, and forgettable. When two dancers are truly dancing with each other, they are dancing a dance that is unique to them.

So it is in early middle game business development. You can follow the well-established routines in making sales calls, presenting your products, leaving your brochures, and offering discounts. Or you can do some things that make you and your company memorable and unique. Early middle game includes the following types of activities—and each has many opportunities for behavioral differentiation:

■ Extending initial contacts and establishing the dialogue

■ Developing and executing tactical account management plans

■ Gathering more information on the customer and exploring how he or she uses your types of products and services

- Providing information on your company

- Gathering intelligence on your competitors' activities

- Determining how the customer is wired—and building a zippered network accordingly

- Building time share and mind share

- Building chemistry with the customer's key people

- Becoming a trusted advisor to customers

- Understanding and managing the political environment

- Testing and valuing your differentiators

- Consulting with the customer on opportunities and threats

Note that these activities should occur *before* a specific business opportunity arises. The fact that you do them will behaviorally differentiate you from your competitors who don't, but the *way* you do these things can also create behavioral differentiation. If you conduct opening and early middle game well, you can establish a powerful, preferential position with the customer before any business opportunities surface, and your competitors who were doing business as usual will be left in the dust.

Establishing the Dialogue

From the moment you establish contact with new, prospective customers, you should be differentiating yourself behaviorally. They are assessing you as a supplier from that moment forward, so your earliest contacts are part of the chemistry test customers use to determine whether they want to work with you. Beyond determining whether you are a good business fit for them, customers are judging your responsiveness, interest, care, and commitment to serving them. To pass the initial chemistry test, you should demonstrate:

■ That you are interested in them and their business, which you show through your knowledge of their industry, their company, and their value proposition to their customers; and through your persistence and the lengths you are willing to go to meet with them.

■ That you are highly responsive, which you demonstrate by meeting as soon as they are willing; by promptly returning telephone calls and other messages; by sending whatever information they request as soon as possible; and by answering their questions fully, even the ones that are difficult to answer. Further, if you don't know the answer, you say so and then find the right answer and give it to them as soon as possible.

■ That you care about them and their business, which you show through your thorough preparation for meetings, through the types of questions you ask, through your patience (i.e., not trying to close the sale because you need to make your numbers), through your empathy toward them and their business, and through your earnest desire to help them solve their problems and meet their needs—all of which signals that you put their interests ahead of your own.

■ That you are committed to serving their needs, which you confirm by having your senior leaders available for early meetings with customers' senior leaders, by devoting the resources necessary to explore their needs and understand their problems, by taking the time to diagnose their value proposition to their customers and adding insightful suggestions where you can to improve that proposition, and by taking the long view of your growing relationship with customers and acting like a partner rather than a vendor.

David Maister, author of *Managing the Professional Service Firm*, observed, "How you behave during the interview (or proposal process) will be taken as a proxy for how you will deal with me after I retain you. Unlike the process of qualification, which is predominantly rational, logical, and based on facts, the selection stage is mostly intuitive, personal and based on impressions."[5] During early middle game, you may also need to demonstrate your competence and credibility as a supplier, but you are always undergoing the chemistry test as well. When potential customers are getting to know you, they ask themselves these kinds of questions: "Can I trust this person and this company?" "Would they be good to work with?" "Do they know their stuff?" "Are they honest and straightforward? Reliable?" "Will they be there when I need them?" "Is this someone I want to work with?" Unless you are the sole provider of your types of products and services, which is unlikely, and assuming that you are competent to serve the customer's needs, then the principal test you must pass early in a developing customer relationship is the chemistry test. By the way, if you fail that test, you may never know why because most customers are reluctant to be that candid with suppliers they don't want to work with. It's too much trouble. Instead, they'll be unavailable for meetings, or stop returning your calls, or pass you off to someone else, usually at a lower level, who will let the communications die.

So to win early middle game, you first have to demonstrate high interest, high responsiveness, high care, and high commitment. Bear in mind that in early middle game you are not competing for a contract. An opportunity hasn't surfaced yet. Rather, you are competing for the customer's time, that finite number of minutes the customer allocates for meeting with outside providers. Only when you win that time-share competition—getting more of the customer's hours than your competitors do—can you begin to build mind share, which is how you build preference prior to endgame. To build time share, you need to be extremely responsive to customers' requests for information. Give them more than they ask for, and do it promptly. Further, customize the initial information you send to them. Avoid boilerplate materials, standard brochures, and cookie-cutter presentations. Those tools look like the labor-saving devices they are, and the message they send is that the customer isn't worth the trouble to do more. While you are devoting the time and spending the money to create customized materials for the customer, take heart. You are studying for the chemistry test, and most of your competitors are probably not investing the time you are, so they are likely to receive a lower grade.

Since your goal is to extend your reach inside the customer's organization and establish an ongoing dialogue about his or her needs and problems, you should also involve others in your company. Senior-level networking is most critical, so if you can interest your CEO, CFO, COO, and senior executives in meeting with their customer counterparts, you will be taking strides that many of your competitors will not be taking, which will differentiate you. However, contacts at all levels are important in building the kind of zippered network that provides value to both organizations. So try to get more people in your company involved in early customer meetings and calls: executives, engineers, project managers, technical experts, and so on. Demonstrate—rather than just state—your interest in the customer's business through as many conduits as possible.

Tactical Account Management

Account management is a business development discipline many companies know they should practice—but few do so with the degree of consistency and intelligence that would behaviorally differentiate them from their competitors. We said in the preceding chapter that you can initiate strategic account planning during the latter stages of opening game when you have targeted prospective customers who have the potential and attractiveness to make good strategic accounts if you can win them. When you make contact with those accounts in early middle game, you should shift your strategic account focus to the kinds of tactical account management activities that help you build your position in the account. You could form an account team, for instance, and develop and implement action plans for extending your network throughout the customer's organization; establishing the dialogue; demonstrating high interest, responsiveness, caring, and commitment; gathering information on the customer; and telling the customer more about your company and products. You could learn how the customer is wired (which we will discuss later in this chapter) and implement a contact plan for systematically developing the right relationships.

You could do many of the early opening game strategies we discuss in this chapter through an account team responsible for penetrating the account and surfacing viable business opportunities. What we are proposing here is not rocket science, nor is it an original idea, but it can differentiate you behaviorally because few companies do it regularly or well. It's one of those business development disciplines that most people agree is useful and productive—but few practice because, they argue, they don't have the time or the resources. It reminds us of the old saying, "I didn't have time to do it well, but I did have time to do it over." Except that in business development, when someone else has won the contract, you can't do it over. In the mid-

1980s, we worked for one of the world's largest engineering firms. We were talking to the head of one of its business units one day about bidding selectively, and he said, "Hell, we'll chase anything that moves, and if it doesn't move, we'll kick it to see if it'll move, and then we'll chase it!"

Another business unit in this same company submitted nearly one hundred proposals in a single fiscal year and didn't win anything. After several days of off-site planning, the company's president announced the strategy for the new year—submit two hundred proposals! With that sort of thinking, the company could fully expect to double its win rate. It goes without saying that bidding indiscriminately is bidding stupidly. There are better ways to throw money around, and one of them is to be selective about which customers you want to pursue (and later which opportunities to pursue, and which to pass by) and then devote the time, energy, and resources to the most attractive and rewarding customers and opportunities. When you're not spread so thin, you have time to do things right, including tactical account management during early middle game.[6]

Gathering Information on the Customer

A sensible guideline when you are developing a relationship with a customer is never to ask a question about his or her company or business that you could have answered from another source. Consider the impression you convey when you ask the customer the obvious fact-finding questions: "I didn't have the energy to look this up myself. I haven't thought about you until this meeting. I was too busy to take the time. You didn't have anything better to do than answer my questions, did you?" In this age of information glut, not doing your homework before you talk to customers is inexcusable. Of course, there's nothing wrong with confirming something you are unsure of, filling in the gaps, or asking questions about areas that are not public knowledge, but failing to do your homework is admitting to a degree of carelessness or laziness that is likely to result in negative BD. At a minimum, gather all the publicly available information you can find on customers before meeting with them the first time. Download their Web site and study it. If they are publicly traded, read their annual reports for the past three years and news or magazine articles about them. Know who they are, what they do, what markets and customers they serve, how they differentiate themselves, what their strategies are, what problems or challenges they've had lately, who their key people are, how they are organized, etc.

The smartest companies we've seen create "prospect books" that detail everything they can discover about a prospect before they make that first contact. Included in these books is an *intelligence needs list* that identifies everything they want to know about the customer. They convert this list into a set of questions for forthcoming meetings or telephone calls with the customer. In those meetings, they *look* more informed because they *are* more informed, and they behave accordingly. They ask better, more insightful questions and avoid the simple fact-finding questions that annoy customers and waste time. The result is behavioral differentiation. Here's a quick self-test: How many times have you gone into a meeting with a prospect knowing very little about the person? How many times have you and your colleagues decided how you were going to approach the meeting in the elevator on the way up to a prospect's office? Whatever your answers are, we are confident that this happens regularly. Many people have told us so.

> ♛ *Inexperienced players are too often impatient. They want to get to the end quickly, and jib at the time spent in a complete analysis of the position, with the result that they do not fathom its peculiarities, the differences between their game and that of their opponent, the weaknesses, threats, the chances on either side, etc. Failing to do this, they often lose a game which, with a little care, they might otherwise have at least drawn and perhaps won.—Eugene A. Znosko-Borovsky,* How Not to Play Chess

Particularly important in your initial information gathering is understanding the prospective customer's culture and self-image. One often-effective way to behaviorally differentiate yourself is to go into those early meetings already knowing how the people in this organization think about themselves, what's important to them, what they individually and collectively value, and what their dos and taboos are. Knowing their operating principles and mentioning them during your meetings is impressive to most customers. Knowing and using customers' language and matching their operating style says that you are adaptable and are striving to be compatible with them. Knowing customers well from the outset says that you care enough to make the effort to learn. It says that you are a thoughtful potential supplier and will probably be a thoughtful partner. It says that you pay attention to details and want to get them right. Even something as mundane as gathering information during your initial customer meetings can be a rich opportunity to differentiate yourself behaviorally from your competitors.

Beyond those initial meetings, knowing your customers and their industry well is a prerequisite to building the kind of trust and credibility with customers that encourages them to seek you out as a thought partner and counselor. In professional services firms like Heidrick & Struggles, knowing clients well is a professional responsibility and the foundation of long-term client relationships. Michael Flagg, managing partner of H&S's global communications practice, observes how being a thought partner to clients is a differentiator: "You differentiate yourself with clients by providing deep and independent thought. You must have the conviction to speak your mind, even when you aren't asked for your opinion, and to suggest in the politest but firmest way what you think the client should or should not be doing. Sometimes, you have to push them pretty hard because at the end of the day you have to own the problem. If you are not willing to go toe-to-toe with your clients on sensitive issues, you limit your value."[7] Clearly, you are in a privileged position relative to your competitors if your customers think of you as a trusted counselor and advisor. You behaviorally differentiate yourself when you have done your homework, know the industry, know the customer, and use the wisdom that comes from your experience and knowledge to add insight during your dialogues with customers. You ensure that value is flowing in both directions, which creates quality face time. In short, you win the battle for customer mind share.

Providing Information to Customers

Traditional sales calls occur during early middle game. In these calls, salespeople typically gather information on customers and their needs and wants, and they provide information to customers about their company and the features and benefits of their products and services. It's a moment where you can win your customers' hearts and minds through behavioral differentiation or leave customers with a bland or even negative impression if you do more telling than asking and more pitching than listening. Because so much has been made of the virtues of consultative selling in the last thirty years, one would think that salespeople today would "get it," but clearly many still don't, including some who sell sales training! We were reminded of this by Joanne Kincer, formerly director of leadership development for Encompass Services Corporation:

> While in the process of evaluating potential sales training vendors, I met with representatives from a number of training organizations attempting to sell their wares. Of course, evaluating sales training vendors is interesting in that while meeting with salespeople representing sales training products, I presume that I will have an opportunity to see the skills and tools they teach in action (after all, they are selling to me, right?). Typically, my assumption is that if I am not comfortable as a customer during the sales process, I would not want to teach my salespeople that same process and use it with my company's customers. Since much of sales is relationship building and a process of first uncovering and then fulfilling needs, I find it interesting that most sales training sales representatives go right into a pitch about their products and all the wonderful features they offer. Unfortunately, few of the so-called "sales professionals" who are attempting to sell sales training as a consultative process actually use the consultative selling process themselves. Most I met with took no interest in first uncovering my needs before attempting to sell something off the shelf and make it fit. There was one exception. One sales training organization that I met with actually spent one and a half hours of our first face-to-face meeting asking questions and verifying information that they had uncovered during prior discovery. They never went into a pitch; rather, they attempted to uncover what we were looking for, both in terms of training and training outcomes. This "no pitch" approach was not only comfortable to me as a customer but also made me feel as though the organization truly wanted to fully understand our situation and needs before asking us to sign on the dotted line. This was, in fact, the process we wanted to bring to life in our own sales organization and, consequently, this is the process we embraced. Not only was it the sales process we were

looking for, but the representatives of the process were living testi-monials of its effectiveness. This company was awarded our busi-ness.[8]

One commonsense lesson from this is that you have to practice what you preach. Your behavior must reflect your message, which is a form of symbolic behavioral differentiation. Another lesson is that you should not pitch your products early in the relationship-building process. Selling is not telling. Few customers today want to be *sold*. Most would rather *discuss, explore,* and *be advised* before coming to their own conclusions about what is best for them. Salespeople who approach customers this way are *facilitating* the buying process rather than selling. It's an important distinction, and it can behaviorally dif-ferentiate you from the pack of salespeople who are hawking their wares. So how do you provide information to customers? You start by imagining that you're in a "no-pitch" zone. You listen and ask questions first. Then you talk about your company and products only in response to customers' questions. When they ask about you, tell them, and then return to your questions rather than staying on a long telling track. In your early meetings with customers, you should observe the 80/20 rule—spend 80 percent of your time asking and listening and only 20 percent of your time telling. The foundation you want to lay is that what customers have to say is far more impor-tant than what you have to say. Most salespeople know this, and most don't do it. In addition, you can do the following to behaviorally differentiate yourself while providing customers information about yourself:

■ Have your CEO, president, or other senior executives present your company's capabilities to the senior leadership in the customer's or-ganization. Additionally, they could be present during other presen-tations or send letters or e-mails expressing their commitment to the customer.

■ Gather the customer's questions and then respond with *customized* executive summaries, brochures, interactive software, Web sites, or presentations. Don't use anything off the shelf; it sends a *commodity* message.

■ Prepare a living executive summary for customers that links their needs, problems, or opportunities with your ways of helping, showing how you can add value and improve business or solve their problems. Avoid strong pitches, and don't try to close the sale with this tool. Be patient. If you sent them your first iteration of a living executive summary during opening game, then this one would be your next iteration.

■ Use symbolic behavioral differentiation in packaging the information you send to customers. Send messages in a form and manner that reflects their products, values, or messages. Besides sending information to customers about yourself and your capabilities, you can inform them about industry issues or matters that could impact their business and help them make smarter decisions. In Chapter 5 we discussed the role of market communications in opening game. In middle game, too, there are numerous opportunities to communicate with customers in ways that behaviorally differentiate you and add value to them. Hall Kinion does this well. It surveys its customers on issues relevant to technology and human capital and publishes the results in a free publication called *Talent Economy*. According to Hall Kinion's Jeffrey Neal, "This magazine creates a lot of value for our customers. They feel some ownership for the magazine, they learn what's happening more broadly among technology managers, and we use it to communicate current issues and trends to our sales force. Our publication of *Talent Economy* shows that we are investing in our customers, our technology, and human capital."[9]

Building a Zippered Network

Gideon Sundback, a Swedish immigrant and electrical engineer who worked for the Universal Fastener Company, invented the "Separable Fastener" in 1917, though the term *zipper* originated with the B. F. Goodrich Company when it used Sundback's invention on a new design for galoshes. Apparently, Goodrich felt that "separable fastener" was too clumsy a term so it chose one with more zip. Goodrich might be surprised today at how we are using the term to describe networking between supplier and customer organizations, but it's an appropriate metaphor. A "zippered network" is one that extends from top to bottom across both organizations—with links between senior executives, between relevant managers and departments, between technicians and support people and those they support, and so on. What binds these multiple levels together is mutual interest in serving the customer's needs. Zippered networks are not born; they are made. And having huge gaps in them is as undesirable in customer networking as it would be in a pair of trousers.

In our experience, most B2B companies do not build zippered networks as thoroughly as they should, so being more disciplined about networking can be a behavioral differentiator. Practically speaking, how does one do that? First, you have to understand how customer organizations are wired, and here we are going to borrow another metaphor from Gideon Sundback, who, you may recall, was also an electrical engineer. Companies have formal organization structures and reporting relationships, which are generally shown on organization charts. But the truth about how companies work—how the juice *really* flows—is never apparent on an organization chart. What's missing are the lines of actual communication between people and groups; the power relationships based partly on hierarchy and position but largely on each person's knowledge, reputation, influence, and working relationships; and the dynamic ebb and flow of those who are rising in the organization, those who are on a plateau, and those whose star is dimming. In effect, this is how the company is actually *wired*—how the work gets done, how priorities are set, how influence is exercised, and how decisions are made. In short, how the power flows.

To network effectively within any customer organization, you have to comprehend how the place is wired, and you have to build relationships with the people who are making or influencing the buying decisions today, as well as those who will be making such decisions tomorrow. Further, if you want to know what's *really* happening inside the customer's organization, you have to be talking to people at all levels—from the executive suite to the project offices and from the cubicles to the lunchrooms. Hence, the importance of building a zippered network.

This is particularly important in global customer organizations where decisions are usually decentralized and there are multiple centers of power and influence. John Gardner, vice chairman of Heidrick & Struggles's board services group and managing partner of the firm's office of the chairmen, advises being systematic in developing global client relationships:

You have to look very broadly at a client's organization and business issues and be part strategist and part psychologist. You also need to know enough about the industry to know the DNA of the competing companies and the implications of their differences. What is unique about your client? What are they trying to accomplish with the resources and leadership they have? Then you reach out and penetrate the client's organization, mapping the terrain, so to speak, knowing who's who in senior management and human resources globally. You match your depth and capability with the client's organization and needs, and then you actively develop the key relationships.[10]

Effective networks don't just happen. You have to be systematic in mapping the terrain, as Gardner said, and then be proactive in establishing contact and building the relationships.

You also have to take the long view about customers. Initially, you should operate in the "no-pitch" zone, striving to come across as a thought partner rather than a vendor trying to close the sale. Some tools you might use to bring the right people together from your company and the customer's organization include seminars, customer forums, idea exchanges, brainstorming or problem-solving meetings, team-building events, private trade shows, product launch events, and social gatherings. Of course, a number of companies do use such tools, but we have not seen many that are as systematic and thoughtful about using these tools as they could be. Some sales managers make good use of them; others use these tools haphazardly if at all. Farther up the high-technology food chain are virtual networks using WebEx, eRoom, or similar platforms to create online chats, discussion boards, document repositories, and so on. Some companies have also created proprietary Web sites that give customers private information or enable them to track shipments or projects, monitor order status, and configure their solutions.

Of course, the key to building an effective network in the customer's organization is not technology, which is only an enabler. Rather, it's having both the personal and the institutional skill and will to do the networking in a systematic and disciplined way—and doing it so that it is visible and valuable to customers. Most companies lack the skill and the will, so you can differentiate yourself behaviorally by following a few simple guidelines:

■ Make networking a formal and deliberate part of your relationship-building process. Manage it and measure it. Develop and use contact plans to make your network building systematic. Include a "Value Provided" field on your contact plans so that you can create and document your effort to establish quality face time in every interaction with the customer. Most companies know this, but few do it. Doing this alone will differentiate you from three-quarters of your competitors, who will not have the contacts when they need them, won't gain as much intelligence on upcoming opportunities, and don't have as much influence in the customer's organization because they lack the broad zippered network you will have built.

■ Create bios of the customer's key people and refresh your memory before meeting with them. Know as much as you can about the people before coming face-to-face with them. As you talk to them and learn more about them, remember the facts of their lives (birthdays, children's names, favorite sports or books, where they've vacationed) and inquire about them from time to time.

■ While you're interacting with customers, disclose some things about yourself, not only the facts of your life but what you like and don't like, your operating style, your weaknesses and pet peeves. Be human with people, and you'll form stronger bonds.

■ Include the assistants and secretaries in your network. They know more about what's going on in the organization than many other professionals. Treat them well, remember their names, and don't ever condescend to them or be rude. Believe it or not, *this* will differentiate you from many of your rivals. There are people who have thinly veiled contempt for those they consider beneath them. Happily, these fools are the behavioral contrast that makes your kind and respectful treatment of *everyone* in the customer's organization a positive differentiator for you. Secretaries, receptionists, and assistants will talk to their bosses about you. They'll say when you have been friendly, helpful, respectful, kind, and understanding—and they'll go out of their way to baste you if you've been unfriendly, gruff, dismissive, demanding, and rude. Remember that *every* customer touch point is an opportunity for behavioral differentiation.

■ Find every reasonable opportunity to meet with the key people in your network informally (during meals, sporting events, social occasions, industry social gatherings, and so on). Informal contacts help build personal bonds.

■ Be absolutely responsive to them at all times. Return telephone calls and e-mail messages promptly.

We know that the advice we're offering here is not new. It goes without saying that you should return phone calls as quickly as possible. These tips have been bandied around in sales books, articles, lectures, videotapes, and sales meetings for decades. Nonetheless, although the advice may sound old hat, the fact is that many people don't do these things consistently. These old saws keep recycling through sales courses and books because they are best practices that aren't practiced universally, and the people who *do* practice them tend to be the stars. When asked for the secrets of their success, the best-in-class people and companies invariably cite these kinds of practices. What do we make of this? Simply that *practicing* the best practices is bound to differentiate you behaviorally from a number of your competitors who know what they should be doing but don't do it— and aren't holding anyone accountable for doing it. Indeed, a great deal of what we're discussing here as behavioral differentiation in early middle game can and should be integrated into a company's sales management and performance review processes.

Building Time Share and Mind Share

The purpose of relationship building is to build time share and mind share with customers. As Figure 6-3 illustrates, when you spend more time with customers—when you create more time share for yourself—you eventually build more mind share, which means they think of you first when they have problems or needs you can help them resolve. Greater mind share leads to greater wallet share, meaning that you get proportionately more of their business, and greater wallet share among the many customers you serve means greater market share. To increase your market share, you must first increase your time share with the customers you serve, and this means spending more time with them than your competitors do during early middle game. Building and then working a zippered network is the best way

FIGURE 6-3. Time share to market share. To build your market share, you must first build time share and mind share with individual customers.

to ensure that you are building time share, but it won't happen serendipitously; you have to manage it actively, encourage your people to spend time with their counterparts in the customer's organization, and sustain the initiative throughout the life of the relationship with the customer.

Kyung Yoon, a vice chairman of Heidrick & Struggles, has been recognized as one of the top two hundred executive recruiters in the world in Nancy Garrison-Jenn's book *The Global 200 Executive Recruiters*. She talked to us about actively building mind share:

> You have to be relationship driven and very transparent about that. The key is demonstrating to clients that you care about them, that you're knowledgeable about their business, and that you're willing to put yourself in their shoes and commit to and invest in the relationship. Over time, you will do much better than consultants who are transactional and only care about closing searches. One of the reasons I have been able to develop such great client relationships is that I articulate that from the beginning. I tell clients I'm looking for a long-term, value-adding relationship on both sides. Then I invest myself in their business so I can understand it enough to give them an objective view about what's going on and what problems and opportunities they might have. They come to see me as an in-house advisor, somebody they're really comfortable with, and call me when they want to talk. You have to be in their mind when they have problems or needs. That's how you build mind share.[11]

Investing in the relationship is critically important, as Kyung Yoon says. You can't show up only when an opportunity surfaces—doing so says that you're only in it for the transaction. You have to invest in the relationship even when there are no business opportunities on the horizon. Here are some other best practices from people who are best-in-class at building long-term customer relationships:

■ Extend your zippered network outside the customer's organization, too. Build connections and relationships with key partners, allies, and other suppliers who serve the customer where such connections are useful and appropriate. Add value to the customer by bringing those other network partners into your discussions as appropriate.

■ Ensure that your face time with customers is always quality time for them. If you can't add value, don't impose on their time. Know what value you are adding every time you interact with them.

■ Find appropriate social opportunities to increase time and mind share with customers, but play by the rules. If business talk is expected, fine; if not, avoid it.

■ Make yourself available for important events in the customer's business, such as new product rollouts, new office openings, and new ad campaign rollouts. If you are invited, attend. If not, send a card with a personal congratulation. The same is true for important personal events (weddings, birthday celebrations, etc.) if you have developed a strong personal relationship with a customer.

■ Notice other important events in the lives of your customers, such as book or article publications, televised appearances, or awards presentations, and send a congratulatory note. Being present in their lives doesn't mean being intrusive, but it does mean paying attention. They will remember who noticed.

■ Find ways to add value through knowledge sharing or problem solving. Be proactive about using industry surveys, research, technical expertise inside your own company, and innovative solutions your company has developed to help them improve their business. One sure way to build mind share is to become an indispensable thought partner with your customers, to add business value none of your competitors adds.

■ Where appropriate, establish personal relationships with customers, but ensure that they are genuine, nontransactional, and unimposing. Not everyone can do this well. Not everyone can avoid the conflict-of-interest implications of friendships with customers because they have trouble keeping their personal and business lives separate. The point is not necessarily to build lifelong friendships as much as it is to create a degree of interpersonal comfort that allows you to establish a human connection. Customers should like you in the sense that they enjoy doing business with you. They should feel that you are honest and forthright, that you are a pleasure to work with, that you bring real value to them, that you don't try to impose on them or sell them things they don't want or need, that you are an interesting person, that you know helpful and useful things, and that you are enjoyable to talk to.

■ Commit valuable face time to the customer even during periods when you are not serving them. This shows that you are in it for the long haul, that you are committed to them through thick and thin. If you can do this, even Superglue couldn't create a stronger bond.

■ Institute a *high-touch, high-care* attitude with everyone in your company who touches customers, either face-to-face or otherwise.

These kinds of practices will not necessarily differentiate you behaviorally from your competitors; it depends on what your competitors are doing. However, these kinds of behaviors will help you build time share and mind share, which will help increase wallet share. In our experience, however, there is a considerable disparity between the amount of face time companies have with customers. Several years ago, we had lunch with the CEO of a large industrial manufacturer who had once led the business development group for an engineering and construction firm that was reputed to be best-in-class in marketing. We asked him how much he expected his salespeople to be out in the field in front of customers, and he said, "Four days a week." Later, we surveyed another firm in this industry, one with a far less successful record in business development, and discovered that its salespeople had on average only about six hours of face time with customers each week. It should be obvious why the former firm was best-in-class. Quality face time is a behavioral differentiator. Lackluster performers don't have enough of it—and it's not because customers won't meet with them; it's because they don't make the effort. To maximize customer contact, you have to set high face-time expectations for the sales group, have the leadership to drive those expectations, and have salespeople skilled enough to add value in every customer interaction. Increasing value-adding face time builds time share; more time share leads to more mind share, which builds wallet share, and this in turn builds market share. Of course, it's not quite as simple as this, but it's awfully close. Quality face time is a powerful behavioral differentiator.

♟ The desire for efficiency and productivity, and the struggle for organizational viability, have increasingly influenced the development of large-scale service enterprises engineered to process masses of customers with speed, consistency, and profitability. . . . This new revolution in service has resulted in a depersonalization of interactions between providers and customers. Depersonalization involves treating customers like numbers, rather than human beings with unique needs and interests.—*Wendy S. Zabava Ford,* Communicating with Customers

---

Building Chemistry

To be well positioned with customers, you must pass the chemistry test, which means they have decided to work with you, regardless of whether they have any immediate needs. Throughout this book, we've noted that being a capable supplier is not enough to get work these days. There are plenty of capable suppliers. As middle game progresses, customers aren't asking whether you can do the job; they're asking themselves whether they prefer to work with you or with someone else. For you to win more than your fair share of work, you must have better chemistry with your customers than your rivals do.

Chemistry has three ingredients, as shown in Figure 6-4: credibility, trust, and compatibility. It would be difficult to assert that any of these ingredients is more important than the others, but credibility is certainly the first gate you must pass through. Before you can have a serious dialogue with customers, they must believe that you are capable of doing the job. As they assess your *credibility*, they are in effect asking these questions:

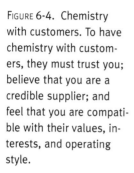

FIGURE 6-4. Chemistry with customers. To have chemistry with customers, they must trust you; believe that you are a credible supplier; and feel that you are compatible with their values, interests, and operating style.

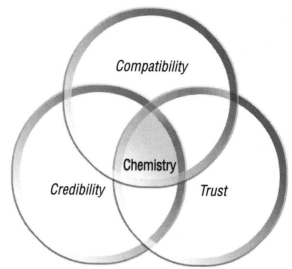

■ Do you belong to a reputable company?

■ Do you have the requisite education, experience, and expertise?

■ Do you know what you're talking about?

■ Do you speak confidently?

■ Do your answers to our questions reveal deep knowledge of the subject?

■ Do you ask knowledgeable and insightful questions of us?

■ Have you worked in our industry before?

■ Have you seen the kinds of problems or opportunities we're facing?

■ Has your previous work for other customers been successful?

■ Do you have the same quality programs and standards we do?

■ Are you a lean manufacturer or service provider? Are your operations as efficient as ours?

■ Are you cost conscious? Do you work vigorously to take costs out of the supply chain? Can you prove that you have saved money or lowered costs for other customers?

■ Do you understand our needs and have good ideas for how we can meet them?

They may ask you these questions directly, but more often these are the unspoken questions running through their head as they talk to you, ask you questions, listen to your responses, and learn more about you and your company. Credibility is the table stake. Without it, none of the rest of this discussion matters. However, it's difficult to behaviorally differentiate yourself in matters of credibility because your key competitors are likely to be just as credible. Much of credibility is tied, directly or indirectly, to capability, and your first-tier competitors have as much as you do. There are more opportunities to differentiate yourself behaviorally in matters of trust. Credibility is largely a matter of the head, but trust is a matter of the heart, and business decisions are rarely based on logic alone. Here are the kinds of questions customers ask about you as they are considering whether they can *trust* you:

■ Are you honest and worthy of trust? Will you always tell me the truth?

■ Do you keep your promises and commitments? Will you do what you say you will do and deliver what you promise?

■ Will you be candid with me, even if it means giving me bad news?

■ Will you treat me fairly?

■ Will you look out for my interests first? Will you do what's right for me?

■ Will you avoid high-pressure sales tactics or manipulative gimmicks that are blatant, self-serving attempts to entice me to buy your products whether I need them or not?

■ Will you work transparently with me and not go behind my back and attempt to influence my boss if things don't go exactly as you'd like?

■ Will you bill fairly and honestly for your time and materials?

■ Will you avoid surprising me with problems or costs I hadn't counted on?

■ Will you keep any secrets I tell you? Will you be discreet?

■ Will you be there when I need you?

Arguably, these elements of trust are nothing more than sound professional behavior toward customers. One would expect to see them in every customer interaction from every B2B supplier. Of course, you don't always see them, which is our point. As fundamental as these behaviors are, many people in business don't behave this way consistently. The customers' interests don't always come first. Companies do promise more than they deliver, and as the Enron collapse showed us, companies can be dishonest, and company leaders aren't always candid about bad news. Integrity isn't a given, and even when companies do act with the best of intentions, failing to be candid with customers can be interpreted as a lack of integrity. It is especially important to be candid in delivering bad news.

Emeric Lepoutre, managing partner of Heidrick & Struggles's Paris office and head of the firm's international legal practice, spoke to us about the importance of honesty and candor. He met with a potential client, a second-tier law firm in Europe, to discuss its search for a new partner. This firm wanted to attract partners from first-tier worldwide law firms like Clifford Chance and Skadden Arps, but in Lepoutre's judgment, it was not ready to attract the finest legal talent from the best firms. "I met with them for three hours," Lepoutre told us. "I said to them, 'If we were to work together, we must be honest with each other and know where you are starting from. You have a lot of work to do. Your lawyers are far from being as good as those at Clifford Chance, and there are many other areas where you need to improve.' My competitors were telling them it would be no problem to search for partners from the best firms, but this was a lie, and it would be revealed later when there were no candidates from Clifford

Chance or Skadden Arps. You should never hesitate to say the truth. Being honest and transparent can differentiate you."[12]

Trust and credibility are necessary conditions for building chemistry with customers, but they still aren't sufficient. Many suppliers are trustworthy and credible. To build the kind of chemistry with customers that differentiates you from your rivals, you need something more. You and the customer must be *compatible*, which the dictionary defines as "existing together in harmony." We believe that harmony operates on several levels. The first is purely personal. People are harmonious when they have similar views and values, enjoy the same things, have the same interests, share a sense of humor, or have something else in common. Robert Cialdini, author of *Influence: The Psychology of Persuasion*, argues that similarity has a powerful effect on how people respond to each other: "We like people who are similar to us. This fact seems to hold true whether the similarity is in the area of opinions, personality traits, background, or life-style."[13] When we like the people we are doing business with, we are inclined to continue doing business with them because it's a more pleasant experience. Salespeople know this and some try to use it to their advantage by faking similarities: "The Yankees are my favorite team, too." "You're a Texan? I lived in Dallas for a while." And so on. This charade occasionally fools an unsuspecting customer, but most people see it for what it is and lose trust in the salespeople who use this tactic—as well they should. But for all the charlatans, there are scores of professionals who behave genuinely with customers and who have discovered mutual interests that make them compatible on the personal level.

Harmony between buyers and sellers operates on the business level, too, and ultimately this is the more important of the two. As customers assess how *compatible* you are as a business thought partner, they ask themselves these kinds of questions:

■ Do you have a genuine interest in me and my success? Do you care about my company and its fortunes?

■ Do you share my perspective about how business is done? Do we have similar views about appropriate business behavior?

■ Do we have similar interests in business topics? Do we read the same kind of business literature, or watch the same business programs, or follow the same issues?

■ Do we have any commonalities in our business experiences? Do we know some of the same people? Do we belong to the same associations?

■ Are you interested in my industry? Are we curious about the same things? Do we have insights to share with each other?

■ Do you understand my operating style and preferences, and are you willing to adapt? Will you work with me the way I want? Will you communicate with me the way I like to communicate?

■ Do you know what's important to me, what my priorities are? Are those your priorities as well?

■ Do I enjoy working with you, not just because you're a nice person and we have some common personal interests, but because you add value to me as a businessperson?

Achieving this level of compatibility with customers requires a great deal of skill and professionalism and a significant investment of time and energy. Not everyone is up to it, which is why it's a powerful behavioral differentiator when it's done well. Nor can everyone create chemistry with every customer. Credibility and trust should be established in all customer relationships, but compatibility is a matter of fit. Even the most charismatic builders of customer relationships won't hit it off with every customer, so smart companies try to match the personalities, operating styles, backgrounds, and interests of their people with those of the customer.

Becoming a Trusted Advisor

Throughout this discussion, we've used the term *salesperson* as a convenience to describe who in your company is building customer relationships, but in truth every executive, project manager, service technician, and other employee who interacts with your customers at key touch points should be trying to establish credibility, build trust, and be compatible with the customer's representatives. The pinnacle of customer relationships is to be viewed as a trusted advisor. Customers who view you as a trusted advisor are more likely to call you when they need help, accept your recommendations and solutions, refer you to others inside or outside their company who could use your help, give you more time share and mind share, and consider you a long-term business associate and friend. When customers have problems or questions and they call you, you have achieved the kind of trust that maximizes mind share. David H. Maister, who has written extensively about professional services firms and coauthored a book entitled *The Trusted Advisor*, usually associates trusted advising with people in the professions: lawyers, accountants, consultants, and so on. However, whether your business is potash, pizza, parrots, or professional services, you can aspire to be viewed by your customers as a trusted advisor. It's largely a matter of mind-set and behavior, as the following best practices suggest:

■ First, think of yourself as an advisor rather than an executive, project manager, account manager, engineer, service technician, or customer service representative. The mind-set is important. If your employees think of themselves as vendors, that's how they'll behave. If they think of themselves as advisors, they'll act like advisors. Of course, they'll need the skills, too, but it begins with their self-concept and their concept of the company, its mission, and their role relative to the customers you serve.

> *To mature from subject-matter expert to trusted business advisor, you have to adopt a student mindset. You need a knowledge acquisition strategy that takes you well beyond your core expertise and utilizes multiple methods of learning. Client learning has to be a central focus of your efforts: depth and breadth of knowledge, together with an intimate understanding of your client and his world, form a powerful combination that will fuel your ability to be insightful and consistently add value.—Jagdish Sheth and Andrew Sobel,* Clients for Life

■ Then you have to build the credibility and trust needed for customers to see you as a trusted advisor. Belonging to a trusted firm or company helps, but trust as an advisor must be earned individually and with every customer. As Maister, Green, and Galford note: "The key point is that trust must be *earned* and *deserved*. You must do something to give the other people the evidence on which they can base their decision on whether to trust you. You must be willing to *give* in order to *get*."[14]

■ Use a consulting approach with customers—ask more questions, do more listening, and help them find the answers themselves. This is in stark contrast to the typical transactional salesperson who tells, pushes, and tries to close. Be patient, act in customers' best interests, and don't do work for customers that you should not be doing or sell them something they don't need.

■ Take a broader view of customers' business, focusing not only on the segments or needs you serve but on their overall business. Search for ways to help them beyond the scope of the work you are doing.

■ Schedule breakfasts, lunches, dinners, or other away-from-work events to have open dialogues with customers, where you can talk about anything of interest to them regarding the business. Ensure that these discussions are confidential from your standpoint—and don't treat these as sales calls. Don't push your own agenda.

■ Find opportunities to add value, especially as a thought partner, when you have nothing to gain, when your reason for adding value is simply to help the customer.

■ Continue to think about customers' problems even when you are not meeting with them or serving them. Call them with ideas when you have something of merit to suggest.

■ Share your own best practices with your customers. General Electric excels at this. Its customer workouts, which we described in *Winning Behavior*, are outstanding behavioral differentiators. Very few companies demonstrate GE's commitment to helping customers improve their businesses.

Clearly, to be viewed as a trusted advisor, you must have something of value to share with customers, some insightful questions to ask or some credible advice to give. Best-in-class companies develop insight deliberately, as part of their corporate strategy, and they invest the time and resources to ensure that it happens. They assign strategic account managers to their key customers—to develop and manage the relationship, to ensure that those customers are well served and their needs are met, and to develop enough understanding of them to provide added value. Some companies analyze their customers' value chains to understand and increase their value-added contributions and to share their insights into how their customers can improve their businesses. Some companies invest in research and educational initiatives to develop more knowledge about their customers' businesses and industries. Whatever your particular path to developing insights for your customers, it's clearly useful to have such insights and use them to educate your employees so they are better able to add value during their customer interactions.

We have devoted considerable time in this chapter to discussing the importance of building zippered networks with customers, increasing your time share and mind share with them, building chemistry, and being thought of as trusted advisors because these are intelligent and competitive ways to build differentiated customer relationships during early middle game. The evidence from most industries would suggest that the majority of companies don't make the investments in relationship building that we have discussed. Many companies have a far more transactional attitude toward customers. They are driven to make the next quarter's numbers, so they emphasize the short term. They create incentives for salespeople to close sales, not build long-term relationships. They busy themselves with internal matters and don't devote the executive time and energy to building customer relationships. Their internal reporting systems place a premium on billable hours; in some companies there are no charge codes for nonbillable "relationship-building hours" with customers. These practices militate against making the kinds of investments in customer relationships that can behaviorally differentiate. Mind you, we're not condemning these practices. There are sensible reasons for each policy decision that reinforces a transactional attitude toward customers. However, companies have to balance their short-term and long-term perspectives, and most emphasize the short term, which creates a spectacular behavioral differentiation opportunity for those few companies that choose to change the balance.

Managing the Political Environment

In the previous chapter, we talked about the need to understand the political environment in your industry and to position yourself by making the right political connections. In opening game, you should develop the kinds of political connections that are likely to be helpful with any customer you might serve. Now, in early middle game with a customer, it's crucial to develop the political connections that are most needed with this particular customer. So an important early middle game challenge is to map the political landscape in which this customer operates. Which governmental connections are important? Which agencies? Which regulators? Which elected officials? Which agents, associations, clubs, special interest groups, and other affiliations?

Mapping the political landscape means comprehending the often-hidden sources and lines of influence and communication in the business and social environment in which the customer conducts its affairs. Comprehending this, you work to build connections in the right places. Having those connections gives you the potential to be a high-value-added partner. Where possible, ethical, and appropriate, you can use your knowledge of the political environment to prepare the way for customers, perhaps by helping them understand what needs to be done; by introducing them to the right people; or by using appropriate influence to facilitate the processes of review, oversight, and approval. We are not advocating doing anything illegal or unethical through political influence, but it would be naïve to assert that you should never help your customers. Within legal and ethical bounds, helping customers politically is good business—and it's how business is done. If you have a better appreciation for the customer's political environment and have useful connections, you will behaviorally differentiate yourself from your competitors who lack those connections. At the same time, making unethical use of political connections may differentiate you negatively and cost you more than you gained. It's a slippery slope, so it's best to differentiate yourself by being ethical and politically savvy at the same time.

Testing and Valuing Your Differentiators

In *The Marketing Imagination*, Harvard's Theodore Levitt makes this cogent point: "Customers attach value to products in proportion to the perceived ability of those products to help solve their problems. Hence a product has meaning only from the viewpoint of the buyer or the ultimate user. All else is derivative. Only the buyer or user can assign value, because value can reside only in the benefits he wants or perceives."[15] So another important early middle game activity is to test your product, service, and behavioral differentiators with customers and determine what value they place on them. It's easy to deceive yourself about your differentiators—to assume that some things differentiate you when in fact they don't, to place more value on them than your customers do, or to undervalue something customers consider important. Clearly, it's important to get this right, so the best practice is to ask customers what's important to them and to test what you perceive as your differentiators. You might do it by asking these kinds of questions:

■ In purchasing our types of products or services, what is most important to you? What do you expect from the product or service and from the supplier? What would exceed your expectations?

■ What do you like about our products or services? What annoys you about them? What would make them a better fit for your needs? What do you wish we would change?

■ What do you like about doing business with us? What annoys you about doing business with us? What could we do to make the business relationship better?

■ What do we do for you that our competitors don't? What do they do for you that we don't? How important are these differences to you?

■ In your view, what differentiates us from our competitors? How important are those differences? What business value would you place on them?

■ What could we do differently that you would value more?

■ If you were to rate us as a supplier or partner, on a scale from 1 to 10, with 10 being the highest, what score would you give us? If we're not a 10, what could we do to reach 10?

> ♘ *Most companies measure and monitor the significant factors affecting their businesses: sales and profits, customer growth and defection, support costs by product line, inventory turns, profit margins, and so forth. On your website you're probably measuring hits and clicks, traffic, page views, and unique visitor sessions. You're probably also monitoring click-throughs, conversion rates, navigation paths, and abandoned shopping carts. But none of these metrics matter to your customers. They can't help you improve your customer's experience in doing business with you.—Patricia B. Seybold,* The Customer Revolution

Even asking these questions is bound to differentiate you behaviorally because few companies are diligent about testing their differentiators and asking customers to value them and their products. We suspect that some people are reluctant to ask the questions as directly as we are suggesting because the news may not be good or because customers may want more than you can reasonably and affordably provide. But in our opinion any answers to these questions are valuable. If you're not as highly thought of as you'd like, it's best to know that now so you can fix it, and if customers want more than you can affordably provide, then you at least have engaged them in a dialogue that can lead to a better understanding between you. Finally, if the customer does not perceive that you are differentiated from your competitors or doesn't value your differentiators, then you at least know where you stand and know that you have work to do. Being unaware that you're undifferentiated, however, means that you'll be beaten down relentlessly on price and won't understand why business is getting so tough. Smart companies test their differentiators with customers and learn how customers value those differentiators. Then they build product, service, and behavioral differentiation from an informed position and are well positioned for mid–middle game when business opportunities arise.

Consulting on Opportunities and Threats

You have succeeded in early middle game when you are well positioned for any opportunities that emerge—when the customer considers you a preferred supplier, when the customer looks for opportunities to work with you before specific needs arise, when you have built a strong network throughout the customer's organization and have established good chemistry with the customer's key people, when you thoroughly understand the customer's needs and have shown how the customer's needs are aligned with the value you offer, and when you have established ongoing dialogues with the customer's key decision-makers and influencers. As we've discussed throughout this chapter, there are numerous ways to differentiate yourself behaviorally while you are building customer relationships. Doing so improves your position and makes you a more attractive supplier. When opportunities do emerge, you should not be on a level playing field with your competitors—even if they are as capable as you are and provide products or services that are indistinguishable from yours. If you have won early middle game, you will have created a favorable bias in the customer's mind and you will win more than your fair share of work if you are also adept at the remaining stages of middle game and at endgame.

The final way to differentiate yourself behaviorally in early middle game is to be proactive about identifying or discovering opportunities for customers to improve their business—through process improvements, better systems or solutions, more creative approaches, and so on. Consider the most common experiences customers have with most would-be suppliers:

■ They receive brochures in the mail or unwanted e-mail promotions. There may or may not be a telephone call following up these mailings.

■ A salesperson drops by now and then, leaves samples and the latest brochures, and asks if they have any needs.

■ A salesperson arrives, sometimes with a team and sometimes at the customer's request, to make a presentation on his or her company's latest products. This presentation includes some testimonials from other satisfied customers and an impressive list of the features and benefits of the company's products.

■ The customers announce that they have a need, and they are quickly besieged by legions of interested suppliers, including some they haven't heard from since the last time they purchased this product or service and some new would-be suppliers they hadn't known about until this moment.

Contrast this picture with behaviorally differentiated suppliers who work with customers over the long term whether or not there are immediate needs for their products or services, who look for opportunities for customers to improve their business, and who help create opportunities that meet the needs of both organizations. Which type of supplier would you rather do business with? There are few downsides to being proactive unless your initiative taking is entirely self-serving, in which case customers should be suspicious of you. However, if you have your customers' best interests at heart, being proactive and finding opportunities is one of the best ways to position yourself for the next phase in the business development cycle—mid-middle game, where opportunities surface and customers start moving toward a purchasing decision.

CHALLENGES FOR READERS

1. How effective is your company at building relationships with customers in early middle game? Do you invest as much in relationship building as you should early on, or do you tend to wait until opportunities surface? How well positioned are you by the time you start pursuing real opportunities?

2. To what extent do you behaviorally differentiate yourself following your initial contacts with new customers? Do you immediately demonstrate your responsiveness, interest, care, and commitment to serving them? Whatever your impression is, how do you know for sure? If you have a large sales force in the field, how do you think they come across? How could you find out?

3. Do you ever create prospect books or something similar on customers before you meet with them the first time? Do you do your homework and avoid asking them the obvious fact-finding questions?

4. Do your salespeople really use a consultative or facilitative sales process? Or do they go in and pitch your products and not listen to customers as well as they should? This is in some ways a trick question because, as we showed in this chapter, even some companies that sell sales training don't embody what they teach.

5. Do you have a strong zippered network with all of your major customers? Who in your company is responsible for building and maintaining those zippered networks? How well are these networks being managed?

6. Do you have a disproportionately high amount of time share and mind share with your customers? If not, what should you do to build it? On average, how much face time do your salespeople have with customers or prospects each week? How much face time do your senior executives have?

7. Building strong chemistry is a key to creating powerful behavioral differentiation during early middle game. How effective are your people at establishing credibility, trust, and compatibility? Don't answer this question too quickly. You are likely to have some people who do it well and some who do it poorly. How do you ensure that your stars are working at the most critical touch points? How do you help them share their best relationship practices with others in your company? How can you build your company's overall skill level?

8. The best kind of relationship to have with a customer is to be viewed as a trusted advisor. To what extent are you and your people viewed as trusted advisors by individual customers? What more could you do to ensure that your people earn and deserve the trust necessary to be viewed as advisors by your key customers?

9. Do you deliberately test and value your differentiators with your customers? If not, use or adapt the list of questions we provided to survey your customers' views of your differentiation. What does that survey tell you? How can you increase your differentiation in ways customers value highly?

CHAPTER 7

Middle Game:
Building a Powerful Position

The side that forces its ideas on a reacting opponent is said to have the initiative.—*Jeremy Silman,* The Complete Book of Chess Strategy

■

Being part of a football team is no different than being a part of any other organization—an army, a political party. The objective is to win, to beat the other guy. You think that is hard or cruel—I don't think it is. I do think it is a reality of life that men are competitive, and the more competitive the business, the more competitive the men. They know the rules, and they know the objective, and they get in the game. And the objective is to win—fairly, squarely, decently, by the rules, but to win.—*Vince Lombardi*

■

Any salesman who says he won a contract based on lowest price should be ashamed of himself.—*Dave Tappen, Retired CEO, Fluor Corporation*

Banker, lawyer, and U.S. senator Dwight Morrow said, in a letter to his son, "The world is divided into people who do things and people who get the credit. Try, if you can, to belong to the first class. There's far less competition." Known for his wit, Morrow was the U.S. ambassador to Mexico when, in 1927, he invited Charles Lindbergh to visit that country and introduced the aviator to his daughter, Anne. During one of his talks with Lindbergh, Morrow observed, "We judge ourselves by our motivations and others by their behavior."

The truth of Morrow's observation became painfully apparent to the president of a large construction company, which we'll call Acme General Contracting Company (AGCO), when it lost a series of bids with a customer it had served for many years—and did not even make the shortlist on the most recent opportunities. Frustrated by this turn of events, the president met with the members of his sales team to diagnose the problem, but they couldn't understand it either. Their prices were competitive, they had competent people, they knew the customer well, they had the experience and expertise to do the work, and their competitors had not introduced anything new or lowered their prices. Have you been doing anything differently, the president asked? Yes, they told him, in the past year they had included Chuck, one of AGCO's most experienced project managers, in their meetings with the customer. Surely, he can't be the problem, they reasoned. Chuck is articulate, knowledgeable, competent, and has more than thirty years of experience running projects. Officially, the customer had no comment, but after another painful loss, some friends inside the customer's organization approached the AGCO president and asked to speak to him confidentially. They told him that Chuck was in fact the problem.

"In a lot of meetings he slouches down in his chair or he leans back and doesn't make eye contact. Sometimes he stares at the ceiling while we're talking, and he taps his hands on the table constantly. Your people may not notice it. They're probably used to Chuck, but he comes across to us as if he doesn't care, doesn't know anything, or would rather be somewhere else. Frankly, if he's acting this way *before* we sign a contract, how much worse is he going to be *after* we've signed?"

In this true story, AGCO was able to help Chuck see how his behavior was harming the relationship and got Chuck and the relationship turned around. The lesson from AGCO's experience is that even inadvertent behaviors can negatively affect customers' perceptions of your company and cost you money. As Dwight Morrow observed, people judge others by their behavior, not by their intentions. Customers interpret business development behaviors as delivery behaviors. They assume that you are on your very best behavior while seeking work, so any negative behaviors will be at least ten times worse once you get the work and are no longer trying to impress them. The negative or positive impacts of behavior are felt most strongly in mid–middle game—the phase of the business development process when customers' needs emerge that result in business opportunities for you.

Once they identify a need, customers typically go through a period where they define the need, explore possible solutions, discuss options with potential suppliers, commit the budget, write specifications or requirements, and then move toward formal purchasing. The exact course of this process depends on many factors—what they need, whether they've had this need before, whether they have standard procedures for meeting the need, and so on. Whether mid–middle game lasts for months, weeks, or days, it can present an extraordinary opportunity for you to position yourself to win through behavioral differentiation. However, as our cautionary AGCO tale illustrates, you can also blow the deal in a heartbeat with negative behaviors. Moreover, you probably won't even know you've blown it—few customers will be that candid with you—and you will waste time and money trying to win work you have no hope of winning.

Mid–Middle Game Goals

To build a powerful position in mid–middle game, you need to achieve the following four goals: pursue the right opportunities intelligently, gain alignment with the customer on his or her needs, position your solution, and preempt the competition, if possible. You accomplish these goals by surfacing opportunities, exploring and aligning with the customer's needs, assessing opportunities, gaining material advantage, building time and mind share, influencing the solution, specifying the requirements, ghosting your competitors, positioning your team, and preselling your solution.

The first of these goals presents an unusual behavioral differentiation opportunity—differentiating by being more selective about the opportunities you choose to pursue. This advice may seem counterintuitive, especially during economic downturns. Indeed, in tough times and out of sheer desperation companies often pull out all the stops and bid on every opportunity they can uncover, whether it's marginal or not. Moreover, some business consultants recommend chasing more bids during economic downturns. But if you chase everything that moves, you dilute your resources and won't have the time to invest as early as you should in the opportunities that really are worth pursuing. Smart companies pick their battles wisely, in good times and bad. Then they have the time and the people they need to do the things that will behaviorally differentiate them and increase their odds of winning the work they really want.

> ♞ *If I am able to determine the enemy's dispositions while at the same time I conceal my own then I can concentrate and he must divide. And if I concentrate while he divides, I can use my entire strength to attack a fraction of his. There, I will be numerically superior. Then, if I am able to use many to strike few at the selected point, those I deal with will be in dire straits.—Sun Tzu, The Art of War*

Surfacing Opportunities

The first chance to be smart is when you learn of a new opportunity. Did you know it was coming? Better yet, did you identify the opportunity for the customer? Has the customer's need just emerged, or has the customer been thinking about it for a while? Do any of your competitors already know about the opportunity? Have any of them been working with the customer to explore solutions? The word of a new opportunity is like a powerful magnet dropped into a bucket of nails—it tends to attract a lot of attention and galvanizes hordes of would-be suppliers into action. Obviously, it's better to lead this group than to lag it. If you are late in learning about an opportunity, you will be well behind your more proactive competitors and will be breathing their exhaust as you start meeting with the customer. The suppliers who surface opportunities early and are proactive in meeting with customers and helping them explore potential solutions to their problems will behaviorally differentiate themselves through their awareness, initiative, persistence, counsel, and ongoing commitment to and investment in the customer. Contrast that with the behavioral message sent by those suppliers who aren't paying attention, don't discover the opportunity until much later and therefore contribute little to the customer's problem solving, and then waltz in with a boilerplate presentation of their capabilities and a few of their standard brochures. This happens far more often than you might imagine. We have seen numerous companies that bid on federal government programs but don't learn about many opportunities until they are published in the *Commerce Business Daily*. This is like buying a ticket to a Broadway musical and then not arriving at the theater until the final song. You will probably have lost your seat and will certainly have missed the show.

Figure 7-1 illustrates what happens in most companies. Imagine that companies have a radar system to alert them when new opportunities are approaching. Typically, their distant early warning system is the salesperson assigned to that customer, although it could be an engineer, a project manager, or someone else who is currently working with the customer on another project. In any case, someone in the field learns of the new need and passes it on to sales. The responsible salesperson calls on the customer and explores the need. At some point, a sales manager is told about this new opportunity and may or may not support the salesperson's decision to pursue it, depending on how attractive an opportunity it is. If it's pursued, this opportunity is entered into the company's lead tracking system and is watched by the sales manager and perhaps others in management who monitor the sales pipeline and forecast sales volume. If the opportunity is exciting enough, it begins to attract attention from other people in the company, and a loose team is assembled to pursue the opportunity, which at some point attracts enough attention to become a high

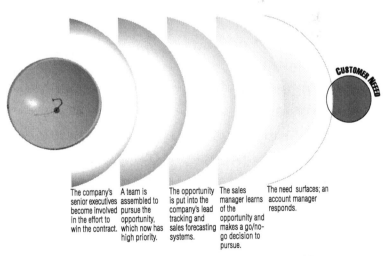

| The company's senior executives become involved in the effort to win the contract. | A team is assembled to pursue the opportunity, which now has high priority. | The opportunity is put into the company's lead tracking and sales forecasting systems. | The sales manager learns of the opportunity and makes a go/no-go decision to pursue. | The need surfaces; an account manager responds. |

FIGURE 7-1. The typical opportunity radar screen. For often-legitimate reasons, most companies do not aggressively pursue new opportunities the moment they surface, which diminishes their ability to behaviorally differentiate themselves.

priority and to develop interest among the company's senior executives, who may or may not offer to meet with their counterparts in the customer's organization and express how committed they are to the customer's business. Does this sound familiar? It will to many readers because this is how it works in most companies.

There are a number of perfectly legitimate reasons why many companies respond this way to new business opportunities:

■ At the distant early warning point, customer needs and opportunities often exist in a fog. The needs are undefined or ill defined, even in the customer's mind. It's not clear *what* they are or *how real* they are. Some needs materialize in the fog and then vanish. Other needs linger, batted around in the customer's organization, debated and redefined, sometimes for months or years before they assume their final form. The salesperson's job is to chase these phantoms until they become real opportunities—and only then sound the alarm and involve others in the company.

■ If the resources the company has for pursuing new opportunities are spread too thin, it may not be able to jump on new opportunities the moment they arise. This is the zero sum situation, and it becomes a question of priorities. To chase *this*, you have to give up *that*. Salespeople are going to chase the opportunities that are most real, most attractive, and most urgent, and with only twenty-four hours in the day, they may have to ignore emerging customer needs until those needs are better defined, more attractive, and more urgent. Of course, the price companies pay for being spread too thin is not getting a head start on emerging opportunities, but the salespeople may have no choice. There are only twenty-four hours in a day.

■ Sometimes companies don't get started earlier because they require consensus on which new opportunities to pursue. Generally, they have a bid review committee or similar oversight group that reviews all new opportunities and decides which ones to pursue, but of course this process takes time. The salesperson has to get the right people together and get them to agree, and those people may be hard to find. They're out fighting other fires.

Sometimes, companies are so operations driven that they focus the vast majority of their time and attention on executing current work.

This makes sense. Executing with excellence is clearly a very high priority, but people frequently assume that if they execute well, new work will magically walk through the door—and sometimes it does. However, in hard times, new work stops walking through the door, and then the companies that have grown to depend on getting new work through excellent execution suffer because they lack the systems, knowledge, skills, and discipline to surface new opportunities proactively and to close sales in this more competitive environment. If you rely on excellent execution to bring in most of your new business, sooner or later you will be eating dirt in a buyer's market and wondering why it doesn't taste like ice cream.

Figure 7-2 shows an opportunity radar screen that *can* behaviorally differentiate you and help you build a powerful position in mid–middle game. In this scenario, you create an account plan in opening game that gives you the initial intelligence on the customer you need to put in place a sound customer development strategy. You have an account team already assigned to the customer before any needs emerge. That team is continually scouting for business improvement opportunities. When needs emerge, you quickly identify and develop them. A rapid-response team swings into action, meeting with the

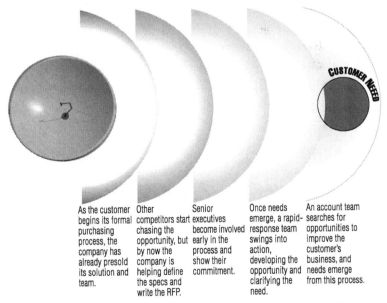

| As the customer begins its formal purchasing process, the company has already presold its solution and team. | Other competitors start chasing the opportunity, but by now the company is helping define the specs and write the RFP. | Senior executives become involved early in the process and show their commitment. | Once needs emerge, a rapid-response team swings into action, developing the opportunity and clarifying the need. | An account team searches for opportunities to improve the customer's business, and needs emerge from this process. |

FIGURE 7-2. The behaviorally differentiated opportunity radar screen. Smart companies help customers discover opportunities to improve their business and rapidly respond to emerging needs, which positions them to win.

customer, clarifying and exploring the customer's needs, and helping the customer think through the options. Ideally, this occurs before your competitors become aware that the need has emerged. We have used the term *rapid-response team* as though it were a formal entity, but in best-in-class B2B companies like Centex Construction Company* and Hall Kinion, such teams are more often loose confederations of people who come together quickly in response to the emerging opportunity.

In the best of circumstances, these rapid-response teams either include senior executives in the company or are joined by them. Having senior executive presence early in the development of an opportunity is a strong behavioral differentiator because it sends a powerful message of commitment to customers—and because it's so rare. By the time other competitors learn about and start chasing the opportunity, your team should be helping customers define their requirements and technical specifications and, ideally, write the RFP. In the best of circumstances, you will have presold your solution to the customer before your competitors become seriously aware of the need. It's not uncommon for customers to preempt a competition and award their preferred supplier a sole-source contract. Clearly, this utopian outcome can occur only when you are well positioned through early middle game, when you are proactive in seeking opportunities, and when you respond rapidly once new customer needs emerge. If your competitors are not equally proactive, you will behaviorally differentiate yourself through your initiative; your demonstrated commitment to serving the customer and improving the customer's business; and the thoughtful assistance, counsel, and information you provide. Of course, this may come at a price because it's difficult to commit this level of resource to every emerging customer need, so you have to choose your battles wisely. That's why being more selective about the opportunities you pursue can be a behavioral differentiator.

Exploring and Aligning with the Customer's Needs

In one important respect, mid–middle game is like playing poker—at each new opportunity to place a bet, you have to assess whether your

---

*Centex Construction Company is a particularly interesting example. Former CEO Bob Moss insisted that pursuits be done as we have described here; consequently, the company was meeting its revenue goals one year ahead of schedule.

hand supports further investment in the pot. No matter how much money you've already bet, you should be willing to fold if the cards turn against you. So it is in business development. Smart companies revisit their decision to pursue an opportunity at various points during mid–middle game, and they stop pursuing the opportunity if they learn that their position has deteriorated or that the opportunity has changed in some way that diminishes its attractiveness. This can be one of the toughest parts of being smart because it's all too easy to be swept along by raw sales enthusiasm—that cockeyed optimism of never give up, never surrender; it's always darkest before the dawn; clouds and silver linings; and so on—manifested behaviorally by an almost genetically encoded resistance to facing reality, saving precious resources from a futile pursuit, and saying, "No go. We've either already lost it or we're so far behind that winning will cost us more than the deal itself is worth."

We might think of these decision points during mid–middle game as gates. To continue chasing an opportunity, you have to pass through a series of gates, and the first one occurs when you initially learn of the opportunity. Here are the kinds of questions companies should ask at this point:

■ When did we learn of this opportunity? Are we ahead of or behind the pack?

■ What is this opportunity? What does the customer want or need? Who is involved? Where did the need originate? How broadly is the need recognized and supported throughout the customer's organization, particularly among the key decision-makers and influencers?

■ How good is the fit between the customer's needs and our solutions? Is this an attractive opportunity for us to pursue?

■ How well do we understand the rationale behind this emerging need? What is driving it? Why is it surfacing now? What is the customer's business case for purchasing a product or service that would fulfill this need? How does the customer value the solution?

■ Are we currently positively or negatively differentiated from our competitors in the customer's mind? Can we build greater preference during middle game? Can we reduce or eliminate any negative differentiation?

As you explore the customer's needs, it is wise to engage the key contacts throughout your zippered network—inquiring about the need with everyone at every level in the customer's organization who can provide insight and who may be instrumental in shaping the solution and selecting the supplier. It's important to ascertain how they've solved such problems or met such needs in the past; what's important to each key person about the solution and the supplier; what requirements they are likely to have; how open they are to considering innovative, value-added solutions; and what criteria they typically use to select their supplier. It's also important to know whether any of your key competitors has an installed base with the customer, or is already in a preferred position, or is well connected with influential people in the customer's organization. A complete list of the questions you might ask while exploring an emerging opportunity would take more room than we care to devote to it, largely because the questions themselves are usually not behavioral differentiators. Suffice it to say that a thorough exploration of the customer's needs requires an exhaustive inquiry and far more *asking* than *telling*—which does bring us to a key behavioral differentiator during this part of middle game.

When opportunities emerge, it's common for salespeople to switch into a *sell and tell* mode far too quickly, especially when customers ask them for information about their company and their products or services. On the theory that their competitors will be aggressively presenting their capabilities and that they must be equally aggressive, salespeople (and the executives, project managers, and others who support them) often have a compulsive need to tell their story, no matter how much they've learned about the value of listening. In the sell and tell trap they fall into, they talk mostly about themselves, don't ask enough questions, miss important clues, and behave in a manner that suggests to customers that what they have to say is much more important than what the customer has to say. Don Traywick, vice president of sales for BE&K, notes the danger of the sell and tell trap:

> Traditionally in the engineering and construction industry the classic approach to selling involves citing a laundry list of strengths: track record, safety, people, references, low risk, schedule and budget vigi-

lance, customer focus, value-added, and so on. Well, that approach is all but dead for one simple reason—all our first-tier competitors have these strengths, too, and they trot them out as often as we do. Customers have heard it so often and for so long that they end up concluding we're all basically the same. And when we let that happen, price unravels the deal for all but the lowest bidder who, more often than not, doesn't end up meeting the customer's needs as well as we could have. The only problem is—we lost the opportunity to prove it.[1]

The self-serving, self-focused behavior endemic to the sell and tell approach is what most customers experience from salespeople enough of the time that the alternative is a refreshing contrast. What is the alternative? It's the facilitative selling approach that many people advocate but few actually practice, and it has these basic principles:

■ *Seek to understand before seeking to be understood.* The cardinal attitude to have when you begin a dialogue with a customer about an emerging need is that what the customer has to say is more important than what you have to say. Furthermore, if you run off at the mouth about your capabilities and wonderful products and services, you risk frustrating customers (who don't feel listened to) and talking about the wrong solutions to the wrong problems. Until you completely understand their perspectives, you should refrain from even discussing your company and your capabilities. Seek to understand them first—and you do this by asking questions and listening. It's simple, but few people do it well.

■ *Sit on the customer's side of the table.* Beyond merely understanding their perspectives, you have to be able to see the world from their side of the table. You have to be able to empathize with them. Forget your company for the moment. Forget your products and solutions and the great things you have to offer. Forget features and benefits and selling solutions and all the other buzzwords, frameworks, and gimmicks. Early in the dialogue, you should release your own agenda so completely that you are free to experience the world through your customers' eyes. What would it be like to be in their position? How would it feel? What would be important and unimportant? What would seem urgent? What is at stake? What is the big win for them, and what are they afraid of losing? Whom should they include in their decisions? Who should be excluded? What does their political environment feel like? What's worrisome? What are the risks? What's exciting? Sitting on the customer's side of the table doesn't mean giving up your own place; it just means allowing yourself to connect with the customer at the emotional level where personal and institutional needs commingle—and where most buying decisions are actually made.

> ♜ *Great client advisors are superb listeners. Their ability not only helps them gain information critical to their work, but gives their clients breathing space and allows them to think through the issues on their own. Empathy also underpins their personal and professional relationship with the client and helps it grow over time.*
> —*Jagdish Sheth and Andrew Sobel,* Clients for Life

■ *Follow the customer's agenda.* Too often, salespeople and company executives go into a meeting with customers with a firm sense of what they want to accomplish in the meeting, and they push their agenda no matter what response they get from the customer. Polite customers, who sense that you are driving your agenda and won't deviate from it, may be patient and appear to be listening, but in their minds they are writing you off. Less polite customers often show their discomfort—or downright hostility—and may throw you out or cut the meeting short. When this happens, you are losing time share, not winning it, and you have done your competitors a huge favor. You have managed to create negative BD that makes them look better than they might have otherwise. (They should send you a thank-you card for your efforts on their behalf.) A far more positive behavior is to abandon your agenda the moment you sense that customers want to deviate from it. When you begin the meeting, ask them what they want to get out of the meeting, and then follow their agenda throughout the meeting. Yes, this could mean that you don't discuss what you had hoped would be discussed; you may need to pursue those things in later meetings or phone calls. Sometimes, the best outcome of a meeting with customers is getting them to agree to another meeting. Your positioning may take time. Think of it as a process, not an event.

■ *Go through the open doors.* When you try to push your line of thought and encounter resistance, it's best not to keep pursuing that line of thought. Think of the dialogue as a long hallway with a number of closed doors along the corridor. Behind each of those doors is a topic for discussion. If you knock on a door and the customer opens it (i.e., seems willing to discuss that topic), you can go through that door and continue with your discussion. However, if you knock on a door and the customer doesn't open it (doesn't want to discuss it), don't keep knocking on the door. It annoys the customer and frustrates you. It's far better to go through the open doors and engage customers in areas they are most interested in and are open to talking about than to pound on the closed doors or, worse yet, try to knock them down with a battering ram (we've seen salespeople do this, and we're willing to bet that you have seen them, too).

■ *Stay in the "No-Pitch" zone.* When you pitch your wares, you are clearly motivated by self-interest and you come across as a vendor. If you want to build trust with customers, you have to stop pitching and start acting like a thought partner—someone who's genuinely interested in helping them solve their problems, whether or not you gain from it. If customers perceive that you are determined to make the sale, no matter what, then they will have good reason to distrust you. On the other hand, if they perceive that you have their best interests in mind and are helping them think through their needs and explore the alternatives from an un-self-serving perspective, then their trust in you will grow and you will behaviorally differentiate yourself from the hawkers and vendors. Most salespeople start pitching far too early in the process.

■ *Ask insightful questions.* During mid–middle game, most salespeople ask the standard, fact-finding questions: *What do you need? When do you need it? How many do you need? Where should it be delivered?* And so on. A somewhat more enlightened set of questions would be: *Why do you need it? Why now? What would happen if you didn't get it? Would something else be better?* The typical salesperson asks questions to qualify the opportunity (e.g., *Do the customer's needs match our product line? Are they open to buying from us?*) and to learn enough about the situation and the customer to know what to pitch and how best to pitch it. The behaviorally differentiated approach is to ask the kinds of questions that stimulate customers to think more deeply about their problems, opportunities, and needs. The framework we've found most helpful in asking insightful questions is GAIN, which stands for *Goals, Achievement Value, Issues,* and *Needs.* In the GAIN framework, you would ask these kinds of questions:

GOALS

What are you trying to achieve? What is your vision? What is the ideal outcome for you? In the best of circumstances, what would success look like? What business purpose are you trying to accomplish? What opportunities do you want to pursue? What's the optimistic view? If there were no obstacles, what would be possible?

ACHIEVEMENT VALUE

What will it be worth to you when you achieve your goals? What are the business implications of solving this problem or capturing this opportunity? Why is this goal important to you? Why are you pursuing it instead of something else? What investment do you anticipate in pursuing this goal, and what is your projected return on that investment?

ISSUES

What is your current situation? What is standing in the way of your achieving your goals? What are your concerns? What's keeping you up at night? As you think about achieving this goal, what roadblocks do you see? What avenues of possibility? What have you tried before? What haven't you tried? As you analyze the situation, what do the numbers tell you? What do your customers tell you? What do your own people tell you? What will happen if you don't solve this problem or achieve your goal? What's the risk of doing nothing? What's the risk of trying something and failing? What's the upside of achieving a spectacular success?

NEEDS

What would help? What do you need in order to solve this problem or capture this opportunity? What are you missing? Why are you looking for help? What other approaches, products, or services have you tried or considered? Why did you reject them? What's the most effective way for you to approach this? What's most important to you? How would you prioritize your needs? If you could find the ideal partner or supplier, what would that company do you for? What is the ideal outcome of the help you receive from any supplier?

What differentiates the GAIN model is that it focuses on customers and is intended to be as helpful to them as it is to the salesperson or executive asking the questions. Further, GAIN is not just an interviewing model; it's a behavioral model. It raises your customers' expectations of what a valuable exchange with a provider should look like and accomplish. When that happens, you have not only raised their expectations, you have raised the bar on your competitors. GAIN is not intended to create demand, increase customers' discomfort, or convince them that they need your products or services. On the contrary, GAIN is intended to provoke a thoughtful discussion of customers' needs, and it's an excellent way to behave like a thought partner instead of a vendor. When you ask Goal questions, you are trying to understand the gap between customers' current situation and some ideal future they envision. In this ideal future, the problem has been solved, the needs met, the opportunities captured. In essence, you are trying to understand their dreams. This is what they wish would come true.

In asking Achievement Value questions, you are trying to link this potential buying decision with customers' business needs and objectives. They are thinking of buying something you offer or engaging your services. Why? What value would such a solution add to their business? In asking this question, you can help them think through the value of various alternatives, including some of the value-added solutions you might propose. The Issues and Needs questions help customers think through the ramifications of their current situation and of the various alternatives they might consider. These questions also help them prioritize their issues, concerns, and needs. The answers tell you what's most important to them, how they are thinking about solutions, what they value (and don't value), and where they are open to considering value-added options. In effect, using the GAIN framework to explore customers' needs helps you and them build the business case for the solution and determine the urgency and scope of their needs. It should be clear how this approach to a customer dialogue is more helpful to customers, can position you as a thought partner with them, and can behaviorally differentiate you from your competitors who use the traditional *sell and tell* approach.

With GAIN, you replace the *selling is telling* behavior with a suite of behaviors that are customer focused, engaging, and insight provoking.

Assessing Opportunities

After you learn enough about the opportunity and the customer's needs to make an informed pursuit decision, you pass through another of the go/no-go gates we spoke of earlier. For some companies, the most formal pursuit decision occurs once they have completed a thorough analysis of the opportunity. In truth, opportunity analysis is a hit-or-miss affair in most companies. Some lack the structure and discipline to impose formal procedures and decision rules for making the bid/no-bid decision, but others have learned from experience to put a formal structure and process in place. Clearly, we favor the more formal approach, largely because bid and pursuit dollars are too precious to waste on bad opportunities, and we've seen companies waste millions of dollars pursuing pipe dreams and phantoms—opportunities they had no hope at all of winning and would not have been able to execute profitably had they won them. In bad economic times, salespeople get desperate and start chasing jobs that in better days, using better judgment, they wouldn't give a second thought—and that's just throwing good money after bad.

The smarter move is to be disciplined and systematic about assessing every opportunity once you know enough about it to make sensible decisions. Many companies have formal bid/no-bid decision criteria. Some require salespeople to submit opportunities on a form that requires them to take a disciplined look at the pros and cons of each potential bid, and this is smart business. It helps prevent the wild goose chases that waste valuable time and money, and it helps ensure that you devote the right amount of time to the opportunities you do choose to pursue. Even if you decide not to pursue an opportunity, you can use your decision as a chance to differentiate yourself behaviorally. You can explain to customers why this opportunity is not right for you and them, why other suppliers—who don't offer what you do—might be a better match for them this time. So you can use your no-bid decision to position yourself for the next opportunity, and in some cases to convince customers to rethink their needs or redefine their requirements so you *are* right for this opportunity. In either case, you show that you are being thoughtful about what you pursue and choose to pursue only when you are a best fit for the customer's needs and have the best solution to offer. There's no downside to this posture, and when you don't chase bad opportunities, you preserve your resources for investing in the better ones.

If you decide to pursue an opportunity, another part of being disciplined in mid–middle game is to develop a pursuit strategy that addresses these kinds of questions:

■ What should we do to position ourselves most favorably during the rest of middle game?

■ How can we ethically build bias in our favor? How can we influence the customer's decision-makers and influencers and add value to them during middle game?

■ How should we engage our zippered network and ensure that the right same-level or cross-level contacts are being made?

■ How can we presell our solution and our people?

■ How can we behaviorally differentiate ourselves from our competitors?

Many companies try to accomplish these middle game goals, but relatively few are as disciplined and systematic about it as they could be, and those who fly by the seat of their pants are really trusting everything to luck. Being disciplined enough to develop and implement a pursuit strategy helps ensure that you are being thoughtful about what you should do to position yourself for the win and helps you avoid the woeful Monday morning quarterbacking one often hears following a loss: "We should have done this, or we should have done that." The smart move is to force yourself to create a pursuit strategy and then to work the strategy systematically, using all the resources at your disposal. The smartest move is to include in your pursuit strategy ideas for behaviorally differentiating yourself during middle game. What can you do—or avoid doing—that will positively differentiate you from your competitors? How can you behave in ways that demonstrate greater responsiveness, interest, care, and commitment to the customer? Behavioral differentiation is generally not the result of serendipity; it results from being thoughtful and self-conscious about your customer behaviors during every touch point.

> ♜ *Never doubt that a small group of thoughtful, committed citizens can change the world; indeed, it is the only thing that ever has.—Margaret Mead*

Gaining Material Advantage

In chess, middle game is the scene of pitched battles where pawns, knights, bishops, rooks, and queens are slain. Victory does not always go to the player with the greatest *number* of surviving pieces—board position and the *value* of the surviving pieces are also crucial—but if you are a betting person, you would be wise to bet on the player who has the advantage in material when the middle game carnage ends. As Jeremy Silman notes, "A material advantage is a wonderful thing to have because it influences all phases of the game. In the opening and middlegame, the side with extra wood possesses more units of force—his army is larger. In the endgame, the side with the material deficit usually goes into a deep depression. In fact, this endgame nightmare is often felt in the middlegame; the material-down defender is basically giving endgame odds and this severely curtails his possibilities."[2]

In business development, you gain material advantage in mid–middle game by having better relationships with more of the customer's key people than your competitors do, by building more time share and mind share than your competitors have, by investing more in the relationship, and by having more influence with the people in the customer's organization who will make or contribute to the buying decision. In practical terms, you show more willingness to go the extra mile for customers, and this can take many forms: sharing proprietary research with them, writing special white papers, customizing your products or solutions, being flexible in your approach to serving their needs, being open to alternative financing arrangements, being more reasonable on terms and conditions, making services available that they would have to pay for elsewhere, sharing your best practices where appropriate, and so on. Of these ideas, flexibility may be most important. What many customers experience is a "take it or leave it" attitude among some suppliers. If you show that you are more open to new ideas, more flexible in your approach, and more willing to customize your solution for them, you score a lot of behavioral points.

Building Time Share and Mind Share

In the preceding chapter, we discussed building time share and mind share during early middle game while you are developing the relationship with the customer *prior to* the surfacing of any specific opportunities. *After* an opportunity surfaces, you must determine how the opportunity is wired—that is, who will be making or influencing *this specific decision*—and build time share and mind share with those key people. Since human beings decide who should receive a contract, you must have relationships with the right people in the customer's organization in order to build position and preference. This is self-evident, but the implications are important:

■ First, you have to know who the right people are, and this is not a trivial requirement. Sometimes, no matter how well you know the customer, you can't be certain about who will make the final decision. Other times, you do know the decision-maker, but you are unlikely to know everyone who will *influence* the buying decision. The influencers may include advisors to the decision-maker (usually other high-level executives); the people who will manage or use the product or service being purchased; the gatekeepers who conduct the purchasing process; and perhaps some external advisors, such as consultants, lawyers, bankers, or government officials. The network of power and influence in any organization is dynamic and complex. It is often difficult even for insiders to comprehend all the influences on a decision, so it is certain that outsiders will have only a proximate view of the situation. Moreover, the group of people advising and influencing the decision-maker is likely to change from one contract to the next. So, although you may know who influenced a previous contract, you are unlikely to know everyone who will influence the next buying decision. Now, in mid–middle game when you are pursuing a particular opportunity, it's critically important to know how the power flows in the decision-making process; how the customer is wired, which we discussed in Chapter 6; and how that wiring leads to winning this deal.

■ Second, relationships do not spring to maturity overnight. It takes time to build a good relationship with anyone. So the implication of having the right relationships is that you had to have built those relationships over time and *before the opportunity surfaced*. This is why getting work with new customers is harder than getting more work with existing customers. It's also why many companies have strategic account management programs, the purpose of which is to ensure that they have the right relationships established long before key opportunities arise. If you decide to pursue an opportunity and do not have established relationships with any of the key people on the opportunity—but your competitors do—you will at best be a long shot. You may still decide to pursue the opportunity, but you should be realistic about your odds.

■ Third, resting on your laurels with people is likely to lead to permanent rest. You can't depend on existing relationships to carry the day. You have to work those relationships actively while the opportunity develops. This means engaging or reengaging with the people in your network, asking GAIN-type questions about the opportunity, exploring their needs, and consulting with them on potential solutions. Your goal should be to presell yourself and your solution. You do that by testing it ahead of time, discovering what works and what doesn't, and seeing what excites them and what leaves them cold.

> ♚ *Speed is the essence of war. Take advantage of the enemy's unpreparedness; travel by unexpected routes and strike him where he has taken no precautions.*—*Sun Tzu*, The Art of War

Let's take stock. When an opportunity surfaces, you can behaviorally differentiate yourself by responding immediately and in force— not just with a lot of people but with a lot of the *right* people from your company. Remember that in chess having a material advantage depends on having more of the most powerful pieces—the queen, rooks, knights, and bishops. In business development, having a material advantage means attacking the problem with more of the right people, including technical experts, highly experienced project managers, other key people the customer knows and respects, and senior executives—your CEO, if possible. You must quickly establish contact with the opportunity decision-maker and influencers and understand how they view the opportunity and what's important to them. Further, you must demonstrate your interest in and commitment to their business by being more responsive, more thorough, and more persistent than your competitors. If the opportunity is real but must still be sold internally, then you can offer help in making the sale—preparing presentations for your customer contacts, doing capabilities demonstrations, creating simulations showing the results of the project, and so on. In essence, you can partner with the customer's key people in making the case to their senior executives or whoever else must be convinced. The companies that are best-in-class at building time share and mind share in mid–middle game also do the following kinds of things:

■ Develop and execute opportunity contact plans, which enable them to be more systematic in identifying and meeting with the right people, not only in the customer's organization but also potential teaming partners, agents, special interest groups, consultants, lobbyists, financiers, and so on. The best contact plans include a behavioral differentiation component and a value component. The former identifies how you will create positive BD with the customer's people. The latter identifies how, in each contact, you will create quality face time by ensuring that value is flowing in both directions.

■ Intensify executive-level contacts, especially some face-to-face meetings that focus principally on the opportunity at hand.

■ Coach customers on a range of issues—from new technologies and innovations, product uses, maintenance and service, and safety and reliability on the one hand, to personal effectiveness areas like leadership, organizational effectiveness, communication skills, and career planning on the other. Coaching on the personal areas requires a great deal of trust and credibility, but if you have this kind of relationship with a customer, it is a powerful behavioral differentiator.

■ Ask customers for an education on how they are using similar products now, how they are evolving their methods or technologies, and how their priorities and perspectives are changing as their own markets evolve.

■ Conduct product or solution familiarization workshops and demonstrations with customers that educate them on options or technologies they have not used or were not considering.

■ Conduct problem-solving or brainstorming sessions with customers to explore their alternatives or improve their risk management.

■ Conduct joint surveys of the customer's markets and consumer needs.

■ Determine whether the customer has preferences on the use of local resources or suppliers, if this is relevant, and then connect with and start building relationships with those preferred entities, engaging in joint discussions with them and the customer.

■ Help the customer obtain any local permits or waivers or meet other requirements essential for the success of the project.

■ Help the customer meet with bankers, venture capitalists, or other funding sources and obtain financial support if necessary.

■ Help the customer with the public relations aspects of the customer's initiative or project if media or public interest is anticipated and you have PR expertise or sources who could be helpful.

■ Work together on the political challenges of the opportunity, jointly lobbying where necessary to gain political support for the project. Helping customers navigate the political landscape can be particularly differentiating if you have the right contacts in the relevant political communities. Your competitors may not have those contacts or may not consciously think about the politics until you have already proven yourself an invaluable resource to the opportunity decision-makers. Being there early and being helpful are prime ways of conditioning the customer and creating a bias in your favor.

Each of these activities can build opportunity time share and mind share if your competitors are not equally active in working with the customer during the early days of opportunity development or they are active only in the old *sell and tell* mode. The secret, if you will, is *adding value while the opportunity is developing.* This is not news, but neither is it the norm because many companies treat mid–middle game as a *selling* phase, not a *value-adding* phase. You will build greater time share and mind share if you find creative ways to add value to customers while helping them define their needs and explore solutions and potential suppliers.

Influencing the Solution

The object of all business development efforts through opening and middle games is to build preference for you and your products and solutions so you are more likely to be selected as the customer's supplier. You really don't want a "level playing field," as it is sometimes called. You want a field tilted heavily in your favor. Having said this, we hasten to add that you should try to create preference in a principled and ethical manner. As Vince Lombardi said about football, "The objective is to win—fairly, squarely, decently, by the rules, but to win." In business, you sometimes behaviorally differentiate yourself through your scrupulous honesty and integrity. If your competitors bend the rules or behave in ways suggesting that they are willing to overlook certain improprieties, then your candor, forthrightness, and uncompromising integrity will stand in sharp contrast.

We take it as an article of faith that business should always be done in an ethical and legal manner. Bearing that in mind, your goal in mid–middle game is nonetheless to influence the solution—to persuade customers to favor your technologies, approaches, products, locations, people, and services as they think about how to solve their problems or meet their needs. Indeed, this is the goal of all selling efforts. It's obviously more critical when your customers are purchasing a product or service they haven't purchased before, when their problems are unique and require an innovative solution, or when their needs have changed and the solutions they've been using no longer apply. In these circumstances, you behaviorally differentiate by being there when they need you, by being willing to consult with them—even if this means "free" consulting—and by helping them think through their alternatives. You differentiate by becoming a valued resource to them, one they would not want to be without.

Customers may need help, first, with their aspirations for meeting their needs. Because they know less about your technologies, options, and economies than you do, they may set their aspirations too low—or, alternatively, they may think they can get more than is possible with the budget they have in mind. In either case, you should help them set their aspirations at the right level. Can they do more than they realize? Are they aiming too low? Are more things possible than they imagine? Alternatively, are there constraints, risks, or barriers they should be aware of? Are there inherent limitations in the solution as they currently envision it? Think of this as "right sizing" the solution. You can be helpful in solution development by advising them on their options and on helping them see alternative solutions that are appropriate for their problems, needs, situation, and budget. Your assistance will not be entirely selfless, of course, because you'll be demonstrating your products and services, showing how you approach meeting needs like theirs, and applying the same problem-solving logic to their problems that you used in creating the kinds of products and services you chose to offer. Your competitors may be attempting to do the same thing you are, so you behaviorally differentiate yourself by being a thought partner instead of a vendor, by putting customers' interests first and helping them find the right solutions to their problems, whatever those may be. That attitude will differentiate you from competitors who, like the car salesman who always tries to sell the luxury model (even to buyers who want and can only afford the standard model), push their products and solutions whether or not they are a good fit for the customer's needs. Here are some of the best practices we've seen for influencing the solution. They have the potential to differentiate you behaviorally if your competitors are not doing them:

■ Help customers solve the technical aspects of the problem. Show them different technical approaches and the pros and cons of each. Observe their operations and offer assistance to their superintendents, supervisors, or other operations managers where you see opportunities for improvement.

■ Invite customers to see how your proprietary technologies or solutions can give them competitive advantages in their own markets, solve technical problems they are having, or improve their business operations. Create customized technology demonstrations that prove the concept.

■ Introduce customers to the experts in your company (or in partner companies or affiliated consultancies or academic institutions) who can educate them on options and help them explore potential solutions.

■ Conduct a joint technical risk assessment to help customers understand issues, challenges, or barriers they had not foreseen and learn how to assess and mitigate the risks of various alternatives.

■ Help customers identify and explore innovative approaches to their business, manufacturing, marketing, or other business processes that help them add value to their customers.

■ Mock up potential solutions and beta-test them with customers. Conduct joint after-action learning events that help both you and them identify areas for improvement or innovation.

Essentially, these ideas are all about being active problem-solving partners with your customers. There may be nothing new about doing this. Some companies do this well already, but there are many industries and companies where this degree of presales commitment to customers is uncommon, so this may represent an opportunity for behavioral differentiation.

Specifying the Requirements

As the opportunity develops, customers' requirements take shape. They have explored the alternatives and have begun to reach conclusions about what they need and want. When they reach this point, they often formalize their requirements as a set of written specifications. If this is relevant to your business, you can be proactive by offering to help customers define or write their specifications, scope of work, budget, terms and conditions, contingencies, and schedule.

Doing so is generally an outgrowth of a counseling or consulting relationship. If you haven't already established this kind of relationship, you are unlikely to be invited to help write the specifications, and any such overtures on your part are likely to be turned down, which is another reason for starting early and building a trusted advisor relationship from the start. If you participate in writing the specs, you should avoid being too self-serving (i.e., specifying requirements that only your company can meet), but you may already have presold requirements that only your company can meet exceptionally well.

You can behaviorally differentiate yourself by writing straw-man specifications even before your customers reach this point. Take the initiative and create a set of specifications for the solution you have discussed with customers and give them those specs, preferably in electronic form so they can modify the requirements as they see fit. You can also offer to review their specifications if they write them internally. If they consent, be timely and diligent in your review and avoid being overtly self-serving in your suggestions. Beyond the technical specifications, you can also offer to draft or review the RFP. If you are allowed to do this, you can help ensure that the RFP accurately reflects what customers need and that there are no surprises in it that would cause you grief. In some venues, such as federal government procurements, this level of assistance is prohibited by law and regulation, but in most commercial bidding situations providing customers with this kind of assistance at this point in the purchasing process is not prohibited and is not inherently unethical.

Ghosting Your Competitors

We haven't discussed your competitors at length, but unless they are truly asleep at the wheel they will also be active, in varying degrees, during mid–middle game. It's essential not to attack your competitors by name, but you should be aware of their actions and should ghost them where you can ethically and comfortably do so. By ghosting, we mean to "raise the specter" of their weaknesses. If a competitor has a poor safety record, for instance, you can stress the importance of safety and of selecting a provider with a proven record of safety. If the competitor has had equipment failures that resulted in longer-than-average system downtimes, you can emphasize the importance of equipment reliability and the costs of excessive downtimes. Of course, if safety and reliability aren't important to customers, raising these issues won't have much impact. The ideal occurs when your competitors' weaknesses correspond to the customer's most important requirements or selection criteria.*

As chess master Ron Curry observes, "Chess is a game of relative strengths and weaknesses, and every game reflects their interplay. Each player strives to maximize his own strengths and minimize his weaknesses, while attempting to minimize his opponent's strengths and capitalize on his weaknesses. *Every successful tactic, combination, sacrifice, and attack is based on one or more weaknesses.* Without them, no successful tactics can occur. *Winning in chess consists of exploiting opponents' weaknesses!*"[3] Arguably, this is true in business development as well, although the attacks on competitors' weaknesses are usually more subtle than they are in chess. Of course, you can't ghost your competitors' weaknesses unless you know what they are, so it behooves you to understand not only how your competitors' products and services compare with your own but also how their behavior compares. What are they doing to position themselves? What behaviors are having a positive impact on customers' perceptions of them? Are there any negative or distracting behaviors?

You generally cannot observe your competitors' behaviors first-hand, but you can learn about them only indirectly. Your best sources are people in the customer's organization who favor you and want you to win. Generally, these are people you have known for some time and with whom you have an excellent relationship. We refer to these people as your *sponsors*. You have to be careful not to abuse the relationship by asking direct questions about your competitors, but we have found that asking the following kinds of questions can help you discover behavioral gaps:

■ What would you recommend that we do at this point?

■ Is there something we should be doing that we aren't?

■ In your opinion, what are the right next steps?

■ How could we be more helpful to [the decision-maker]?

---

*Likewise, your strengths should correspond to the customer's highest-priority requirements or concerns. When your strengths and your competitors' weaknesses overlap the customer's key requirements, you are operating in the "sweet spot." When the converse is true, you are in the "sour spot."

You might want to revisit our discussion of the living executive summary in Chapter 6. Now, as a specific opportunity is taking shape, is the opportune time to prepare and deliver a brochure executive summary focused on the customer and his or her key issues relative to his or her procurement. Meanwhile, your competitors may still be handing out their generic brochures filled with stock photographs and focused entirely on themselves and their products or services.

Ron Curry said, "Every move alters the position on the chessboard, so pay particular attention to your opponent's last move. Immediately after each of your opponent's last moves, ask yourself: What is the threat? What has changed?"[4] His advice applies to business development as well. Without being paranoid about or distracted by your competitors' actions, you should keep your eyes and ears open. Be aware of how they are positioning themselves and what they might be doing to differentiate themselves behaviorally. If you know what benchmark they are setting, you should have the knowledge required to outbehave them.

Positioning Your Team

If you are proposing a project team as part of your solution, then a potentially powerful behavioral differentiator is to assemble and introduce your team to the customer during mid–middle game. Most suppliers don't finalize their teams until they write their proposals (which occurs in endgame), or even worse, they propose one team and then substitute another, a negative behavioral practice known as bait-and-switch. So introducing your team much earlier can allow you to build a level of trust and confidence with customers that your tardier competitors can't hope to match when the selection decision is made. To maximize the team's BD potential, you should ensure the following:

■ The team has an effective leader—someone who can build the team, give it coherence and direction, and provide leadership both internally and with the customer. The team leader should be someone eminently capable of generating the right chemistry with the customer's key people.

■ The team has the right composition—members who have the requisite skills and experience and who are well matched with the customer's culture and style.

■ There are no interpersonal issues, power conflicts, or other issues that could prevent the team members from working together.

■ The team acts like a team. The members know each other; have worked with each other; and have a common sense of purpose, values, goals, and working style. They collaborate with and show respect for each other.

■ The team members know and understand the customer's specific needs, wants, and requirements, as well as the customer's industry. They should speak confidently and knowledgeably about the customer's business.

The last item is very important. It's not uncommon for suppliers to assemble their teams at the last moment and for their team members not to have participated in middle game relationship building or positioning, responding to the bid request, or creating the proposal. If your team members are recent imports, they are likely to look that way to customers, which does not enhance your credibility or build trust. Smart suppliers assemble their teams early and ensure that they take part in developing the solution and the proposal. Moreover, the members act like a team, and that's what the customer sees. Bear in mind the point we made at the beginning of this chapter: Customers interpret your business development behaviors as delivery behaviors.

As soon as you assemble your team, take the time to educate these people on the customer's situation and needs and on the dialogue that has occurred with the customer since you learned of the opportunity. Ensure that they are experts on the customer's organization, key people, and needs before you introduce them. Finally, demonstrate your commitment to the customer and your seriousness about wanting the customer's business by giving him or her the best team possible. This last point can be difficult because your best people usually aren't sitting on the bench waiting for new opportunities—they are out executing current work. But most customers are remarkably adept at spotting your substandard performers and sense when the team you're parading before them is suboptimal. You send a powerfully negative signal when you field your "B" team. There are no "B" projects for customers, so consider the message you send with the people you choose to constitute your proposed team. Assuming you have a solid team assembled, here are some things you can do to position your team with the customer during mid and late middle game:

■ If the team members haven't worked together previously, do some team building before they meet with the customer. Even if the group of people who will serve the customer are not technically a "team," do some team building anyway.

■ As early as possible, introduce customers to the people in your company who will serve them if you get the contract. Do this as a way to test their chemistry with customers and to develop stronger, trust-based relationships. If you discover that some team member is not developing good chemistry, replace that person. Do it sooner rather than later.

■ Have your key people participate in important middle game meetings with the customer. Prep them for these meetings so they are adding value and building their credibility as individuals.

■ Try to have your key people participate in some social events with customers if this is appropriate so they can get to know each other informally. The bonds they build create preference.

■ If you give any presentations during middle game, have your team members lead or participate in these presentations and field customers' questions. Furthermore, keep in mind the three rules for a successful team presentation: Rehearse. Rehearse. Rehearse.

■ Ensure that your team leader or project manager has a special amount of face time with key customers and that this person passes customers' chemistry test with flying colors. It's critical that your project manager walk through the project with customers, participate or lead the problem-solving efforts, and help customers think through their challenges and opportunities, as well as identify places where they might save time or money or otherwise derive more benefit from what they intend to do.

If you are not proposing a team but will have people in your company who will regularly meet with or serve customers' needs or provide after-sales services, these best practices apply. Your presales behaviors are strong indicators of what it will be like to work with you. If the people you introduce customers to are credible, trustworthy, and committed; know the customer; have helped shape the solution; and act like a team, you will create an impression that strongly differentiates you from suppliers who might talk a good game but don't walk their talk. As we said in Chapter 3, your behavior is the purest form of the expression of your intent, your priorities, and your feelings. No matter what language you use to describe yourself, no matter what promises you make, no matter how sincerely you tell customers you want their business, the truth about you will always emerge in how you behave.

> ♛ *Most games are decided in the middlegame by attacks against Kings and tactics which win decisive material. Strategy and tactics dominate, and attack and defense are the main activities. Checkmate, the ultimate goal, is always first priority.—Ron Curry,* Win at Chess!

Preselling Your Solution

The ideal outcome of mid or late middle game is to presell your solution and preempt the competition by having the customer award you a sole-source contract. In business development, as in chess, it doesn't have to go to endgame—and sometimes doesn't. Although not a common occurrence, securing the contract and thereby keeping the RFP off the street happens often enough that you should explore the possibility with each customer. If you can make it work, everyone wins except your competitors, and that's the best tilt you can put on the playing field. At the very least, you want to have sold the customer on your solution even if the customer proceeds with formal purchasing. Sometimes, though some key people may already have made their decision, they have to go through the motions of formal purchasing. But whether they are going through the motions or proceeding with a good-faith effort to fairly assess all the bidders, your goal should be to convince them to select you before they formally release their bid request document or RFP. Our experience suggests that this is feasible more often than not if you have played middle game well.

In part you presell your solution by having crafted it with customers—by having worked with them so thoroughly in defining their needs and exploring alternatives that they have gained an extraordinary level of comfort with you, your people, and your products. In part you presell by taking the initiative and being more present, more helpful, and more engaged than your competitors have been, which demonstrates more commitment to customers—a commitment they are inclined to repay through the simple social mechanism of reciprocation. Of course, your solution must be excellent; it must solve their problems or meet their needs in ways that are technically and financially sound and competitive. But if all else is equal, your superior commitment to customers during mid–middle game will behaviorally differentiate you and position you for the win.

CHALLENGES FOR READERS

1. How selective are you in chasing opportunities? Do you channel your resources into the best opportunities or do you squander resources on opportunities you have no hope of winning or couldn't execute profitably if you did win them?

2. When do you typically start pursuing opportunities with enough force and commitment to send a strong behavioral message? Look again at Figures 7-1 and 7-2. Which of these radar diagrams is most like you? If your picture is more like Figure 7-1, what could you do to engage new opportunities sooner and with more resources?

3. In this chapter, we contrast the *sell and tell* approach with a facilitative selling approach. Which of these approaches is more characteristic of your company? What behavioral message do you send while you are exploring the customer's needs and developing the opportunity?

4. Do you have a formal process for assessing opportunities and determining which ones to pursue? Do you create pursuit strategies that include ways to differentiate yourself behaviorally during mid–middle game? If you don't develop pursuit strategies now, what would it take to implement this practice in your company?

5. How much customer time share and mind share do you typically have during mid–middle game while the opportunity is developing? What could you do to increase them?

6. To what extent do you typically influence the solution? How often do you help customers draft the specifications or the RFP? If you are rarely invited to participate in these mid–middle game activities, what are you doing wrong? And what can you do to fix it?

7. Finally, how well do you position your teams during mid–middle game? How effectively do you presell your solution? Do you go into late middle games and endgames already positioned for the win? Or do you typically get started late in middle game and find yourself chasing your more proactive competitors? Most companies win or lose B2B competitive contracts in middle game. What could you do to improve your behavioral differentiation during this crucial part of the business development process?

CHAPTER 8

Late Middle Game Positioning

> *Generally, he who occupies the field of battle first and awaits his enemy is at ease; he who comes later to the scene and rushes into the fight is weary.*—*Sun Tzu*, The Art of War
>
> ■
>
> *As soon as the play shows signs of leading into an endgame, reconsider the position from that point of view. If you feel uneasy about it, defer the endgame as long as you can and utilize the time gained in improving your chances for the ending. If, on the contrary, your chances are good, bring about the endgame as quickly as you can.*—*Eugene A. Znosko-Borovsky*
>
> ■
>
> *Dear, dear! How queer everything is to-day! And yesterday things went on just as usual. I wonder if I've been changed in the night?*
> —*Lewis Carroll*, Alice's Adventures in Wonderland

In business development, the rules of engagement can change radically once late middle game begins and customers begin their formal purchasing process. Sometimes the people who have been talking to you are no longer allowed to talk to you. The communication channels that had been so open and helpful—for both you and your customer—are sealed tight and the flow of information becomes measured and prescribed. This is the *Realm of Procurement*, and if you have had a close and productive relationship with the customer, late middle game can seem as strange as falling down a rabbit hole and having tea with the Mad Hatter and the March Hare.

If your customers do not have formal procurement processes with well-defined rules and procedures about how major products or services are purchased, then our analogy may seem far-fetched. However, if you sell to federal, state, or local governments, or to corporations that do have formal purchasing processes, then our allusions to Alice in Wonderland will make perfect sense. For the benefit of all readers, here's how it often works.

Communication with suppliers is typically very open before the start of the formal purchasing process. Then, at some point, the specifications, scope of work, and bid request documents are prepared, approved, and ready to be issued. The budget is approved, and the purchasing request moves into the customer's purchasing department, where it is assigned to a purchasing agent whose responsibility is to manage the process from that point forward according to the laws, rules, regulations, or guidelines in force. At this point, the need has been formalized and has left the hands of the people and departments where it originated. Those people will have found it useful to talk openly with suppliers while they were exploring their needs, but in many formal purchasing situations they become incommunicado once the requirement is dropped into a purchasing manager's lap. The reason for the sudden stonewall is procurement integrity, and in federal procurements, preserving the integrity of the system is—like gravity—more than just a good idea, it's the law.

This process has thousands of variations and may not apply at all in your industry or with your customers. Sometimes, there is a discernible shift in mood and tone once formal purchasing begins but you still have access to the customer's key people and can continue positioning your solution. Sometimes, only a reduced field of providers continues to have access. If you are among those excluded, you may get a message that says, in effect, "Thanks for your interest, and better luck next time." In other cases, the door is slammed shut on everyone. When that occurs, you lose access to key people and can no longer effectively influence the outcome, which is another reason why you should start early in middle game to condition the customer and position yourself to win. If you wait too long, you will lose the opportunity to presell your solution and will probably have lost the contract. In any case, the circumstances of late middle game vary considerably, so bear in mind as we discuss this phase of the business development process that there is no *average* situation. Whether or not you can do any of the things we suggest will depend on your customers, their particular purchasing process, and how much access they grant you to their key people as they begin formal purchasing.

In this chapter, we also discuss how you can recover from a weak middle game position and defend yourself if your competitors have done a better job of positioning and behavioral differentiation prior to late middle game. Be forewarned, however, that most late middle game defensive actions are truly a shot in the dark. If you wait until late middle game to start chasing an opportunity, prayer may be more helpful to you than behavioral differentiation because your behavior will already have communicated to customers that you were not very interested in meeting this need.

Late Middle Game Goals

Assuming that you arrive at late middle game having done a decent job in the opening and early parts of middle game, these are the typical late middle game goals: Consolidate your position, gain alignment on the right answer, test your selling strategy, and recover from a weak position if you are in one. What customers generally want to see in late middle game is a strong commitment to their program or project, so it's important to maintain a high level of contact with their key people in the final days before the RFP is released. Many of your also-ran competitors, knowing they are late to the game and fearing that if they don't leap into the fray they'll lose for sure—a reasonable fear—will likely intensify their presence, or try to, during those final days. From the customer's perspective, this may look and feel like a shark feeding frenzy, but you should not disappear just because there are so many new fish in the water. Two psychological principles are important here—the laws of primacy and recency. Other effects notwithstanding, customers will tend to remember best those who were first (primacy) and last (recency). You should figure prominently throughout middle game, but it's important to be there first and to maintain your presence through to the end.

> ♟ *Play the board, not the person. If you're facing a higher rated opponent, don't change your style out of fear. If you're facing a lower rated opponent, don't play below your ability due to overconfidence.*—*Jeremy Silman,* The Complete Book of Chess Strategy

Bear in mind that as middle game ends, customers are forming their final impressions of the potential suppliers. Of course, the proposals and presentations characteristic of endgame also affect the selection decision, but the tools of endgame tend to *confirm* rather than *form* impressions. Moreover, as the RFP release nears, customers are generally not groping to discover who can provide what they need. By this point, they already know that all the front-runners are capable of doing the work. That's no longer an issue. What still may be an issue, at least for some people who will influence the selection decision, is which of the front-runners they prefer. Others are likely to already know whom they prefer, at least subconsciously. So in late middle game a key behavioral differentiator is to be present and accounted for in the customer's hallways, offices, hearts, and minds—maintaining your zippered contacts; continuing to be helpful; remaining engaged and enthusiastic about the project; and sustaining high-quality meetings, demonstrations, presentations, and other communications. What could differentiate you negatively is assuming you have the contract already won and resting on your laurels. The customer's final impressions of you are critical. If there are any undecideds in the waning moments of middle game, then like good politicians on election day, you want to make that final positive impression as they head for the polls. The challenge is to be fully present without overdoing it and making a pest of yourself, turning what should be positive behaviors into negative ones. The only guideline is to use common sense. Each person in the customer's organization is likely to have a different "relational threshold," so you must judge, person by person, whether more contact will help or harm the relationship and the customer's impressions of you.

Rehearsing for Endgame

Legendary college basketball coach Bobby Knight said, "The will to succeed is important, but what's even more important is the will to prepare." As middle game draws to a close, smart companies rehearse their win strategy and selling messages in much the same way that a professional theater troupe conducts dress rehearsals before a live audience. The purpose of this preparation is to test the audience's reactions—to know whether the effects you have planned actually work, whether people respond the way you want them to respond, whether they laugh and applaud at the right moments, and whether your stagecraft is likely to result in a hit or a flop. It wouldn't make sense to open a new Broadway play without any rehearsal beforehand. It doesn't make sense in business development either.

In business development, the rehearsal process begins with a close look at your audience. You should know by now who, in endgame, will be reading the proposals, reviewing the bids, receiving the presentation, and influencing and making the selection decision. Who are these people? What are their roles in the process? More important, what do they think is *essential*—both in the technical solution and in the supplier they choose? Beyond the essentials, the *must haves,* what else would they like to see? What trade-offs are they willing to accept? From their perspective, what are the *ahas* and *oh-ohs*—the things that delight them on the one hand, and disturb them on the other? A best practice in late middle game is to map these elements person by person and then consider how your solution is going to play with this audience and their sets of expectations. It's easy to fall in love with your own products, technologies, and solutions—why wouldn't you? If you don't think you have the latest and greatest, why should the customer? But you're not the audience, and if it doesn't play in Peoria you won't have a hit.

As you reflect on your audience, try to anticipate their questions and concerns. When you and your team meet with them, don't just respond to customers' questions, write them down as well. Collect them from all customer sources, and map their questions on a sheet of paper showing who is asking which questions and who is expressing which concerns. You can often detect patterns that indicate how you should prepare for meetings with particular people (and who to take to those meetings) or what to include in correspondence going to them. Where are they uncertain about a product or service feature? What are they still questioning? Where do they remain unconvinced? The point of this is to anticipate their questions—*now*, in your pre-endgame meetings, so you don't have to guess later, when you are writing your proposal or preparing for your presentation.

Many of the customer's questions and concerns will not appear in the RFP. No RFP has ever been so complete that it tells the whole story. Your goal should be to develop insight into the customer's personal and business issues and concerns, the story that underlies the purchasing decision and the requirements that will appear in the RFP.

That story is rarely told in a complete form anywhere. So you have to piece it together, like a jigsaw puzzle whose box has no clues and no picture to work from. You have to take the pieces you are given—and the ones you can discover—and build a coherent picture. If your competitors have not been as diligent as you in discovering the hidden pieces, they will suffer from an incomplete picture as they try to write a response, price their offering, and show that they understand the customer's needs. Demonstrating that you have greater insight into the customer's needs and wants is a powerful behavioral differentiator in endgame—and you set the stage here in late middle game as you probe deeper, ask more insightful questions, are more thorough in your coverage, pay more attention, and are more disciplined than your competitors who got started late and have time to develop only a superficial understanding of the customer's needs before endgame begins.

Once you feel that you have a thorough understanding of the customer's questions and concerns, prepare your answers and the supporting materials you need to present them, including visuals or graphs, presentation slides, tables, research, data, photographs, histories of previous projects, and résumés. It's best not to wait until proposal preparation to create those materials. Create them now and test them with the customer. Use them to educate not only the customer but also the people in your company who will later be fielding the customer's questions and will have to explain the elements of your offer.

Testing Your Selling Strategy

As we said in Chapter 6, the ultimate goal of middle game is to presell your solution—to begin endgame having already sold the customer on your company and your solution and to establish a bias in your favor that your competitors will be unable to overcome. To feel confident that you have presold your solution, you need to test your selling strategy before endgame begins. First, you test the elements of your solution, the features you intend to offer in response to the customer's needs and wants, the project approach you think is best, and the service configurations that you think give the customer the best value for what the customer needs and is willing to spend.

"Here's what we're thinking of proposing," you might say. "What do you think of this? Is this responsive to your needs? Does this fill the bill? If not, how should we modify it?"

If you sense resistance—or just plain boredom—try to understand why. The time to convince customers is now, not in the proposal or final presentation. The worst mistake, which occurs over and over again, is arrogance—assuming that you know more than customers, that you understand the problem better than they do, that you have all the right answers and the cross you have to bear is putting up with ignorant people. We've seen this attitude in countless companies, and it's a deadly negative behavioral differentiator. Truly intelligent behavior is listening carefully to customers' questions, concerns, and perspectives and understanding the basis for their uncertainty. Often, they really do understand what you're saying but have some unrelated objection, which if you *hear* it can lead you to greater insight about how they view their situation and what they think they need. Then, if you still think they are missing something, you should try to educate them gently and provide substantiation for your position. A great outcome of testing your story with customers is to discover that your solution is perfectly aligned with their business goals, key issues, and program or project requirements. But, frankly, if you discover that you're not perfectly aligned, that's a good outcome, too. At least now you know you're not aligned and can try to fix it before going into endgame. The *ideal* outcome of testing is to confirm that you are not only aligned with customers but that they prefer you and will sing your song in the selection committee meetings to come.

You should also test your product differentiators. It's easy to deceive yourself on the existence and value of product differentiation, so a best practice is to test your differentiators during middle game:

"We think this is a unique feature of our product. How do you see it?" or "We aren't aware of any other supplier offering this particular feature. Is that what you've seen?"

Another way to test your differentiators is to ask open questions:

"What do you see as our differentiators?" or "In your view, what is uniquely better about our products?"

♞ *Practice means to perform, over and over again in the face of all obstacles, some act of vision, of faith, of desire. Practice is a means of inviting the perfection desired.—Martha Graham*

It's important to understand where you are actually differentiated and where you're not. You may think you have a unique feature and then discover that one of your competitors has just introduced the same thing or something superior. Worse yet, you may *not* discover it and make a big deal of this feature in your proposal and presentation only to learn later that you were highlighting how similar you and your competitors are. It's also important to know how much value your customers place on your differentiators. They may place even more value on a differentiated feature than you realized or less value than you think they should. In any case, you should ask questions like: "How important is this feature to you?" or "What would this feature enable you to do?" and "What would the bottom-line impact of that be?"

It's best not to ask for different comparisons between yourself and your competitors. Many customers are uncomfortable making such comparisons, and some find it downright tacky if you ask. The customers who are inclined to offer comparisons of your company and products with your competitors' companies and products will do so voluntarily. However, it's completely kosher to ask how they think you are differentiated from other suppliers and how much they value those differentiators. It's also acceptable to ask if they perceive that any other suppliers are differentiated from you, if their products and services have unique and highly valued features that yours don't. Finally, you should test whether your customers are willing to pay for the areas where you are differentiated. You may have some powerful product differentiators that customers see as *nice-to-haves* but that are unaffordable.

A best practice is to treat opportunities the way the U.S. Navy runs an aircraft carrier. The navy wants no surprises below or on the flight deck, so it tests every component, system, and procedure—over and over. It thoroughly trains every crew member, runs drills until actions and reactions are second nature, and practices emergency procedures so everyone knows not only what he or she should do but also what everyone else should do as well. It trains and tests constantly as a way to ensure flawless execution every time. Should you be as diligent as the U.S. Navy? It depends on how important the business is to you. In the past twenty-five years we have seen hundreds of opportunities with clients where big wins saved business units and jobs or losses led to downsizing and outplacement. Fortunes have been made and dreams dashed based on how favorably a customer viewed a supplier's offer that may have taken the supplier months and hundreds of thousands of dollars to produce. Consider the Joint Strike Fighter (JSF), the stealthy, multirole fighter aircraft commissioned by the Pentagon for the U.S. Air Force, Navy, and Marine Corps and for the U.K. Royal Air Force and Royal Navy. From 1997 through 2001, teams led by Boeing and Lockheed Martin were fiercely competing for this contract, which is the largest in U.S. history—worth $200 to $400 billion over the life of the program. Given the magnitude of the contract, both teams worked hard for years to develop their aircraft concepts and position themselves with the Pentagon. In October 2001, the Lockheed Martin team, which included Northrop Grumman and BAE Systems, received the award. Here were some of the effects on Boeing:

■ Following the Pentagon's announcement of the award to Lockheed Martin, Boeing's share price fell by more than 10 percent, which amounted to a loss of nearly $3.3 billion in market value.

■ The company cut 12,000 jobs on October 12, 2001, and another 2,900 jobs on November 27 as part of a downsizing in its defense business that was expected to total 30,000 jobs by June 2002.

■ Boeing expressed hope that it might have a subcontractor role on the JSF program, but by January 2002 those hopes appeared to have been dashed. As one Boeing spokesman said, "At this point we're more pessimistic than optimistic."

■ In December 2001, Lockheed Martin and Northrop Grumman began advertising for workers in St. Louis (Boeing's home turf) and in January held a job fair to lure Boeing's highly skilled workers to the JSF program. Lockheed sought to hire 2,500 people, and Northrop, 1,000.

■ In late January, *The News Tribune* in Tacoma, Washington, reported that if the end of 2001 was tough for Boeing, 2002 was likely to be much worse, and *The Economist* argued that Boeing had a bleak outlook in the years ahead.*

---

*This story has another interesting lesson about middle game. In November 2001, after Lockheed Martin had won the award, Vago Muradian, reporting for *Defense Daily International*, revealed, "Lockheed Martin two years ago emerged as the frontrunner in the

Boeing will no doubt survive this contract loss but clearly not without significant pain. When individual opportunities can have such a profound effect on your business, it behooves you to manage the most important of those opportunities as though you were the U.S. Navy operating an aircraft carrier, and that means scrupulous attention to detail and testing, testing, testing.

In effect, you want to turn your customer into a coach. You do this by checking with the customer on your solution, your differentiators, and your team. Naturally, if you have any sponsors in the customer's organization (sponsors are the people who want you to win), you should rehearse your selling messages and solution with them, but it's advisable to have a rehearsal with every key customer contact. How does this behaviorally differentiate you? For one thing, your competitors are not likely to be as meticulous as you are. We have met some account managers and executives who are as thoughtful about the process as we are describing, but there are many more who are undisciplined, don't think to ask the questions, don't listen as well as they should, and propose their own standard solutions no matter what the customer really wants and needs. In many cases, the outward effort to win actually slows in late middle game as a company ramps up internally to receive the RFP and crank out a proposal. The account team implodes, concluding that it has done everything it could to position the company and presell its solution. When this happens, a competitor who's at the top of its chess game can make the critical pre-endgame moves that will pay huge post-RFP dividends, and those are the moves we are advocating here.

Rehearsing as we have described will help you be better aligned with your customers and will help you present solutions and selling

multibillion dollar Joint Strike Fighter (JSF) competition on the performance of its proposed jets, particularly after rival Boeing (BA) was forced to comprehensively redesign its aircraft, but senior Pentagon officials concluded that the contest between the two must continue to ensure against Lockheed becoming complacent and drive the companies to deliver better proposals, according to former government officials." Later in this article, Muradian claimed, "Although some senior Pentagon officials saw the competition as imbalanced, they wanted to ensure continued competition and so in public consistently maintained that the two teams were equally matched and that the outcome of the contest was uncertain." What's fascinating in this story is the difference between the public and private positions the customer took. Middle game is often won by one of the competitors, but the customer—for legal, political, or public relations reasons—will assert that the contest is still open, the winner undecided. In fact, Lockheed Martin won this contest in middle game; the rest was window dressing, including two years of continued effort by Boeing at a cost of hundreds of millions of dollars. For further details, see Vago Muradian, "Lockheed Seen as JSF Leader Two Years Ago, but DoD Kept Competition Going," *Defense Daily International* 3, no. 1 (November 2, 2001): 2.

messages that you know resonate with them because you have pre-conditioned those messages and adjusted them according to the responses you received during your late middle game testing period. Furthermore, because you have been listening well, you should be better able to identify and address the customer's hidden issues and concerns. The point here isn't just about appearances. You will in fact be better informed and more in sync if you behave in the ways we are suggesting—and that's how you behaviorally differentiate during late middle game, assuming you still have good access to the customer's key people. If, in your industry, you are routinely denied such access during late middle game, then you should do your testing and rehearsing in mid–middle game while you can still meet with key customers.

> ♜ *Bad moves come in all shapes and sizes, from simple oversights to hideous blunders. They are usually caused by inexperience, lack of skill or just plain fatigue.* —*Larry Evans*, The 10 Most Common Chess Mistakes

Defending a Weak Position in Late Middle Game

In *The Complete Book of Chess Strategy*, international chess master Jeremy Silman says, "At times a blunder will immediately be fatal, but often it will deprive you of a hard-earned edge and will force you to start the beginning process (i.e., building up an advantage) all over again."[1] Whether or not you have blundered, you will occasionally find yourself in a weak position going into late middle game—you may be facing a competitor with a strong incumbent position, or competitors with well-placed customer sponsors, or a smart competitor who has played an excellent middle game and outfoxed you to this point. Beyond prayer, what can you do to recover from a weak late middle game position? Fourth-quarter come-from-behind victories do happen. Joe Montana pulled it off many times as quarterback of the San Francisco '49ers, but to accomplish what he did, you need enough time on the clock, supporting players as good as wide receiver Jerry Rice, and a lot of luck. In business development, this usually means having a solid technical offering, customers who are open-minded enough to give you a fair hearing, competitors who have become complacent, and enough time before endgame begins for you to work some magic. Here are some thoughts on how you can behaviorally differentiate yourself in these circumstances and perhaps find victory. As in football, the best defense is a good offense:

■ First, do a candid and realistic assessment of the situation. Is it hopeless or just bad? If it's hopeless, what do you stand to gain by pursuing this opportunity? Is that gain worth the investment? If so, you should be clear about what you're trying to achieve (it could be positioning for future opportunities rather than winning this contract) and shoot for that. If the situation is simply bad, then, like army doctors treating casualties during war, you should perform triage on the survivors: Ignore the customers you cannot save and focus on those who are most likely to respond well to treatment. You may be able to build enough support to generate serious interest among the customer representatives who were neutral or antagonistic toward you earlier.

■ Look for technical or behavioral blunders by your opponents. Are there any openings for you? As Jeremy Silman so eloquently notes, "Everyone blunders."[2] An opponent's misstep can open the door for you, but your response should be timely and professional—respectfully silent toward competitors and immediately helpful to the customer.

■ Look for changes in customers' needs or expectations that you may be able to exploit. Competitive bidding situations tend to be fluid in middle game and fixed in endgame. Customers' requirements may change as they learn more, explore more, and syndicate their views among themselves. Changes in their needs or their expectations of the supplier they choose may suddenly favor you, and you should be poised to take advantage of such changes.

■ Intensify your efforts. If you want to win the contract, you can't be fainthearted; this is a time to be bold. You may need to take risks you are not used to taking and do things you are not used to doing.

■ Look for ways to pleasantly surprise customers and get their attention. If, for instance, you can introduce a new technology, process, product, or innovation of some kind that dramatically increases the value to customers, you may get their attention in a way that changes their mind about what they want. When you start from behind, you generally must do something dramatic to get people to notice, something your competitors cannot quickly or easily copy.

■ Intensify your efforts at the top. If you can engage your C-level executives with their counterparts in the customer's organization—and mirror their intensity with contacts of your own at the working levels of the customer's opportunity decision process—you may be able to recover lost ground. The danger is that customers will be suspicious about your sudden high level of interest and dig in their heels against you. So your best option is to be candid and explain why you were not more active earlier. Being human and candid about your mistakes can be disarming if it is genuine. As Thoreau said, "Nothing so amazes a man as plain speaking and honest dealing."

■ Finally, you can roll up your sleeves and work hard to make up for lost ground. It's been done, generally when none of the competitors has successfully presold their solution and established a strong position earlier in middle game. If none of you has behaviorally differentiated yourselves to date, then that opportunity may still exist in late middle game.

We offer one final caution. If you are in a strong position coming into late middle game, don't presume that it's in the bag. In *The Middle Game in Chess*, Russian chess master Eugene A. Znosko-Borovsky advises players to attack opponents who have foolishly dropped their guard: "The player who, after sustained effort, has won some material, is naturally inclined to relax; having realized his intentions, he is not in the best condition for the immediate conception of another plan requiring further efforts. This is the moment when we should try to assume the initiative and create as many difficulties for him as possible. Passive acceptance of the situation almost certainly leads to disaster."[3]

CHALLENGES FOR READERS

1. In your industry and purchasing environment, how much latitude do you have to communicate with customers during late mid-

dle game after formal purchasing begins? How do the rules change once your customers initiate formal purchasing?

2. If you are permitted to do so, do you routinely maintain a strong presence in your customer's hallways and offices during late middle game? Do you maintain your intensity as RFP release nears? If not, why not? In your estimation, do you do a good job of impressing management as endgame approaches?

3. To what extent do you rehearse your solution, differentiators, and selling messages with customers during late middle game? Do you consciously test your customers' responses to each of the elements of your offer?

4. Do you behaviorally differentiate yourself in late middle game? If so, how? In what ways does your behavior demonstrate more understanding of customers' needs, more awareness of their hidden issues and concerns, more commitment to serving them, and greater alignment with their goals?

5. How effective are you at defending a weak late middle game position? What could you do to increase your behavioral differentiation during these difficult circumstances?

Endgame: Conditioning the Deal

> *Four things come not back—the spoken word, the sped arrow, the past life, and the neglected opportunity.—Arabian proverb*
>
> ■
>
> *You will find that a lion's heart and a fighting spirit can overcome tremendous difficulties on the chessboard. Never give up, hang on like grim death, and force your opponent to play like a genius if he's going to drag you down.—Jeremy Silman,* The Complete Book of Chess Strategy
>
> ■
>
> *The game is now nearing its end; threats are less numerous but more intense.—Eugene A. Znosko-Borovsky,* The Middle Game in Chess

Suddenly, the waiting is over. The RFP hits the streets. The clock is ticking. It's the last lap, the final round, the two-minute warning, the bottom of the ninth. When customers formally request a bid, tender, or proposal, you are in endgame. Now there is a deadline for bidders to submit their proposals. After customers evaluate the proposals and short-list the front-runners, they often require the bidders to present their offers, a process sometimes colorfully known as a *shoot-out*. From these contests emerges a winner, chosen but not quite home free because there are still negotiations ahead. If those are concluded successfully, the winner signs the contract and moves on to happy days; if not, the winner may be eclipsed at the finish line by a runner-up who is more open to the customer's terms and conditions, more willing to deal, and therefore more positively differentiated in a behavioral sense during the negotiations.

In endgame, the die is cast. The requirements are fixed, and the procedures and criteria are in place for selecting the winner. The most important artifact of endgame is the proposal, which can vary from a short and simple letter proposal to an elaborate, multivolume tome that requires months; hundreds of thousands of dollars; and armies of engineers, writers, editors, and graphic artists to produce. Earlier in this book, we argued that endgame accounts for only about 10 percent of your win probability, that most contracts are won or lost in opening game (with 20 percent of win probability) and middle game (70 percent). But it would be a mistake to treat proposals as a pro forma exercise. Some companies do. They behave as though the proposal is an annoying requirement, part of the administrivia of contracting, a mere formality, and they devote only as much time and attention to their proposals as is absolutely required. Sometimes they get away with it, but often they don't. When they don't, they tend to blame their losses on price and don't examine or discover the real reasons for their low win rate.

Proposals do generally *confirm* the impressions you made during middle game, rather than *form* new impressions of you. But it's best to think of proposals as the final lap in what might be a close race. It's not time to let up yet. When your competitors are nip and tuck with you in the final lap, you can win by having a little more endurance, a little more speed, and a little more determination. Consider Stefania Belmondo. She won the first gold medal awarded in the 2002 Winter Olympics in Salt Lake City. In the women's 15-kilometer cross-country ski race, Stefania was skiing with the lead pack when, at the 10.5-kilometer point, she broke a ski pole and started falling behind. She struggled for the next 700 meters, was passed by skiers who'd been trailing her, and lost seven seconds to the leaders. As she was about to lose hope, a team trainer ran to the course and handed her another pole. She regained her composure and, driven by a powerful will, began closing the gap. With just seconds remaining, she caught the leader and, in the last 20 meters of the race, surged to victory. The competitors who have superior will in endgame often win close races. Had Stefania Belmondo not skied well until her pole broke, she would not have been in position to catch the leaders, but it took a fierce determination to carry her across the finish line once she was back in the race. Likewise, a splendid proposal may not be able to raise you from the ashes of a poor middle game, but if you've played middle game well and some key competitors are close in the final stretch, a great proposal can lift you ahead of the pack.

Conversely, a poor proposal can cost you the victory even if you are well positioned when endgame begins. The fact is, if you are poorly positioned after middle game, a great proposal will rarely help you win, but even if you play an excellent middle game, you can lose in a heartbeat with a poor proposal. What you need in endgame is both skill and will—the skill to create outstanding proposals and presentations and the will to see them through—because if you coast at the end, someone like Stefania Belmondo is going to pass you at the finish line.

> ♛ *I think it is rather fine, this necessity for the tense bracing of the will before anything worth doing can be done. I rather like it myself. I feel it is to be the chief thing that differentiates me from the cat by the fire.—Arnold Bennett*

The Goals of Endgame

In *The Complete Book of Chess Strategy*, Jeremy Silman offers this advice to chess players: "Learning the basics of endgame play is of extreme importance. I can't implore you in strong enough terms to correct your flaws in this area. By doing so you will find that your opening and middlegame play will improve, whole new strategies will suggest themselves, and a newfound confidence will enable you to enter endgames with the strongest of opponents."[1] Successful endgames require a great deal of skill. Well-written proposals and well-delivered presentations are not accidents, and they aren't produced by amateurs, no matter how skilled those amateurs might be in other parts of their professional lives. If you intend to do well here, you must invest here. So what are the goals of endgame? First, you are trying to position yourself to win, to bring successful closure to the customer's decision, and you accomplish that by creating superior proposals and presentations. Next, if you win, your goal should be to achieve a mutually acceptable exchange of value in the negotiations. Finally, you should prepare yourself to execute the contract in a manner that delights the customer. Throughout endgame, there are numerous opportunities for behavioral differentiation. The first occurs in how you organize and manage the proposal development process.

Behavioral Differentiation in the Proposal Process

German historian Oswald Spengler said that the secret of all victory lies in the organization of the nonobvious. The behavioral difference between companies that excel at endgame and those that don't lies in how well they organize and manage their proposal efforts. They treat proposal creation as though it were a profession (which it is) that requires knowledgeable, educated professionals. The best-in-class companies we have seen hire or develop proposal professionals—proposal managers (who often act as internal proposal consultants), writers, editors, and others who specialize in designing, creating, and producing customer-oriented proposals. First-rate proposal managers are particularly important. They must know how to lead virtual teams of engineers, project managers, scientists, technicians, and others to create proposals that are responsive to the customer's proposal requirements while telling a compelling story of their offer. Success in proposal management depends very much on what, to outside observers, would look like the organization of the nonobvious.

In and of itself, outstanding proposal management does not behaviorally differentiate because customers generally do not witness it. However, it's like Bishop George Berkeley's famous philosophical conundrum: "If a tree falls in a forest and no one is there to hear it, does it make a sound?" Certainly, you won't hear the tree fall if you are not present when it falls, but if you walk by it later you will observe that it's fallen down. Similarly, though customers don't observe the behind-the-scenes management of proposals (the "nonobvious," as it were), they will experience the effects of good proposal management as behavioral differences in your team's understanding of their needs; responsiveness to their issues and concerns; compliance with their requirements; and outstanding storytelling that links their goals and key issues with the features, benefits, and proofs of your solution. In short, your proposal becomes the documentary evidence of your behavioral differentiation.

In the past forty years, spurred largely by advances in the proposal art from the large aerospace and defense contractors—who had to learn how to produce outstanding proposals or perish, while pursuing some of the largest contracts ever awarded—a body of best practices has emerged that includes the following items. Collectively, these best practices in proposal management can help you create outstanding, behaviorally differentiated proposals:

■ First, treat proposal development professionally. Many companies treat it as a necessary evil, and it shows in the ad hoc way they assign people to proposal projects (often, they are the ones who can be spared rather than the best and most knowledgeable people) and in the low-visibility proposal efforts received from top management.

■ Assign proposal managers early—as early as mid-middle game when the opportunity first emerges—and ensure that these proposal managers know what they are doing. Managing proposals is not like managing every other kind of project; it requires the special skill that comes from education, mentoring, or long experience. You can't assign someone willy-nilly to manage a proposal and expect a great outcome. By and large, it won't happen.

■ Ensure that the account managers who have been working with customers in middle game participate in the proposal project. We have seen companies in which the account manager, who has most of the customer knowledge prior to the proposal project, throws the RFP over the transom and then disappears, leaving the proposal manager and team to discover for themselves the customer's priorities, key issues, and concerns, and other matters not evident in the RFP. This behavior will differentiate you, but not positively. Instead, it causes an information and strategy disconnect between middle game efforts to presell and endgame efforts to do the same thing in the proposal. Ultimately, the communication breakdown is a behavioral breakdown.

■ Try to dedicate the proposal writers to the project. Often, the engineers and other contributors to proposal efforts are not released from their normal responsibilities, so proposal work is an overload, and it shows in what they produce, no matter how good their "best effort" might be. The finest proposals come from dedicated teams of writers who understand how proposals differ from technical documents. (The difference is that although proposals typically contain abundant technical matter, they are essentially not technical documents. They are sales documents.)

■ Begin organizing the proposal in middle game. If you wait until endgame to initiate the proposal effort, you will lose valuable time and frustrate the proposal team. Before the RFP arrives, the proposal manager should have coordinated with sales and account managers, gathered intelligence, contributed to middle game positioning, organized the proposal team and the project, developed a proposal win strategy, created the major themes that will be woven throughout the proposal, and prepared for the proposal project kickoff meeting. So full are proposal managers' plates during mid-to-late middle game that many companies have created detailed checklists to help them manage the process systematically.

■ Use a kickoff meeting to launch the proposal project. The moment the RFP hits the streets, the proposal manager should analyze it; build a compliance matrix; develop a detailed outline of the proposal; create a win strategy and themes; develop the proposal format; organize the writing of the proposal sections; prepare for reviews; and then conduct a kickoff meeting in which the members of the team are brought together, oriented on the effort, and given their assignments. The most effective kickoff meetings are big deals—not quite the fanfare of a Hollywood opening but darn near. Senior executives should attend, as well as key operations or manufacturing managers, sales managers, and others whose presence communicates that this is a major opportunity for the company—an investment of time, money, and energy that the company considers very important.

■ Use the full desktop-publishing capability you already have at your disposal. One of the most telling negative differentiators in a proposal occurs when the words declare that your company is state-of-the-art, committed to quality through and through, best-in-class, the industry standard bearer, the recognized leader in innovation, etc., and it's all being said in a document at least ten years or more behind in current desktop-publishing capability. Those claims become little more than sales noise in the customer's head because the physically observable behaviors of proposal design, format, and finish communicate a very different message.

■ Ensure that executives in senior management are present throughout the proposal effort. By their presence or absence, and by the amount of attention they pay or don't pay to the proposal effort, your CEO and other senior executives behave in ways that communicate how important they consider this business-building effort to be. In some of the companies we have seen, these senior executives never show up; in others, they pay a perfunctory visit during the kickoff meeting and are never seen again. While working for Hughes Radar Systems, however, we witnessed a vice president who, for the entire sixty-day response period, rolled up his sleeves; went into the proposal area; and worked on strategies, themes, graphics, and text—right alongside the beleaguered technical experts, writers, and proposal specialists who were sweating bullets to win the contract. The result was a unified team effort, supported at the top, and a proposal that made competing proposals look like what they were—substandard documents signed by vice presidents who did not get involved until it was time to sign the cover letter. Hughes won the deal hands down, and the vice president hosted a huge victory party for the entire team. That's behavioral differentiation in endgame.

Behavioral differentiation in proposal management is often the result of a proposal manager's creative approach to communication. Some years ago, we worked with a proposal team in a division of Honeywell. The proposal manager, whom we will call Fred, had an innovative solution for driving their selling themes through every section of the proposal. In this, as in all good proposal efforts, the proposal manager identified the primary selling messages or themes of their offer before the proposal project began. By late middle game, Fred knew that they needed to emphasize five major themes and around twenty minor themes throughout their proposal. Twenty-five messages may seem like too many, but in a multivolume proposal of a thousand pages or so, this is not unusual. Fred's problem was that he had a team of about eighty writers working on the proposal, and he knew that simply asking them to stress these themes in the appropriate places in the document would be fruitless. Fred was no fool—he had managed proposal efforts before—so he knew he had to do something dramatic.

His solution was to ask their on-site printing facility if they could print his twenty-five messages as bumper stickers. This proposal was written in the era when bumper stickers were popular, and the printers said, sure, they could do that. What colors did he want? So Fred had his themes printed in lime green, competition orange, florid purple, canary yellow, and other vibrant colors. He organized his thematic bumper stickers as individual packets for each of the eighty writers. Each pack contained only the bumper stickers with the themes each writer needed to emphasize in his or her sections. In the kickoff meeting, Fred's packets had the kind of puzzled and then delighted effect he'd hoped for, and in the weeks to follow you could walk into any writer's cubicle and see a rainbow of theme statements taped to the wall above the desk. Fred's solution captured their attention; ensured that they would remember what they were supposed to emphasize as they wrote their sections; and resulted in a winning proposal in which messages to the customer were clear, strong, and repeated throughout the document.

> ♛ *I've never known a man worth his salt who in the long run, deep down in his heart, didn't appreciate the grind, the discipline. . . . I firmly believe that any man's finest hour—this greatest fulfillment to all he holds dear—is that moment when he has worked his heart out in a good cause and lies exhausted on the field of battle victorious.—Vince Lombardi*

Proposals are generally written by technical experts in various disciplines or functional areas who can write with authority about their areas of expertise. By and large, these people are not professional writers and do not have a background in sales, so although they can answer the customer's technical questions, they usually do not know how proposals are evaluated and have only the most basic notion of how to *sell* their part of the solution. Further, they tend to write from their own perspective rather than the customer's, so they will say, "Here's what we have," instead of, "Here's what you need, and here's how our proposed solution best meets your needs." Best-in-class proposals are highly customer focused. They center on the customer's goals, needs, issues, and requirements. The supplier's solution is presented as a response to the customer's needs. Customer focus is an easy concept to comprehend, but it turns out to be very difficult to achieve in practice, largely because proposals are written by people who are not proposal professionals and because they tend to write from the standard documents in their work areas: technical descriptions, specifications, process flows, user manuals, standard operating procedures, and so on—all of which were written primarily for internal use. No wonder it's difficult for them to translate this language to something more customer focused and compelling to potential buyers. It's best to think of proposals as an observable set of behaviors that will either confirm or contradict your sales rhetoric. If you claim to be a customer-focused organization, how can you *behave* in your proposals in a way that demonstrates customer focus?

Consequently, one of the proposal manager's principal tasks is guiding this group of independent experts in the creation of a document they do not intuitively understand and very often don't like. To accomplish this, some of the best proposal managers do all they can to make the process more bearable and, ideally, even rewarding. Some have a standing order at the local pizza parlor or hot food delivery service. Some send thank-you cards—not to the people working days and nights and weekends on the proposal but to their friends or spouses and families. In a very classy move, one proposal manager for General Dynamics Fort Worth Division, knowing that the upcoming proposal was a "must win" for the company and would require huge sacrifices from the proposal team, invited not only the team members to the kickoff meeting but also their spouses. He ordered corsages for the women and boutonnieres for the men and included everyone— proposal writers, experts, security guards, administrative assistants, receptionists, custodians—who would be contributing directly or indirectly to the cause through cancelled vacations, lost weekends, or lost family time. When they won the contract, the proposal manager held a huge victory party in which the chairman of the division attended and personally thanked everyone for their contributions. The proposal manager also sent a personal thank-you letter to the partner or spouse of each member of the team.

How do these proposal management behaviors differentiate? To answer that question, we must contrast them with what often happens. First, many companies do not assign a proposal manager until the RFP hits the streets. By then, it's too late. The person they assign is generally well intentioned but inexperienced at managing proposals. Many companies lack the resources that could help make the process easier to manage and more sophisticated—software for analyzing the customer's key issues and developing strategy; tools for stripping the RFP and creating compliance checklists; databases of resumes and project experience; libraries of lessons learned and winning proposals; checklists for kickoff meetings; and procedures for storyboarding, conducting pink and red team reviews, and creating brochure executive summaries. In short, companies that do not manage proposals well lack the skill and the will to do it better. Either their management doesn't think it's important or they are too busy putting out today's fires to worry about tomorrow's business. In either case, they risk creating a proposal product that will negatively differentiate them.

We have been talking about very large companies with the resources to hire or develop professional proposal staffs and to dedicate proposal writers' time to proposal projects. How possible is it to behaviorally differentiate during the proposal development process, however, if you are a smaller company with fewer resources? We think it's a matter of scale, certainly, but also of attitude and commitment. If you consider it important, you can find a way to get started early, to manage the proposal process more professionally, to emphasize the importance of the proposal effort to those who participate in it, to ensure top-management support for and participation in the process, and to create customer-focused proposals using the kinds of best practices we cited.

Superior proposals are not the fruit of serendipity; they result from a disciplined, self-conscious process of clearheaded management and customer-focused execution. As English statesman Edmund Burke said, "There is nothing in the world really beneficial that does not lie within the reach of an informed understanding and a well-protected pursuit." Behavioral differentiation through proposal management will almost invariably yield a behaviorally differentiated product, especially if your competitors are not as disciplined, systematic, and sophisticated in their approaches as you are.

Behaviorally Differentiated Proposals

To appreciate a proposal that creates positive behavioral differentiation, first consider varieties of proposals that negatively differentiate. At the far end of "poor" on the spectrum of proposal quality are the off-the-shelf brochures and price lists. Believe it or not, suppliers sometimes put these in the mail in response to a customer's request for a proposal. Bordering on being disrespectful, these kinds of responses show no insight into the customer's problems and little real desire for the work. They are a convenience to the supplier but signal, correctly, that the supplier has taken no time to learn more about the customer's needs and expended no energy to customize a response.

What we like about them, however, is that they are easy to compete against because it's not hard to behaviorally differentiate yourself if your competitors are this careless.

Next on the negative hit parade are proposals built wholly or mostly from boilerplate, which includes standard descriptions, off-the-shelf résumés and experience write-ups, and sections of previous proposals. Boilerplate is a convenience for proposal writers who argue, reasonably, that reinventing the wheel is a waste of time, but danger is afoot when you beg, borrow, and steal passages from previous proposals. One high-tech company we know of—which wishes to remain nameless—was bidding on a large contract for the U.S. Air Force. It had previously bid on a U.S. Army contract for a similar system, and its proposal team borrowed liberally from the Army proposal as they wrote the one for the Air Force. In numerous places throughout the document they neglected to change the customer's name, although their most egregious faux pas was not misnaming the customer in the text but doing it on the cover. Further, in what can only be described as a suicidal moment, the proposal proudly declared, "We will provide the U.S. Army with the highest possible quality and attention to detail." This story lacks a happy ending, except for the competitors. When we saw what they had done, we were inclined to ask, "Can you spell *interservice rivalry*?" Boilerplate is a convenience, but if you use it, then "paying attention to detail" has to be more than a slogan. You have to ensure that each word, sentence, paragraph, section, and visual actually addresses what your current customer is asking for. Untailored boilerplate is rarely on target, though it can provide the raw material from which to construct an excellent proposal.

Next on the negative ledger are proposals that we would describe as noncompliant descriptions of capability. A surprising number of these kinds of proposals are submitted every year. In these proposals, the authors have looked at the bid request document and tried to provide the information requested, but they have not been meticulous in responding to every request or requirement, and they have focused almost exclusively on their own capabilities and products. These are generally very difficult proposals for customers to evaluate because it isn't immediately clear whether the information customers requested is in the proposal. The biggest problem with these proposals is compliance, and they generally lose because evaluators can't find the information they need, usually because the proposal writers have not answered the mail. These proposals often contain a disproportionately high amount of boilerplate and are not well designed. The signals they send to customers are "We don't care enough to do a better job," or "We're behind the eight ball on your proposal, and, frankly, this is the best we can do. So how will you score us on the chemistry test? How will you translate this behavioral message into how well we will manage your project? What's your conclusion about that commitment to service and quality we kept telling you about in middle game?"

Proposal writers are strongly inclined to tell their story the best way they know how, which is to organize their thoughts in a manner that is logical to them. However, this is often a fatal error. Proposal evaluators do their jobs by comparing each proposal to a set of requirements and criteria, which are typically spelled out in the RFP, technical specifications, or scope of work. In the evaluation process, they look at proposals to see how well each bidder is addressing the requirements or meeting the criteria. So proposals that are organized the way their authors think they should be are often terribly frustrating for the evaluators, who are following the "script" dictated by the RFP and related documents. This leads us to the first of our suggestions for creating behaviorally differentiated proposals: answer the mail. If the customer asks how you would handle areas A, B, C, and D, then be sure your proposal provides information on areas A, B, C, and D—in that order. Although the customer's logic in asking for information may not be apparent to you (or make sense), you are not the audience and you are not the customer. So a cardinal rule of proposal writing is to give customers exactly what they ask for in the order they ask for it. If you did this and this alone, you would make it much easier for customers to read your proposals and would behaviorally differentiate yourself from a great many competing suppliers who don't follow this simple rule.

Being compliant means providing all the information customers ask for. If you fail to comply fully, you have failed the customer's first tests: *Can you listen? Do you understand what we want? Will you give us what we want? Can we trust that your solution will meet our needs?* The finest proposals not only answer the mail; they do it so their compliance is transparent. They are meticulous in following the customer's lead. They are scrupulous in addressing every requirement—in the order the customer listed them. They use the customer's language, and they provide aids to help the evaluators see their compliance more easily. Responsiveness goes well beyond mere compliance. Bear in mind that no RFP can ever fully capture the customer's intent. The RFP writers are human and typically work in a procurement function, which means they are not the end user or even the ultimate buyer of what they are attempting to define and discuss. They may be restricted from describing everything that would be helpful for suppliers to know. Even when no restrictions exist, few RFP writers are skillful enough to convey fully not only customers' requirements but also their goals, underlying concerns, key issues or hot buttons, and values.

In short, what most RFPs lack is *insight*. They present the official and superficial (though usually detailed) picture of what the customer wants, but they generally fail to enlighten suppliers about the more subtle and intangible factors that led to the customer's decision to purchase this product or service and the hopes, fears, and political concerns that will drive the customer's supplier selection decision. Compliant proposals focus on the supplier's capability to deliver what the customer has specified in the RFP. Consequently, they focus on the supplier and the *features* of the supplier's solution rather than the customer and the *benefits* those features provide. They describe, but they don't sell, and there is a powerful difference between the two approaches.

Responsive proposals do more. They demonstrate how the bidder will help customers achieve their business goals, not just their project or procurement goals. The latter goals are not the end. They are the means to the end, and a responsive proposal shows astute awareness of this distinction. What most proposals fail to recognize is that customers are not in the problem-solving business. The millions they are about to invest are just that—an investment—and their ultimate goals define the return on investment (ROI) they must get as a business. Solving the problem is how they will do it. The proposal that maps a clear path through the problem or immediate need to those business goals is a proposal that truly understands what's driving the investment and what's at stake. To write a responsive proposal, then, you must incorporate the middle game insights you discovered while working with the customer into the text and visuals in ways that demonstrate your superior understanding of the customer's needs, goals, and underlying drivers.

Beyond compliance and responsiveness, proposals that behaviorally differentiate you from competing proposals do an excellent job of explaining the logic underlying your offer. In other words, throughout every part of your proposal, you answer four key questions: *Why us? Why not them? So what?* and *How so?* The first two questions remind us that proposals are sales tools. The answers explain why customers should choose you (why your solution is best) and why they should not choose your competitors. It is not good business practice to attack your competitors by name, but you should attack their areas of weakness. When customers have finished reading your proposal, they should understand clearly why you and your solution are preferable and why your competitors' solutions are undesirable. Next, in answering the *So what?* question, you are explaining to customers why you have chosen the solution, products, or features you are proposing. You might say, for example, "Our project team brings 323 years of aggregate experience to this challenge." *So what?* What do those 323 years do for the customer? This is the WIIFM (What's in it for me?) factor. Everything you propose has no meaning except in what it does for the customer, and explaining the *So whats* for every feature of your offer makes the customer's WIIFM clear.

If you could read customers' minds while they assess proposals or presentations, you might be staggered at how often the "So what?" occurs and never gets answered. Furthermore, keep in mind that the people who evaluate your proposals do not award you the deal. They *recommend* you to their decision-makers. So if they try to recommend your company by repeating all the features you trotted out in your proposal—those 323 years of experience—the decision-makers will also respond with "So what?" The evaluators need benefits to answer that question for their executives. A proposal that gives them those answers has behaved exceptionally well, and when the evaluators decide to recommend your company and solution, they have just joined your sales force. Behaviorally, you need to give them what they need to sell you, your company, and your offer, and to unsell your competitors in the process.

Likewise, if you make a benefit-related claim (that your approach will improve the customer's configuration management, for example), then you are obliged to explain *how so*. We have been reviewing proposals for the past twenty-five years, and our experience over that period suggests that 80 to 90 percent of all proposals fail to answer these four questions consistently and well. When they do, they are award-winning knockouts and are dazzlingly effective with customers, but as we said earlier, it's difficult to persuade the engineers, technicians, and scientists who write many proposal sections to think this way. It's just not in their DNA.

The finest proposals also manifest a clear and compelling strategy and a strong and repeated set of messages or themes. The writers are clear about why the customer should choose them. They build themes based on their most powerful differentiators and sales messages, and those themes appear at every appropriate point—in the executive summary, in volume or section summaries, at the beginning of relevant paragraphs, as sidebar comments, and in visuals and captions. The key messages are reinforced in so many ways it's impossible for customers not to get the message, yet in the most artful of proposals, this is done subtly. The themes don't reach out and smack readers in the face; they simply keep appearing, in various forms, understated here and plainly stated there, so the cumulative effect is persuasive and memorable.

Some readers derive most of their information from the words on the page; others are more visually oriented and respond best to visual representations of the major ideas in a proposal. Consequently, the most impactful proposals are about 30 percent visual, which means that on the whole about one page in three or four is visual. Of course, the visuals should be integrated into the text, and many visuals are half-page or quarter-page in size. Still, your proposals will be more effective if they contain a lot of high-impact visuals. Visuals draw the eye and engage the imagination. One articulate visual, presented well, has more power than pages and pages of text. Annotated visuals are especially compelling. These have short captions that draw readers to and explain important parts of the illustration. A well-annotated visual is like a walking tour of the illustration, drawing the reader's eyes to what the bidder wants to emphasize and making the journey more enlightening.

Decades ago the fad among large defense contractors was to produce "visually oriented proposals" in which each page of text was matched with an opposite page of visuals. This stilted format did not last long, but it did emphasize how important visuals are in telling a compelling story—and this is the more important lesson. Imagine the effect if a publication such as *National Geographic* suddenly dropped those brilliant photographs and maps, leaving only the text to be read. Or if it just attached those pictures at the back of each issue rather than integrating them with the articles. The impact would be numbing and perhaps fatal. Similarly, proposals must tell a compelling story. A good story told poorly will lose every time to a good story told well. Assuming all else is equal—that you and your key competitors are credible and acceptable, that your price is competitive, and that each company has good relationships in the customer's organization—the winning team will be the one that has been most compelling in the presentation of its offer. Artistry matters.

> *Art is a human activity consisting in this, that one man consciously, by means of certain external signs, hands on to others feelings he has lived through, and that other people are infected by these feelings, and also experience them.—Leo Tolstoy*

What also matters is the ease of evaluation. Proposals that are easy to evaluate tend to get higher scores because, simply put, the evaluators like them. Of course, you must have a good solution and so forth, but if you give two proposals to an evaluator and one is easy to evaluate and the other hard to evaluate, the former will get higher technical scores even if they propose exactly the same technology, the same products, and the same solution. Why? Because the evaluators are human, and they develop a positive attitude toward proposals that make their lives easier, and vice versa. No matter how objective customers want the process of proposal evaluation to be, the simple truth is that the difference between higher and lower scores depends largely on each evaluator's judgment. So how do you make your proposals easier to evaluate?

■ First, be sure to answer the mail. Be steadfastly compliant. Turn the RFP into a checklist of requirements and make sure you respond to every single request for information. Sometimes, a single sentence in an RFP may include three or four separate pieces to respond to. Respond to each of them. Moreover, as we said earlier, follow the customer's organization. Don't invent your own. In many cases, evaluators will not read your proposal word for word. In fact, if they have to, you're making them work too hard to choose you. So by designing a reader-friendly proposal that emphatically delivers all your key messages—including powerful answers to those four questions discussed earlier—you are, in fact, making it easier for them to choose your proposal, especially if they have to slog through your competitors' proposals. Relatively speaking, yours was a pleasure to evaluate: compliant, responsive, and compelling.

■ **Make your compliance transparent.** Create a "compliance checklist" that shows, side by side, their requirements from the RFP and the page in your proposal where you respond to them. Submit this checklist with your proposal.

■ **Use customers' language.** You may refer to something as a *thingamajig*, but if they call it a *widget*, then you should call it a *widget*. Even simple practices like this can make your proposal easier for evaluators to follow, and it shows more respect than insisting on your own terminology. We once wrote a proposal for a large aerospace manufacturer. After winning, we had a chance to talk to the head of its evaluation team, and he said, "Reading your proposal was like reading my own thoughts." When you follow their structure and use their terms, you increase their comfort with you—in part because it says that you've listened to them, in part because it shows you're not arrogant, and in part because it convinces them that you will deliver what they want. How could it get any better than that?

Proposal specialist DeNeil Hogan Petersen tells an interesting story about making proposals easier to evaluate:

In 1988, I was hired to build a proposal department for a company that sold hand-held computer systems to municipalities and utilities for meter reading and parking ticket management. These systems are common now but were fairly new at the time. The industry practice was for all the competitors to supply the customer with a document called "bid specs" listing the specifications for their hardware, software, and maintenance programs. The customer would then prepare an RFP incorporating the various bid specs (e.g., "the hand-held unit must be waterproof and capable of being dropped from a height of six feet onto pavement," "the software must be capable of identifying and escalating scofflaw information and downloading to the hand-held units for immediate action on the street," or "the vendor must offer prepaid overnight shipping to and from the maintenance facility"). Thus, the typical proposal had a lengthy section entitled

"Response to Specifications." The standard response was a numbered list with yes/no or compliant/noncompliant.

Initially, I repeated the customer's specifications in the response section, with a checklist identifying whether we complied with or exceeded the requirement (which we often did) and a narrative explanation. The customer feedback on our proposals was very positive, especially for the simple act of repeating their requirements, and it wasn't long before we started noticing RFP's asking for a checklist response. The copies of our competitors' proposals and bid specs our sales reps were able to obtain verified they had started doing the same things.

Then one of the sales reps suggested we start supplying bid specs on disk, which was a pretty novel idea for the time. I rewrote ours like an actual RFP, without mentioning our name in the technical specifications, and including proposal instructions. This we presented as an RFP preparation tool, inviting the customer to use verbatim or edit as necessary, and of course they did. Even when they inserted competitors' specifications in place of ours, they tended to use our proposal instructions, forcing our competitors to respond in our format and making the task of preparing proposals a lot easier for us. Again, the feedback on the RFP-style bid specs was extremely positive.[2]

Her experience illustrates not only good proposal practice but also the entropic forces that drive all markets toward commodities. Best practices will invariably be adopted by the market and spread to other competitors. Nonetheless, it is better to lead the pack than follow it. First movers have the behavioral advantage in every kind of market, and if you can behave in innovative ways with customers—even though it may raise their expectations and eventually cause your competitors to copy your practices—you will still have gained the advantage by outbehaving your competitors to start with.

Another in our arsenal of best proposal practices is the brochure executive summary, and this one is a blockbuster. Research on the effectiveness of various practices in proposals has shown that creating a brochure executive summary can more than double your probability of winning. Proposals often include executive summaries but many are perfunctory, uninspired, and uninspiring. We began our work on the brochure executive summary years ago while helping a large telecommunications firm bid on the telephone system for a state's college and university system (we told this story in *Winning Behavior*). Since then, we have seen brochure executive summaries used in countless competitions. If they are well designed and well executed, they can make a powerful difference because, unlike the full proposals, these executive summaries are getting your best messages to the people who will ultimately make the buying decision. Several years ago, we helped a large engineering and construction firm study its proposal wins and losses. The firm isolated a number of potential contributing factors, including the presence or absence of brochure executive summaries, and examined fifty opportunities—half of them wins and half losses. A factor analysis revealed that when the firm included brochure executive summaries with its proposals, it was two and one-half times more likely to win.

The most recent innovations in proposal design are outgrowths of the personal computer and its bombastic cousin, the Internet. In recent years, we have seen proposals submitted on CD-ROM; electronic executive summaries with hierarchical levels of detail that allowed customers to go as deep or shallow on a topic as they wished; and interactive proposals that featured searchable slide show presentations, animated flowcharts, "peelable" illustrations in which customers could peer inside drawings and plant configurations, executive summaries with embedded movies instead of the standard still photographs (so the supplier's key people could "speak" to customers), movies of related projects that showed innovative features and approaches, and other high-tech ways of displaying information so it was more useful, more interesting, and more informative for customers. Some years ago, these capabilities were prohibitively expensive and time-consuming to create, but today's computer technology is making them affordable and within reach of most proposal departments, even in smaller companies.

So, let's summarize. How do you behaviorally differentiate yourself in the proposal itself? First, you ensure that you are 100 percent compliant and responsive. You answer the mail and show insight into the customer's goals, needs, and key issues. Compliance and responsiveness are fundamental. Failing to do this is likely to differentiate you negatively. Next, you ensure that your proposals are customer oriented, focusing on customers' needs and on the benefits to them of your proposed products and services. Answer the four key questions throughout your proposals: *Why us? Why not them? So what?* and *How so?* If you use boilerplate, be sure to customize it (and use the find and replace function in your software to ensure that you change all previous customers' names in the document). Base your proposals on a clear and compelling strategy with themes and messages repeated verbally and visually throughout, and do everything you can to make the proposals easy to evaluate. Finally, use brochure executive summaries and state-of-the-art software tools to make your proposals interesting, informative, engaging, and appealing, especially to your customers' executives.

To customers, your proposals are more than promises of your future behavior; they *are* your behavior. Your proposals are often the first tangible evidence customers have of your quality, your ability to listen, your willingness to be flexible, your attention to detail, and so on. Whether you intend it or not, your proposals are symbols of you, and they have the potential to be symbolic behavioral differentiators—either positively or negatively. So if you claim to be customer oriented, don't submit a "we" proposal. If you say you excel at meeting project schedules, don't request a deadline extension. If you pride yourself on paying attention to details, make sure your proposals are error free. If you claim to be state-of-the-art, prove it in the quality of your proposals and executive summaries. If you say you understand the customer's real issues and concerns, show those insights in the document. Your proposals are not warm-ups for the main event; they are a very real part of the main event. Your behavior doesn't start when you get the contract; it starts back in early middle game—and nowhere is it more important in business development than now, when customers are making the selection decision.

Like all marketing and sales tools, proposals are creators of impressions. Artful proposals shape readers' perceptions and work as much on the intuitive and subliminal level as they do on the rational, descriptive level. Artful proposals persuade on many levels and build the impressions they create from the complex interplay of strategy, knowledge, language, design, emphasis, visualization, and packaging.

Behavioral Differentiation in the BAFO

The next stop in the endgame journey is the shortlist; clarifications; and, sometimes, preliminary negotiations with the shortlisted contenders. Different customers play this part of endgame in hundreds of ways. Generally, however, the suppliers who survive the proposal evaluations are put on the shortlist of qualified suppliers, who may be asked to present their offers orally. Customers may have some clarification questions for them and may invite them to participate in preliminary negotiations. The result is your best and final offer (BAFO), and if customers have not already chosen the winner, the BAFO is usually the final gate before their decision. Occasionally, suppliers who have made the shortlist become overly confident, which in turn makes them bolder and less flexible than they should be. The way to behaviorally differentiate yourself at this stage is to be flexible and to avoid throwing obstacles in the customer's path. That's not what happened to John, however, who works for a large aerospace firm. Here's his story:

> We were fiercely competing with another major aerospace firm on a large multimillion-dollar procurement. We had both invested significant time and money to survive the competitive cut. After the final proposals were submitted, the customer was compelled to issue some modest changes in the requirements and the terms and conditions. They asked both teams to provide written responses within three days. Our team ran to our lawyers, finance people, and contracts managers. They pored over the new requirements in such depth that they asked the customer for two extra days to respond properly. When they did finally respond, they sent a 20-page letter detailing our concerns, offering counter suggestions, and indicating that the new requirements could impact cost and schedule, all of which would have to be given additional thought. Our competitors responded to the new requirements within three hours and said, "No problem." You can guess who won the award. I don't blame the customer. Who would you want to do business with—someone flexible and responsive or a bunch of lawyers? I think we allowed our inbred "cultural reflex" to torpedo this major contract award.[3]

However well grounded your legal concerns might be, you need to consider how your behavior appears to customers and whether your competitors will behave in ways that positively differentiate them. Sometimes, as this next story illustrates, the key is understanding the customer's culture and showing that you can do business with the customer and vice versa. This story is from Dagmar, who works for a large European telecommunications company:

In the strange but true category, we were competing with an American and another European supplier for a contract in Russia. In that country, it is customary to negotiate during the day and go to dinner together in the evening. The dinners often end with a lot of vodka. The day before the final decision would be made, the customer asked all three suppliers to prepare their BAFOs for the next day. Recognizing the importance of the dinner that evening, all three of us suppliers joined the customer for dinner, but our two competitors left early to prepare their BAFOs. We decided to stay and keep partying with our Russian hosts. We wound up drinking vodka until 4 A.M. and were in no shape later to even think about a BAFO, much less prepare one. But when we met the next morning to present our revised offers, the customer announced that they'd already made their decision. We got the contract because, in the customer's words, "They had the best ability to adapt to the Russian lifestyle."[4]

This may fall into the "don't try this at home" category, but it does illustrate the importance of understanding how customers work and behaving in ways that make them more comfortable.

Behaviorally Differentiated Presentations

Both your proposal and your presentation are manifestations of your behavior toward customers, but a presentation is more visceral. You are there in front of them—living, breathing, coughing and sputtering, walking your talk, answering questions, and behaving in ways that instill either confidence or dismay. The presentations by competing suppliers normally occur one right after another, all of them frequently on the same day, and behavioral comparisons are inevitable. When you present your offer to customers, you might as well be stark naked on an Alaskan glacier in the middle of an ice storm—it doesn't get more exposed than that. This is face time at its absolute premium. For obvious reasons, then, the presentation is a prime opportunity for behavioral differentiation. You can win the presentation with behaviors that differentiate your interest in the customer and commitment to the customer's business. Paul Krauss, a retired director of McKinsey & Company, recalls such a win while consulting to a division of BASF:

We were working with the Basic Systems Division of BASF. There was a joint venture between BASF and General Electric to produce audiotapes and disk drives. I got involved in 1975 when GE spun out the joint venture and BASF took it over. BASF's competitors in audiotapes were highly marketed companies like Memorex and Hitachi. At the time, Memorex was saying that when Ella Fitzgerald sings on our tapes glasses shatter, and Hitachi was this super commercial company that went to retailers and said, "At what price point do you have to sell tape? How many feet do you sell? What's the quality? How many times do you promote it? How much would you be willing to pay me for a product that did this?", and so on. Then they would make a deal and go find someone who would make the product.

At that time, BASF was advertising that, "We invented audiotape. We are Germans. We are perfect engineers. We're brilliant." So the Germans were doing 1930s advertising, which is telling you the input rather than the output. They were totally out of date, and the most senior chairman of the board came over to New York from Germany to talk to us about it. I took pages out of magazines and showed him how people advertised in America. The bottom line is that we decided to engage an advertising agency. As McKinsey did with all other services, we told them what criteria they should use for selecting one and then gave them a list of five we thought were good and professional and advised them to interview these agencies and select one.

To protect the names, we'll focus on three and say they were called A, B, and C. The guy from Agency A presented first. He had done the advertising for a big hosiery product, which was super popular at the time. And this guy came in and bragged that he had written that copy and was brilliant and famous and they should hire him.

Then the people from Agency B walked in. They had a famous chairman who had written some best-selling books on advertising, and they came in and talked about their chairman and what a brilliant guy he was and how he had a château in France and had done a lot of famous work, and they basically just talked about him.

Then came an account manager and the chairman of Agency C. The chairman said, "We have an office in Frankfurt, and you are an important company to us. We care about your business, and here is the account supervisor you will be working with if you select us."

Then the account manager said, "We didn't know anything about your product, so we decided to do a little research to find out what consumers think of your product and your company. Here's what we found, and here are the issues we think you need to address." That was the clincher. He didn't focus on their agency's history or what they had done for other people. He said, "We're here to talk about you and your business and what you need to do in the future." The choice was a no-brainer to everyone in the room. You didn't need to fill out evaluation sheets to make that call.[5]

The two losers thought they should talk about themselves and how great they are—that that's what the customer wanted to hear. The winner behaved so differently that it knocked the other competitors out of serious contention. Customer focus is not a new concept, but many suppliers remain trapped in the notion that when they present to customers they have to sell themselves by talking about themselves. Remarkably, it is still behaviorally differentiating to sell yourself by talking about the customer instead. A final obvious point of Paul's story is that the winning agency was curious enough to invest time and money learning about its potential customer—and that's precisely the kind of firm customers want working for them.

> ♘ *So it is that good warriors take their stand on ground where they cannot lose, and do not overlook conditions that make an opponent prone to defeat. Therefore a victorious army first wins and then seeks battle; a defeated army first battles and then seeks victory.—Sun Tzu,* The Art of War

In presentations, *all* your behavior is on display—not only your behavior toward customers, which everyone expects to be solicitous, but also your behavior toward each other. If you are proposing a team, then customers expect to see your people working as a team, and they will observe how your team members interact with each other. After winning the shortlist presentation contest against a major competitor, one of our clients asked the customer's decision-maker what she had found particularly impressive about the team's presentation. The decision-maker said, "I was impressed by the respect your team members showed for each other. I was also impressed by the respect you showed for me and my time by staying on schedule. The other company didn't do either of these things."

By the time you give your presentation, customers already know what you have to offer. They have read it in your proposal. They already believe you are a credible and capable supplier. So what is the purpose of the presentation? It's the final chemistry test. What they are testing is not your credibility but rather their trust in you and your compatibility with them—the evidence of which they find in your behavior. How well do you present yourself? How well do you answer questions? How effectively do you think on your feet? Are you willing to admit when you are unsure of something? How candid will you be with us? How well do you interact with our people? How comfortable are we with you? How well do you work together as a team? What will it be like to work with you for the next six months or a year? Sometimes what they want is that little extra sign of commitment, and sometimes the behaviors that turn the tide are small but significant things, as this next story illustrates.

Dennis Fukai is an assistant professor at the School of Building Construction at the University of Florida in Gainesville. In an article for *Engineering News Record*, he reported something unusual that he observed in a proposal presentation:

> I saw something amazing happen at a recent round of presentations by shortlisted bidders for a construction project that I was involved in at the University of Florida. Despite all the hype from the bidders about their Web sites and technology, the winning and losing came down to one CEO turning off the computer and high-resolution projector, and standing alone in front of our selection committee to promise that he would do everything in his power to make sure that the project went smoothly. He then wrote down his home phone number on his business card, gave it to the committee chairman and earnestly asked to be called if anything did not go according to our expectations. In doing so, he opened himself up to honest, direct communications and won the job.[6]

John Tarpey, president of Centex Construction Company in Fairfax, Virginia, did something similar. His company was bidding on a $70 million project for a federal agency. As they went into the presentations, John learned that one of the key issues for the customer's decision-maker was having immediate and continuous communication with the top executive of the winning firm. The normal behavior would have been to acknowledge the importance of the issue, to say how important it was to the bidder as well, and to promise that the top executive would always be available. But John Tarpey went a significant step further. When he got to that part of their presentation, John handed the customer a cell phone and asked him to press a speed dial number on the phone, which then dialed an 800 number. As John kept speaking, the pager under his jacket began beeping. John pulled out the beeper and held it up. "I have never in my life worn one of these," he said. "But I will wear this one for you for the life of the project. That cell phone is yours, and you alone have this 800 number." That presentation ended around 4 p.m. The call awarding Centex the contract came at 10 the following morning. In the debriefing, the customer said that the use of the cell phone and pager was an especially impressive part of their overall presentation.[7]

Sometimes what seems like a small gesture can have tremendous impact. The secret is knowing what is important to your customers and behaving in ways that symbolize your commitment to meeting their needs and addressing their concerns. As long as your behavior is unique and remarkable to your customers in positive ways, you will differentiate yourself behaviorally. Of course, when John Tarpey's competitors learn what he did, there may be a run on cell phones. Then he will have to invent new ways to behaviorally differentiate himself and his firm.

Behavioral Differentiation in Next Game

Clearly, behavioral differentiation does not end once you receive a contract. The possibility for behavioral differentiation exists at every customer touch point, so throughout the process of executing work, delivering and installing equipment, performing maintenance, providing services, conducting postsales support, or doing whatever else you do for customers, you should be looking for ways to behave toward your customers that distinguish you from your competitors. In all you do to serve your customers you should find ways to remain customer focused; encourage your employees to act with purpose while performing their functions; and communicate more, measure more, and request feedback more often than your competitors do.

Even if you lose a contract award, you can differentiate yourself in next game and position yourself for future opportunities because of your behavioral differentiation. Deke Lincoln of BE&K tells us how:

> We received an opportunity to bid on a project for a company I'll call Global Oil Refining. The project was for NOx emission reduction in the powerhouse. It was a pretty substantial job with some major work to be done later. We had targeted Global as a priority customer because of the hundreds of millions of dollars in capital to be spent there over the next few years. This opportunity was our first with this customer. We had some early communication with them and had done some marketing, but we had not spent enough middle game time with the customer prior to bidding on this project.
>
> Our competition on this job was fierce, including Competitors X, Y, and Z. All had *substantially* more experience and better résumés than we did when it came to refineries and power. In fact, one of the boilers to be modified on this project was a Competitor X boiler. Few in my organization gave us a chance in hell of winning this job. The pessimism was quite amazing, in fact. It was difficult to not be affected by it, but we were determined not to give up or give in to the naysayers who believed that experience and price meant everything. Most importantly, we were determined to be good sports in defeat—if we lost—and to build on the relationship if we felt the customer had good future potential.
>
> Anyway, we ended up losing this job to Competitor X. After a couple of weeks of going back and forth with the customer after they announced the winner, I thought we had an awesome chance. We had put together a really nice proposal that addressed all of Global's key issues, and it came very close to winning. In fact, the project manager, Jim Smith, told me that it was one of the hardest decisions he'd had to make. But he went with Competitor X because they had also turned in a good proposal, and they could self-perform the boiler modeling, something we could not do.
>
> We were disappointed at losing the job, and the internal pessimists made it even more difficult, saying that we shouldn't waste any more time with this customer. Despite the fact that we really improved our relationship with these guys, people were willing to throw in the towel. But we didn't do that. We were sincere in wishing Jim luck and fed him information (articles, vendor information, and technical reports) to help him on the project, despite the fact that we

had not been selected. We also continued to develop our relationship with Jim and other key decision-makers at the plant and continued to show our interest in helping them with their problems.

A few months later, we received several more project opportunities, which we won, and we were single sourced on three more projects (two were from Jim Smith!). Later, we proposed on an $80 million project for Global. We did several things in that bid to try to differentiate ourselves. First, we submitted a really nice, to-the-point, executive summary to the people reading the proposal and others who would be involved in the decision. We were the only company to do this, and they really liked it. We also tried to help them find a supplier of caustic because they expected it to be a problem and were worried about the costs associated with higher demand. Finding a supplier of caustic is not a typical scope item for a firm like ours, but we had contacts and used them to help Global. Finally, we tried to help them improve their relationships with the public and with local regulatory authorities.

We had not performed any projects of this magnitude in the oil refinery industry, and our competition included every heavy hitter in our industry. As the decision came down to the wire, it was between us and Competitor A, which had the edge because of their involvement with the front-end engineering. According to Global, Competitor A thought they had it in the bag. But we won. Afterward, Global told us we won this work because we wanted it more and because they trust us and like us and believe we can execute projects successfully for them. It took a lot of effort to develop that trust, but in the end it is what won us the work.[8]

In the end, as Deke Lincoln's story illustrates, very few buying decisions are purely rational. When customers have equally qualified alternatives, they will go with the supplier they prefer on *emotional* grounds. BE&K won because the customer felt the company's people "wanted it more," and because the customer trusted them and liked them and believed they would do the job. Credibility is clearly fundamental. You must be able to do the work successfully, but many companies can do that. In the end, the difference is desire, commitment, trust, and liking—and those impressions are formed based on your behaviors.

CHALLENGES FOR READERS

1. How effective is your company at managing endgame? Candidly, do you tend to let down then or push ahead harder? How much senior presence do you typically have during endgame?

2. How professional is your proposal management process? Do you assign knowledgeable, qualified proposal managers? Or whoever is on the bench at the moment? Do you develop proposal win strategies? Do you use tools like the kickoff meeting? Storyboarding? Pink and red team reviews? Proposal management checklists?

3. Do you produce customer-oriented proposals with strong and repeated themes and visuals? Do your proposals consistently and effectively answer the four key questions: *Why us? Why not them? So what?* and *How so?* Do you routinely use compelling, brochure-type executive summaries?

4. What do you do to differentiate yourself during your presentations? Do you always rehearse your presentations? Do you rehearse the questions and answers? Do you create good summaries of your key points to leave behind? What do you do during your presentations to symbolize your understanding of the customer's needs and demonstrate your commitment?

CHAPTER 10

Creating a Behavioral
Differentiation Strategy

> *Positive behavioral differentiation has always played a more significant role than technical problem solving in the development of long-lasting relationships. This fact became evident two decades ago when Florida went to a qualifications-based selection process for their construction professionals. Technical differentiation lasts only as long as it takes for the competition to learn of your new approach and offer the same services—often only a few weeks. Behavioral differentiation has shown to last over twenty years, and it will continue to do so as long as a human being makes the buying decision.*—Business Development Director, Construction Company
>
> ■
>
> *We have more ability than will power, and it is often an excuse to ourselves that we imagine that things are impossible.*—La Rochefoucauld

Throughout this book and *Winning Behavior*, we have argued that behavior can and should be managed. It should be evident from our discussion of behavioral differences during opening, middle, and end-game that if you approach business development thoughtfully and behave in ways that customers find uniquely and memorably positive, you can create a behavioral advantage for yourself and improve your probability of winning more business. In our years of working with clients, we have met some enlightened executives who instinctively understood BD and found ways to outbehave their competitors consistently enough to improve their top and bottom lines significantly. We have also met numerous executives who were clueless about the impact of behavior and had not the faintest idea how to use behavior competitively. Unfortunately, there are many more of the latter than the former. The good news, however, is that *anyone* can learn to build a behavioral advantage if he or she has the will to do so.

Being determined to differentiate yourself behaviorally is the first step, of course. Without the will, there is no way. However, even with the will, it is challenging to create and implement a *consistent* behavioral strategy throughout an organization or over the life cycle of a business development opportunity, especially if what you choose to do is beyond what your people normally do. Challenging, but not impossible. It just takes good leadership and the determination to create a behavioral advantage. As Eric Krueger, chief relationship officer for Centex Construction Company, observes, in today's tough markets you may not have a choice:

> Competition is so keen today that the difference between first and second is as close as the winner and runner-up in the Olympic 100-meter sprint. So for us, winning is not about what we can do for customers. Our competitors can do the same things. We're all running a tight race on capability. Rather, it's about *how* we'll do it, and that means it's all about behavior and the strategies we implement to differentiate us with every customer—*during* a business development effort and *after* we win the contract. That may sound simple, but it's not. It's just critically important if we want to get and keep customers. Before and after we win, everyone who "touches" the customer in any way must be empowered to act as a servant leader, be open minded, show empathy, do what's right, and demonstrate superior judgment skills. Otherwise, we're just another runner in an endless race.[1]

We begin with two premises. First, you *can* gain a behavioral advantage if you think strategically about your behavior toward customers. Second, you are unlikely to gain a behavioral advantage *unless* you actively manage how you and others in your company behave. Left to their own devices and instincts, most of your people will behave as they normally do, and you will not differentiate yourself behaviorally because your competitors will probably behave much the same way. So, if you are going to gain a behavioral advantage, you need to develop a thoughtful behavioral strategy and manage your behavior at every touch point in the course of business development and execution.

In this chapter, we discuss how to create a behavioral differentiation strategy. In the next chapter, we explore why some companies have difficulty creating sustainable behavioral differentiation—and why others have no trouble at all.

Developing an Overall Behavioral Strategy

A strategy serves a purpose, so it would be useful to begin by asking what purpose a behavioral strategy would serve. We have been focusing on particular business development opportunities, so one obvious purpose of a behavioral differentiation strategy is to improve your positioning during opportunity pursuits and thus improve your odds of winning the contract. However, more broadly, your purpose may be to improve your business as a whole by differentiating your company more effectively from your rivals whenever you interact with customers. We will begin with this broader purpose and then discuss how to create an opportunity-specific strategy.

We have found it helpful in working with clients to begin developing an overall BD strategy by benchmarking the behaviors in the marketplace—understanding what customers *normally* receive and therefore expect; how those expectations shape their perceptions of your industry, not just your company; and what behaviors they would consider normal, remarkably negative, or remarkably positive. Based on the elegantly simple notion that business development is largely the management of perception, it's important to know where and how you can most affect your customers' perceptions of you. To do this, you need to identify and prioritize the touch points where anyone in your company has an important interaction with a customer. You also need to analyze how your people typically behave at those critical touch points and identify the positive behaviors they should either keep doing or how they should behave instead so they positively differentiate themselves and your company from your competitors. The final step is to prioritize the behaviors you want to change or emphasize and then develop a change strategy to drive these new behaviors through and across your organization.

A short example might be helpful. In pursuing work with customers in your industry, it might be typical for suppliers' salespeople (including yours) to do routine sales calls, inquire about customers' needs, leave brochures behind, try to develop personal relationships with the buyers, and telephone periodically to stay in touch. The more enlightened salespeople may come up with new ideas and technical solutions their company has recently developed. From the customers' standpoint, here's how this supplier behavior normally appears:

■ The supplier's people who are responsible for sales call for appointments.

■ When we (the customer) meet with them, these salespeople seek to understand what we've been doing lately, how their products or services are working for us, whether anything has changed that affects our use of their products, and what we currently need or may need in the near future.

■ If we've never met them before, these salespeople introduce themselves, ask about us and our company, seek to understand how we use their types of products or services, and explain or demonstrate their products. They also explain how they are different from other suppliers (and they usually all say the same thing) and why we should purchase from them rather than their competitors. The worst of them give us a "hard sell" pitch and try to get the order, always concluding with a slightly mechanical, earnest variation of "I want your business" because they learned long ago that good salespeople aren't afraid to ask for the order. The best of them are not so blatant about it, but the message is the same.

■ The suppliers leave behind their brochures, catalogs, product descriptions, samples, or other typical—and generic—marketing materials.

■ Some of these salespeople try to build a personal relationship, and some invite us to lunch or dinner, play golf, go to a ball game, or offer other inducements to spend "informal" time with them.

■ If we give them even minimal encouragement, these salespeople continue to call, try to set up more meetings, and stay in touch in various other ways.

In industries where salespeople are normally more consultative, this may be too "traditional" a picture of typical business development behavior, but let's assume for a moment that this represents the norm in your industry. Your BD strategy, then, would be to behave "abnormally," if you will, *in ways customers would value* to give you a favored position in their eyes. That strategy might include these kinds of behaviors:

■ In many customer meetings, particularly the early ones, the salesperson goes with an executive, technical or operations manager, or professional whose purpose is not to increase sales but to build a mutually beneficial business relationship. That might seem like a subtle difference, but it plays much differently with customers when they realize that you are not acting entirely out of self-interest and that by investing in sending two people, rather than just one, you are demonstrating your commitment.

■ Beyond trying to understand their needs and business objectives, you spend time understanding their business, culture, people, products, competitive climate, etc. The homework you do before meeting with them enables you to reveal some things about their company, competitors, or markets that *they* didn't know. You are proactive in scheduling site visits at your locations and at theirs where both of you can develop a better understanding of each other's business, competitive pressures, challenges, cultures, and cost structures.

■ Your CEO and other senior executives attend some meetings with their customer counterparts, and your senior people devote some ongoing time to face-to-face customer meetings. If there are problems, your senior executives become personally involved in problem solving if the problems are not resolved quickly. These executives pledge their personal commitment to the relationship and validate those words with their willingness to sustain close customer contact.

> ♜ *I think the basic business principle always holds true, above and beyond all else: "People like to work with people they like." This is human nature. Although we still must present a balance of technical excellence, innovation, and relevant experience, what clients remember most are the human elements of fairness, flexibility, responsiveness, integrity, trust, honesty, efficiency, and trustworthiness.—Judy Lembke*

■ Before meeting with any prospective customers, you do your homework and come with considerable knowledge about them and their business. You avoid asking the typical "situation" questions (like "How many offices do you have?") because you have done your homework. Instead, your questions are insightful, focused, and specific.

■ Until the customer asks for a solution or asks about your products/services and pricing, you stay in the "No Pitch" zone. You ask and listen rather than sell and tell.

■ You never leave behind standard brochures, catalogs, product descriptions, samples, or other typical marketing materials. Instead, you bring customized executive summary brochures that focus on *this* industry and *this* customer.

■ You allow personal relationships to evolve naturally and do not try to force these relationships by inviting customers to lunch or dinner, to play golf, go to a ball game, or other things that take their valuable time and do not add business value. If you do these types of activities, it's because they provide the right venue for substantive exchanges, for value moving in both directions. Customers are typically cynical about providers who spend lavishly on entertainment *per se*, especially when their prices are obviously structured to regain those expenditures.

■ You are thoughtful about how customers can improve their business, thinking beyond your own narrow product or service lines. You are proactive about bringing new ideas and solutions to them. You think like a supply chain partner and try to help them take costs out of the system. Furthermore, you try to work closely with their supply chain managers and purchasing professionals.

■ As you learn more and more about their needs, it sometimes becomes clear that you have a great deal to offer but not a total solution. Rather than masking that fact, you bring it into the open, discuss the particulars, and help the customer to find the best total solution to the problem.

Many of these ideas may seem familiar—and you may be doing much or all of this already. In Chapter 2, we noted a number of ways suppliers can make a behavioral difference, and this sample strategy includes those kinds of behaviors. The purpose of a BD strategy is to identify the kinds of behaviors that will set you apart from your competitors. Then the challenge is to implement the strategy throughout your company so that people consistently behave in ways that make a positive difference. As we said above, the first step is benchmarking the normal behaviors in your industry.

Step 1: Do Behavioral Benchmarking

Benchmarking is customarily thought of as a comparison of product or service features, technology or technical solutions to problems, business processes, and other aspects of a business operation where one company's state-of-the-art approach can help other companies raise the bar for themselves by learning the best practices being used. When we benchmark, we establish what the best-in-class is. We normally do not apply the term to behavioral comparisons, except when companies compare customer service practices, which, as we have said, is but a small part of your total behavior externally with customers and internally with employees. However, it's clear that behavior can be benchmarked. It is possible to research and understand what the companies that are best-in-class in behavioral differentiation do to achieve that distinction. We described a number of their practices in *Winning Behavior*.

The key is to understand, first, what constitutes the behavioral norm in your industry. In other words, what do customers normally expect and how are they normally treated by suppliers like you who are currently working with them or are seeking to do so? Clearly, it's easier for B2C companies to benchmark behavior because, as consumers themselves, they have relatively easy access to their competitors' sales channels and can appreciate the consumer's experience firsthand. A car retailer can buy from a rival dealership and experience the sales and service processes that are part of the total experience. Restaurateurs can eat in their rivals' restaurants and experience how diners are treated. It's more challenging to experience the customer's experience in the B2B marketplace, but it can be done. Here are six ways:

1. Survey your employees who have worked for either competitors' or customers' companies. Ask them these kinds of questions:

IF THEY WORKED FOR A CUSTOMER:

■ What was normal supplier behavior? In other words, what did suppliers typically do to build relationships, uncover needs, solve problems, execute work, and so on?

■ What did you expect from all suppliers, no matter who they were?

■ What did suppliers normally do when they were trying to establish a relationship and sell their products or services? What did they normally do when they were performing work? How did they follow up?

■ How did you measure supplier performance? What was the difference between the best and worst suppliers?

■ When suppliers delighted you in some positive way, what did they do? What was delightful? Conversely, when suppliers disappointed you, what did they do wrong? What disappointed you?

■ What did it take for suppliers to become long-term trusted partners with your company? What supplier behaviors built or destroyed customer loyalty?

IF THEY WORKED FOR A COMPETITOR:

■ What did your former company do best in building business and serving customers? What were its best practices in building relationships, making sales, executing work, maintaining equipment or systems, performing customer service, and so on?

■ Who in that company was renowned for having "good customer hands"? Who had the best customer-management skills and talent? What made this person so good? How did he or she behave toward customers that enabled him or her to build strong and lasting relationships?

■ What policies, procedures, or standard practices in that company gave it a competitive edge? What did people in the company routinely do that was different from and better than what its competitors did?

■ What positive feedback did that company receive from customers? What did customers say they particularly liked? Conversely, what negative feedback did customers give? What did the company or its people do that irritated or frustrated customers?

2. Hire as consultants people who have retired from or otherwise left a customer's organization and ask the same kinds of questions as just cited. Clearly, you want to hire people who have intimate knowledge of how you and your competitors interacted with people in the customer's organization and how the customer perceived you and competing suppliers. The best sources are people who have good business sense, are observant, and can offer insights into behavioral differences among suppliers. You want consultants who were on the receiving end of supplier behavior, but beware of hiring the most senior ex-customers simply because they were very senior. They may not have as useful a perspective as less-senior people with more consistent supplier contact.

3. Survey your customers and ask them for behavioral benchmarks without explicitly naming your competitors—or, for that matter, *any* suppliers. First, ask them what they expect from partner suppliers. Then ask them, generically, what their suppliers have done that they liked and valued or disliked and devalued. You don't want names. You just want to know which behaviors they found valuable and which ones they didn't. Finally, ask them what your company and its people have done that they liked or disliked, as well as what you could do to be an even better supplier to them. You have to ensure when setting up this kind of customer survey that they don't see it as an attempt to "dig up dirt on the competition." Your purpose should be to discover how to improve the way you work, to learn how to make it easier for them to work with you, to remove any obstacles or barriers to how you are serving them, and so on.

4. Benchmark other industries. Look for superior behaviors in other fields and consider what behaviors you could adopt. Sometimes, the most innovative ideas come from this kind of examination, but you have to look and think outside the box. You have to be open to ideas that may seem strange or irrelevant at first. What could you learn from Disney's "cast member" concept at their theme parks? Or from Ritz-Carlton's daily line-ups and credo card? What could you learn from Chuck-E-Cheese? Starbucks? Marshall Field's? United Air-

lines? PBS? The Girl Scouts of America? The United States Marine Corps? Clearly, not everything these organizations do is worth emulating, but you can learn as much from a bad behavioral experience or a mediocre one as you can from the best experiences.

We have found that when you begin consciously thinking about behavior, you begin to recognize the behaviors we all take for granted (the ones in the vast middle hump of the bell curve) and the ones that distinguish people positively or negatively. You also begin to see how your own behavior toward customers creates their impression of you and affects their willingness to do further business with you.

5. Examine your own suppliers. Which of their behaviors seem normal to you? That is, which behaviors are unremarkable—neither positive nor negative? How do you expect *any* supplier to behave in normal circumstances? What do they all do that is similar? Then look at your best and worst suppliers. How do they behave differently? What do the best ones do that the worst ones don't, and vice versa? Survey your own purchasing directors and supply chain managers. You can learn a number of lessons about BD by examining how your own suppliers differentiate themselves.

6. Last, examine your own wins and losses, as well as your most successful and least successful program or project managers. It is sometimes difficult to see what the people who are naturally good at BD do that makes them good at BD. You almost have to shadow them and observe their behavior with customers and employees. They may or may not be fully aware of their behaviors that make a difference, so asking them for a list of best behavioral practices is often not useful.

There is nothing earthshakingly new in our suggestions about how to do behavioral benchmarking. Most of this is common sense. The point is to be more self-conscious about behaviors toward customers that are normal and therefore indistinguishable and about those behaviors that are significantly better or worse than the norm. Extremely positive and negative behaviors are blatant enough to leap out at the most casual observer, but it takes a discerning eye to recognize the more subtle behaviors that can have a differentiating impact on customers. Often, as we've said before, the difference is a smile where it wasn't expected, a quick response to an e-mailed question, a thank-you card that no one else sent, a telephone call on a weekend with a sudden brainstorm about how to reduce a cost, a degree of diligence and responsiveness that stands out, and so on.

The word *chiaroscuro* refers to the treatment of light and shade in painting or the use of contrast in literature. In painting, the arrangement of light and dark elements creates a meaningful contrast, and that in effect is what we are trying to achieve as we benchmark behavior. We want to find a meaningful contrast between behaviors that attract customers and those that repel customers, and we want to understand that vast, undifferentiated middle ground where behavior has no discernible effect because it is indistinguishable from how everyone else behaves. The typical outcome of behavioral benchmarking is two lists of behaviors: the positives and the negatives. In effect, you want to create a behavioral bell curve like the one depicted in Figure 3-2, emphasizing the significant behaviors on either wing of the curve. This kind of display of your findings helps people grasp the demarcations between what's normal and what's extraordinary, and it is helpful later when you examine your own behaviors at various customer touch points.

Step 2:
Identify and Prioritize Your Customer Touch Points

To know where and how you are impacting customers behaviorally, you need to understand your touch points—all of those "moments of truth," as Jan Carlzon, former CEO of SAS Airlines (see Figure 10-1), called them. These are the points at which anyone in your company interacts with anyone in a customer organization in any way. You make a behavioral impression at every touch point whether or not you intend to do so. Identifying your touch points can be a difficult and time-consuming process because there may be thousands of them, depending on your business, and your people may interact with customers hundreds of times every day at each of those touch points. Carlzon estimated that SAS had more than 50 million such "moments of truth" every year, and he said that SAS was re-created on each of those occasions.[2]

To make this task manageable, we have found it best to ask each line and staff manager to identify the touch points for his or her em-

Figure 10-1. Jan Carlzon, former CEO, SAS Airlines. Carlzon instinctively understood the importance of differentiating behavior. He turned around SAS Airlines by focusing on exceptional behavior at each of the "moments of truth" when SAS employees interacted with customers—and these occurred millions of times every year. (Photo courtesy of Christer Jansson and SpeakersNet AB. Used with permission.)

ployees. Those touch points often include but are not limited to the following:

Typical B2B Touch Points During Business Development

- Advertising

- Trade shows

- Conferences

- Seminars/workshops

- Community events/projects

- Off-site co-retreats

- Marketing collateral materials and professional publications

- Company awareness-building materials

- Web sites

- Cold calls and letters
- Sales introductory meetings
- Follow-up communications
- Supply chain/purchasing meetings and communications
- Sales meetings
- Sales presentations and leave-behinds
- Product demonstrations
- Site visits/plant tours
- Executive meetings
- Executive follow-up communications (calls, letters, e-mails, etc.)
- Functional meetings (technical, brainstorming, problem solving, information exchange)
- Executive/sales social events
- Qualifications documents and communications
- Proposals
- Proposal clarifications, amendments, and discussions
- Proposal presentations, follow-up communications, and leave-behinds
- Negotiations
- Legal and contractual discussions and communications
- Contract award discussions
- Postproposal debriefings

TYPICAL B2B TOUCH POINTS DURING BUSINESS EXECUTION

- Product/solution design meetings and communications
- Configuration management meetings
- Quality and inspections meetings and communications
- Site inspection meetings and third-party/government meetings
- Packaging and shipping meetings and communications
- Installation, service, and inspection coordination communications

- Delivery and installation or shipping and receiving

- Training and certifying events and communications

- Problem resolution meetings and communications

- Maintenance and service events and follow-up communications

- Project/program management meetings and communications

- Ongoing executive/sales meetings and communications

- Measurement and evaluation, plus follow-up meetings and communications

- Lessons learned/continuous improvement/Six Sigma events and meetings

- Customer satisfaction/delight surveys

- Functional meetings and communications

- Invoicing/accounts payable communications

- Contract compliance reviews

- Order handling and processing

- Project kickoff workshops

- Pre-kickoff team-building workshops

- Project closeouts

> ♛ *The life span of behavioral differentiation is potentially unlimited. It is constrained only by our will to advance the customer's position. Technical differentiation is constantly becoming obsolete and adds value to a customer only if it fulfills a specific technical need. Behavioral differentiation is a commitment to tailor our technical capabilities and resources to add value to a customer's business, or personal, situation.—James B. Hamlin*

Clearly, the number of potential touch points is enormous—and these lists are not comprehensive. When you are developing a BD strategy, it is often helpful to focus first on those touch points where you are now having or could have the greatest behavioral impact on customers and where, consequently, changes in behavior could make the greatest difference. So we suggest identifying the most critical touch points and developing behavioral strategies for them first.

Step 3:
Analyze Your Current Behavior at Critical Touch Points

How are your people behaving at the critical touch points? What behavioral impression are they making now? Obviously, it's best to talk to customers and ask for their impressions. They will have a much broader perspective than you because they also interact with your competitors and will have relevant comparisons already in mind. Some suppliers hire consultants to do "blind" industry surveys where all competitors are benchmarked by name. Such surveys are valuable, but they don't replace the face-to-face discussions you should also have with your customers where you ask them how they think you are doing, which of your behaviors they like or dislike, and what you could be doing better. Blind surveys may be more objective, but customer surveys you do yourself yield much more specific information about how you can improve, and they demonstrate to customers that you care about what they think and that you want to improve how you work with them.

You should come out of this step with a clear understanding of where your current customer behaviors are negative, neutral, or positive. Behavioral benchmarking (Step 1) gives you a general sense of the spectrum of behaviors in your industry. This step helps you establish how you are currently performing and whether your behavior is having a significantly positive or negative effect on customers.

Step 4:
Identify Potential Positive Differentiating Behaviors

What could you be doing differently that would enable you to behaviorally differentiate yourself from your competitors? Now you should identify potential positive differentiating behaviors. Remember that behavioral differentiation is not entirely about having good interpersonal skills, a service orientation, and excellent customer service practices, although these help. A number of the positively differentiating behaviors are related to communication, responsiveness, commitment, and proactive problem solving. Here are some of the supplier behaviors that a variety of B2B customers said had the most positive impact on them. Which of these could you do?

■ You demonstrate your passion for the business by devoting time to it, investing in innovation, sharing learning, bringing ideas to customers, and being committed to the business for the long term.

■ You demonstrate your commitment to customers by sticking with them in good markets and bad. You protect their interests as much as you can during downturns and don't take advantage of them if they can't get products or services when supplies are tight. You never burn the bridge between you and customers, even when they haven't done any business with you for a long time.

■ You show that you understand and care about the ultimate consumer of your customer's products. You invest the time to study these consumers and know how they use your customer's products, what they value, and what innovations they would value more.

■ You show as much interest in your customers' growth as you do your own.

■ You think like a partner, not a vendor. You don't think or act transactionally. You see the bigger picture and act for everyone's mutual, long-term benefit.

■ You give customers your full attention, no matter how much of your business they currently represent.

■ You avoid the *sell and tell* trap. You don't use discounts as incentives to purchase immediately or in greater volume, don't act like a used-car salesperson, and don't routinely ask for the order. Instead, you ask a lot of questions, listen thoughtfully, and act like a partner.

■ You devote the time, energy, and interest necessary to deeply understand the customer's organization, culture, and needs. You spend time on site, listening to the customer's problems, issues, and concerns. You do this regardless of what you have to offer. If you don't have the right solution, you help the customer find one.

■ You keep your key account managers assigned to customer accounts for as many years as possible. You don't continually switch their key contact.

■ You ensure that your senior executives are engaged with your customers. Your most important customers receive a significant amount of your CEO's time and mind share.

■ You think like a partner in your customer's supply chain. You have learned supply chain management principles and are proactive in finding and suggesting ways the customer can take costs out of the supply chain or otherwise make the chain more efficient and productive.

■ You get to know your customer's purchasing directors and don't treat them like gatekeepers. Instead, you treat them like supply chain partners. You know how they think, what their goals and priorities are, and what they value in a supplier partner. You know how they like to communicate, what excites them, and what annoys them. You communicate constantly with them and are fair, open, and honest. You try to achieve a win-win solution in which you don't feel beat up on and they don't feel manipulated. You know what they expect and how you can exceed their expectations.

■ You are highly flexible and adapt to your customers' preferred ways of doing business. In the rare case in which they ask for something you cannot do, you seek a win-win compromise. Your attitude is that their convenience is more important than yours.

■ You are very easy to work with. You survey your customers periodically and discover what they like about working with you and what they don't like. Then you make visible changes that make it easier to work with you.

■ When conflict arises, which in long-term relationships is inevitable, you take the lead in resolving the problems and finding ways to move forward.

■ You are always open, candid, and transparent with customers. You notify them immediately when something has gone wrong that can or will affect them or when something could go wrong that they can plan for if they know about it soon enough.

■ You never surprise customers in proposals, presentations, deliveries, or invoices.

■ You are transparent about your cost structure. You help customers understand the elements of your pricing. You are proactive about helping customers find ways to reduce supply chain costs by changing the way they do business with you or make other adjustments that could take costs out of the total supply chain.

■ You anticipate your customers' needs and help them make wise choices in their purchasing.

■ You are a proactive thought partner with your customers. You are innovative and bring new ideas to them that could save them money or otherwise enhance their business.

■ If extraordinary problems occur that negatively affect your customer's business and you can do something to help, you do it, almost regardless of the extra time and money it takes. You are there when customers need you.

■ You go the extra mile to ensure that your customers are well served. You anticipate their needs and are extraordinarily responsive to them.

■ You follow up on every customer communication or contact. When customers ask for something, you respond as quickly and completely as possible. All e-mail and phone messages are returned within hours, not days.

■ You customize your marketing communications to customers, including your letters, brochures, executive summaries, proposals, and so forth. Whenever you can avoid it, you do not put a generic marketing piece in a customer's hands.

■ You create customized, confidential Web sites for customers that provide immediate, worldwide access to information about their orders, shipments, deliveries, invoices, and other business matters. Your site makes it very easy for them to know what is available at what price and when it can be delivered.

■ If customers do not already have metrics in place to measure your performance as a supplier, you suggest the right metrics and implement them yourself.

■ You provide ready access to your technical people and sponsor seminars, workshops, symposiums, and other events for sharing ideas with customers and advancing the state of the art. You create customer advisory councils that enable customers to work with your engineers and designers on future products that will meet customers' emerging needs.

■ You create ways and means to anticipate customers' technical problems and are often there to "fix" problems before they occur and before customers knew they had the problem.

■ When things go wrong, your senior managers become involved very quickly if the problems are not resolved within a reasonably short time frame.

■ You are very nimble and nonbureaucratic. Your front-line people have the responsibility and authority to resolve customer problems without going through many layers of management to get approval.

■ Your proposals are on time, compliant, highly responsive, easy to read, easy to evaluate, and very customer focused.

■ Your CEO attends key proposal presentations and makes a personal commitment to the customer. The CEO gives the customer's program manager a cell phone programmed with his or her direct line and says, "Call me anytime you need me to resolve an issue or discuss a need."

■ You invest time and energy in understanding the customer's core values and operating principles. You determine the behaviors that would most demonstrate alignment with those values and principles, and you deploy those behaviors consistently across the touch points.

Again, this is by no means a comprehensive list. Furthermore, depending on your business and industry, some of these ideas might not be practicable and some may not differentiate you behaviorally. However, this list is an idea starter. If some of these behaviors will work for you, great. Adopt them. If some are inappropriate or wrong, think about what you could do instead. There are many opportunities to behave in ways that can give you a behavioral advantage. Identify the behaviors that will make the greatest difference and that are the easiest to adopt.

Step 5:
Prioritize the Behaviors and Develop a Change Strategy

In our work with clients, we have found that the most effective strategies for creating greater positive BD are not those that result in gut-wrenching transformations of the organization and its culture but instead focus on a few right changes at a time. As the change management gurus know, wholesale behavioral change in organizations is extraordinarily difficult to achieve in the short term. Sometimes it takes doing only a few things differently to make a big behavioral difference. So prioritize the behaviors you want to change, and focus on the high-impact areas first. Here are other best practices in developing a BD strategy:

■ Start with your senior leadership's commitment to the change. Like any change initiative, a BD strategy needs to be credible and driven from the top (or at least visibly supported by the top). People in the company must understand why the change is necessary and see that senior leaders are driving and supporting it. Furthermore, be sure that your senior leaders have the will to see it through. Some companies suffer from the "flavor of the month" syndrome. Behavioral differentiation will not be sustained if people sense that this is another of those management initiatives that will go away when the leaders tire of talking about it. Sustaining behavioral differentiation requires good leadership, a strong culture, and excellent processes for operationalizing significantly positive customer behaviors.

■ Find early adopters among management who will be passionate torchbearers for BD. They should be visible and respected managers, leaders who are known for walking the talk and performing well. They should coauthor the strategy, be personally committed to it, and drive its implementation. Your strategy should be to get them on board and passionately engaged in the change effort.

■ Look for low-hanging fruit and publicize early wins. This commonsense advice on managing change certainly applies to BD. It's especially important for a BD strategy to include ways of publicizing wins achieved through positively differentiated behavior. You would want to reinforce the positive behaviors and legitimize the change program. For the same reasons, it's important for a BD strategy to have measurable outcomes. Part of your strategy should include ways of measuring customer satisfaction, delight, or loyalty before and after making behavioral changes.

■ Consider cloaking BD changes in a more familiar change initiative. *Behavioral differentiation* is an unfamiliar term to many people, and it may seem too abstract to refer to a "behavioral differentiation" strategy or program. However, people readily understand programs with names like "customer first" and "customer focus." Behavioral changes are generally part of any change initiative, so it may be easier to get people to buy into a behavioral change program if it's given a more familiar label.

■ Look for ways to operationalize behavioral difference. In *Winning Behavior*, we noted that processes are one of the drivers of BD. The key is to identify the positive BDs you want people to do consistently and then make those behaviors part of their standard operating procedures: "This is how we do things around here." If you can operationalize positive behaviors and make them part of your employees' "routine," then you have a good chance of making those behaviors consistent (across a range of employees) and sustainable over time (assuming that employees and managers reinforce the behaviors and insist that everyone does what's expected).

■ Remember that negative BD is sometimes the unintended consequence of policies or procedures that otherwise make sense. For instance, policies intended to provide oversight of ordering and
shipping processes might inadvertently frustrate and confuse customers. We have seen a number of internally focused companies whose
efficient managers put systems, procedures, and policies in place that
make the company's internal processes excellent but negatively affect
customers. You can't be entirely externally focused either, but you
may be able to strike a balance in which your internal systems com-
plement a customer focus. So as part of your strategy, look for
policies, procedures, rules, decision criteria, or work flows that dis-
courage exceptional BD and change them. Enable your employees by
giving them the responsibility and latitude to do something extraordinary for customers—and be recognized and rewarded for it (instead
of punished and castigated).

■ Don't try to mandate too many specific behavioral changes at once.
Ritz-Carlton manages positive BD with a simple "Credo Card" that
identifies the twenty specific ways it wants Ritz-Carlton employees
to treat guests. Twenty is manageable; one hundred would not be.
Instead, create the expectations and conditions that will enable positive behavioral differentiation; ensure that your leaders model those
behaviors themselves; then communicate, teach, and reinforce the
changes until they become second nature.

■ As part of your strategy, look for opportunities to hire people
with superior interpersonal skills or move people with such skills into
positions that involve key customer touch points. Likewise, look for
people who are currently in positions of significant customer interface who lack those skills and move them to areas with less customer
interface. You should try to create the possibility for interpersonal
BD by putting people who are naturally high in emotional intelligence into customer-facing positions. However, that may not be
enough. Your strategy may also need to include training and education in interpersonal skills or emotional intelligence for the majority
of your people who interact with customers. This is especially important in technology businesses or engineering organizations that tend
to hire technical experts who may not be as socially adept as nontech-
nical employees.

■ In communicating behavioral changes, link the *what* with the *why*. At Ritz-Carlton, former CEO Horst Schulze began shaping the culture and instilling BD with the motto, "We are ladies and gentlemen serving ladies and gentlemen." Ritz-Carlton's Gold Standards followed from this precept. The behaviors Ritz-Carlton wants employees to use reflect this motto, and the motto is Ritz-Carlton's strategic purpose.*

■ As part of your implementation strategy, use employee councils, work groups, and implementation teams. Consider creating joint employee-customer teams for identifying and introducing positive behavioral changes. It's crucial to engage employees in these changes and ensure that they feel ownership of the change process and the outcomes. The companies we've researched that are exemplars of BD, like Southwest Airlines, ensure that employees are heavily involved in building and sustaining a culture that enables BD.

> ♛ *We're in the Customer service business; we just happen to provide airline transportation.*—Colleen Barrett, President, Southwest Airlines

■ Ensure that you and your management team are walking the talk. If not, change this immediately. You need congruence between your behavior and your values and messages. Leading behavioral change in organizations is exactly like parenting in that you cannot say one thing and do another. You can't levy rules on others that don't apply to you. If you tell your teenagers not to use curse words, you can't use them yourself. Similarly, you can't tell your employees to be customer focused if you aren't customer focused yourself. A principal function of leadership is to lead people to behave in ways that are congruent with the vision, values, and purpose of the organization you are leading, and to do that you must model the values and principles you espouse. If you want to build sustainable behavioral differentiation, then *you* have to walk the talk 24/7/365.

---

*For more information on Ritz-Carlton, see chapter 5 in Terry R. Bacon and David G. Pugh, *Winning Behavior: What the Smartest, Most Successful Companies Do Differently* (New York: AMACOM, 2003).

■ Remember: *The drivers of behavioral differentiation are leadership, culture, and process.* To develop a successful BD strategy, you must ensure that these are aligned, which implies that your strategy may need to address each of these drivers. Have your leaders bought into the concept of BD? Do they understand it? Are they prepared to do what it will take to drive behavioral differentiation throughout the organization over the long term? Is your culture one that will support BD? If not, your strategy must include ways to begin changing the culture, which can be a long-term process. Do your current systems and processes support BD? If not, how will you need to change them? Creating sustainable behavioral differentiation is not as simple as mandating that employees "start treating customers better." You must have a business purpose and model that support positive BD— and the leadership, culture, and processes to sustain it over time.

Any good business strategy addresses these basic questions: *What* are we going to do? *Why* are we doing it? *Who* will do what? And *what* are the time frames and expected outcomes? It's also useful to specify how you will measure success. A sometimes-neglected element of strategy is how you will implement it and follow it up. So, at the simplest level, a BD strategy would describe what positive behavioral changes you intend to make; why you are making them; who will be responsible for leading, managing, and monitoring these changes; when you will implement the changes; what you expect the changes to achieve; how you will measure the impacts; and how you will implement these behavioral changes throughout the organization. When BD strategies involve widespread behavioral changes—as in a wholesale transformation of the company culture regarding ways of working with and relating to customers—we have found that it's wise to implement the changes in a succession of stages over time; modify systems and processes as a way of reinforcing behavioral change; use training and education programs to enhance emotional intelligence and communicate process changes; and apply comprehensive management oversight, especially during the initial change period of three to six months.

Developing an Opportunity-Specific BD Strategy

The overall BD strategy we have been discussing applies to opening game and early middle game as you are pursuing new business. However, when you reach mid–middle game, and a specific opportunity arises, then you need to develop a strategy for behaviorally differentiating yourself from mid–middle game through endgame. Essentially, this BD strategy forms part of your pursuit or win strategy as you chase the opportunity. A tool that we have found helpful in developing a pursuit strategy is the differentiation needs analysis (DNA), the first page of which is shown in Figure 10-2. The DNA tool consists of this first page, called the "Account Level," and subsequent pages for developing differentiation strategies. The tool has three parts. Part 1 helps you assess your current capability in the three phases of the business development process, where you can achieve the most impact on winning. Part 2 allows you to assess your current differentiation strength and the implications of it (what needs to change?). Part 3 is for developing differentiation strategies, and there may be any number of Part 3 pages—one or more for each domain of differentiation.

The DNA tool has broader applications than behavioral differentiation. It is intended to help business developers analyze and improve their differentiation in *every* domain of differentiation; however, we will focus primarily on the behavioral applications of this tool. Figure 10-2.1 shows the top part of the "Account Level" page, which describes what typically occurs in each phase of the business development process and asks users to rate their current capability in opening, middle, and endgame. As this example shows, the company is most skilled at endgame and has serious deficiencies in opening and middle game, which, together, constitute about 90 percent of the impact on winning.

Figure 10-2.2 shows Part 2a of the "Account Level" page, which is for analyzing your current level of differentiation among all the domains of differentiation (listed at the left). You first select the relevant domains and enter them into the left column. Then you weight the importance of these domains according to their relative importance to your customer or account. In the third column, you enter a score from 1 (worst) to 10 (best) to reflect the customer's current perception of your company. The rightmost column is for entering scores for the customer's perception of the relative importance of each domain of differentiation in your industry. In this example, you think that the customer believes product-service uniqueness is the most important factor in selecting suppliers, so you would rate this domain 10. A score of 8 in the far right column shows that the

DIFFERENTIATION NEEDS ANALYSIS: ACCOUNT LEVEL

Team: Global Account Team

Account: Global Gas Transport Group

Opening Game	Market Analysis / Resource Analysis / Strategic Planning	Business Planning / Account Planning / Brand/Image Management
Condition the Market		

Early — Middle Game — Mid — Late		
Relationship Management — Trust, Compatibility, Credibility, Perceptions, Information	*Opportunity Development* — Opportunity, Definition, Pursuit, Strategy	*Positioning to Win* — Preference, Capture, Strategy
Condition the Customer		

Endgame	Proposal / Presentation / Negotiation / Contracting
Condition the Deal	

▷ CONTACT ▷ RFP/ITT ▷ AWARD

Part 1a. Impact on Winning
Part 1b. Current Capability (1-10)
Part 2a. Current Differentiation

	Opening Game %	Middle Game %	Endgame %
Part 1a.	20	70	10
Part 1b.	4	4	7

Part 2b. So What? (Implications or What Needs to Change)

Domains of Differentiation	Relevant Domains (Select from the list at left)	Weights (1-10) (Importance to Account)	Account Perceptions of Us (1-10)	Account Perceptions of Industry (1-10)	[Opening Game]	[Middle Game]	[Endgame]
Product-service uniqueness	Product-service uniqueness	10	5	8	We are widely perceived to have fallen behind in both inspection and crack-detection technologies. Our total pipeline integrity offering is behind schedule and was publicized too soon; consequently, we are losing credibility in the market.	The customer believes that our integrity solution is on indefinite hold. We are likely to miss the chance to drive the requirements for a forthcoming multi-year, multi regional contract if we can't correct this perception.	In previous proposals, we have not done a good job of emphasizing the unique features we can offer and the unique value to customers. Our product-service solutions appear generic, and we have been under increasing price pressure as a result.
Distribution/ location				50			
Market segmentation/ specialization				80			
Responsiveness pre- and post-sale	People	9	6	8	The market is unaware of the steps we've taken to revamp our engineering and inspection groups. The perception lingers that we've lost too much expertise to competitors. Although in the past year we have initiated Six Sigma and have vigorously trained our people (we now have 32 black belts), we have not communicated our commitment to Six Sigma quality standards to the market.	We tend to start opportunity pursuits too late and not commit more than our account manager until near the RFP release. We now have management's commitment to earlier starts but have not done enough to implement that. On the plus side, we have established a pursuit team for this opportunity and now need a strong pursuit and value-added plan.	We have had differences of opinion about résumés and sometimes submit standard bios with proposals. The commitment going forward is to customize for every proposal, but we haven't done it yet.
Breadth of offerings (full service)				54	72		
Brand	Behavior	5	3	6	We are not doing a good job positioning ourselves in the market. We should be entering middle game with a reputation for integrity and quality, but prospective clients don't perceive that. We are not well positioned politically. With many prospects, we are well behind our competitors on community and political connections.	We've been candid with GGTG about the challenges their timetable presents. We need a highly visible, extraordinary effort toward meeting their needs on their schedule. We typically do not demonstrate our strong desire to win the work. Too often, we come across as "business as usual." As the saying goes, we tend to be more reactive than proactive during early opportunity problem solving.	Our proposed project teams sometimes don't come together until endgame, and it shows in the presentations. We need to do more team building before they present. Our self-perception is that we do what is required in endgame, but we don't do anything extraordinary. We are compliant but nothing more.
Market size/ dominance				15	30		
Price							
People							
Behavior							
Other (write in)							
Best Possible Score		240	119	182			

Total Weighted Scores

DNA-HZ-1.0-0503

FIGURE 10-2. Differentiation needs analysis: Account level. The first page of the DNA tool enables you to analyze your current level of differentiation for a particular customer or account and a particular new business opportunity.

DIFFERENTIATION NEEDS ANALYSIS: ACCOUNT LEVEL

Team: ___Global Account Team___

Account: ___Global Gas Transport Group___

| | Opening Game | Early : Mid : Late | End Game |
| | | Middle Game | |

CONTACT ———— RFP/ITT ———— AWARD

Opening Game
Market Analysis   Business Planning
Resource Analysis Account Planning
Strategic Planning Brand/Image Management

▼ *Condition the Market*

Middle Game
Relationship   Opportunity   Positioning
Management   Development   to Win
— Trust   — Opportunity   — Preference
— Compatibility   Definition   Building
— Credibility   — Pursuit   — Capture
— Perceptions   Strategy   Strategy
— Information

▼ *Condition the Customer*

End Game
Proposal
Presentation
Negotiation
Contracting

▼ *Condition the Deal*

	%	%	%
Part 1a. Impact on Winning	20	70	10
Part 1b. Current Capability (1-10)	4	4	7

FIGURE 10-2.1. Part 1—The business development process. The first step is to assess your current capability in opening, middle, and endgame. Base your score, from 1 (weakest) to 10 (strongest) on this customer's perceptions of your capabilities and on your own knowledge of how well or poorly you differentiate yourself in these phases of business development.

Domains of Differentiation	**Part 2a. Current Differentiation**			
	Relevant Domains (Select from the list at left)	**Weights (1-10)** (Importance to Account)	**Account Perceptions of Us (1-10)**	**Account Perceptions of Industry (1-10)**
Product-service uniqueness	Product-service uniqueness	10	5 50	8 80
Distribution/ location				
Market segmentation/ specialization	People	9	6 54	8 72
Responsiveness pre- and post-sale				
Breadth of offerings (full service)	Behavior	5	3 15	6 30
Brand				
Market size/ dominance				
Price				
People				
Behavior				
Other (write in)				
	Best Possible Score	240	119	182

Total Weighted Scores

FIGURE 10-2.2. Part 2a— Current differentiation. The next step is to identify the relevant domains of differentiation for this customer and this opportunity. Then weight and score these domains according to how this customer perceives you and your industry in general.

customer perceives suppliers in the industry to be fairly strong in creating product-service uniqueness. However, this customer would likely give your company only a 5, suggesting that your company's products or services are not seen as particularly unique.

In this example, you are also disadvantaged in the domains of people and behavior. Overall, your weighted score is about half the best possible score and is well below how customers view your industry, including the other suppliers who compete with you. Keep in mind that you are doing the scoring, not the customer, so these are *your perceptions of the customer's perceptions*, which is tricky to do and will probably not be completely accurate. However, the value is in the process, even if your numbers are not exactly what the customer might have given you. If you know the customer and your industry as well as you should, then your scores will probably be close enough to give you a picture that is at least directionally correct.

Figure 10-2.3 shows Part 2b of the "Account Level" page. Part 2b is a matrix of the intersection between your differentiation status

Part 2b. So What? (Implications or What Needs to Change)

	So What?	Implications or What Needs to Change
We are widely perceived to have fallen behind in both inspection and crack-detection technologies. Our total pipeline integrity offering is behind schedule and was publicized too soon; consequently, we are losing credibility in the market.	The customer believes that our integrity solution is on indefinite hold. We are likely to miss the chance to drive the requirements for a forthcoming multi year, multi regional contract if we can't correct this perception.	In previous proposals, we have not done a good job of emphasizing the unique features we can offer and the unique value to customers. Our product-service solutions appear generic, and we have been under increasing price pressure as a result.
The market is unaware of the steps we've taken to revamp our engineering and inspection groups. The perception lingers that we've lost too much expertise to competitors. Although in the past year we have initiated Six Sigma and have vigorously trained our people (we now have 32 black belts), we have not communicated our commitment to Six Sigma quality standards to the market.	We tend to start opportunity pursuits too late and not commit more than our account manager until near the RFP release. We now have management's commitment to earlier starts but have not done enough to implement that. On the plus side, we have established a pursuit team for this opportunity and now need a strong pursuit and value-added plan.	We have had differences of opinion about résumés and sometimes submit standard bios with proposals. The commitment going forward is to customize for every proposal, but we haven't done it yet.
We are not doing a good job positioning ourselves in the market. We should be entering middle game with a reputation for integrity and quality, but prospective clients don't perceive that. We are not well positioned politically. With many prospects, we are well behind our competitors on community and political connections.	We've been candid with GGTG about the challenges their timetable presents. We need a highly visible, extraordinary effort toward meeting their needs on their schedule. We typically do not demonstrate our strong desire to win the work. Too often, we come across as "business as usual." As the saying goes, we tend to be more reactive than proactive during early opportunity problem solving.	Our proposed project teams sometimes don't come together until endgame, and it shows in the presentations. We need to do more team building before they present. Our self-perception is that we do what is required in end game, but we don't do anything extraordinary. We are compliant but nothing more.

FIGURE 10-2.3. Part 2b—So what? In this part of the DNA tool, you identify the implications of your current differentiation. What needs to change? In this matrix, show the differentiation issues for each relevant domain across each phase of the business development process.

(Part 2a) and the three phases of the business development process. In other words, it shows where you are stronger or weaker in differentiating yourself throughout the whole business development process—and therefore what you need to do to improve your position. This example illustrates the kinds of differentiation issues that may arise during each phase of the business development process. Note, in particular, the behavioral differentiation issues along the bottom row. In this abbreviated example, we have shown only a few of the issues. In actual opportunity pursuits, we have seen dozens of issues listed, including some positive differentiators as well as areas where clients need to change. The purpose of this analysis is to understand how well or poorly you are differentiated—in each of the domains of differentiation—throughout the business development process. Your differentiation strategy, then, is to highlight your strengths and mitigate your weaknesses. Any area where you are poorly differentiated is obviously a call to action.

Figure 10-3 shows Part 3 (differentiation strategies) of the DNA tool. On these pages, you focus on one domain of differentiation at a time and identify the actions you can take at this point to increase your differentiation and hence your win probability. Your strategy consists of your objectives plus the actions required to achieve them. For purposes of illustration, we are showing only the page associated with *behavior*, but a complete DNA analysis for this opportunity would also have pages on the other domains discussed in Part 2: *product-service uniqueness* and *people*. Again, because this form is difficult to read in its entirety, we are also showing it in three parts.

> ♛ *In competitive situations, expected tactics are normally used to confront the opponent. But it is the power created by the use of unexpected tactics—that is, innovative use of people and information—that makes victory certain.—Donald G. Krause,* The Art of War for Executives

Figure 10-3.1 shows the actions you will take to resolve the opening game behavioral differentiation issues cited in Part 2. This part of the DNA tool is intended to be very specific about who will do what by when. This is action planning that can be monitored and measured. The

Part 3. Differentiation Strategies

For (enter a selected domain of differentiation from p. 1): _____ Behavior Objective + Action = Strategy

Objectives should be SMART (specific, measurable, attainable, relevant, and timely).

Opening Game			Middle Game			Endgame		
Objective: By the end of this calendar year, reassure all existing and potential pipeline integrity customers that we are in the game and intend to win.			**Objective:** By the end of this year, demonstrate top-down support for commitments made to GGTG as part of our product-service uniqueness and people differentiation objectives.			**Objective:** Raise GGTG's expectations by breaking from the industry standards for endgame communications with the account, particularly all future proposals and presentations.		
Actions	**Who**	**When**	**Actions**	**Who**	**When**	**Actions**	**Who**	**When**
Deliver information packages to integrity customers in person wherever humanly possible	Account Mgrs (all)	8/19 (GGTG by 7/22)	Arrange for executive sponsors to visit GGTG COO and Regional VPs worldwide to review our product development/roll-out and GGTG implementation plans, discuss their concerns, and establish a regular calendar of meetings.	Acct Mgr	7/29	Gain meeting with GGTG's Dir. of Sales Support to benchmark their best practices for proposals and presentations with their customers.	Don Hicks	8/15
Collaboratively develop value plans for all key customers	Acct Mgrs (all)	8/26 (GGTG by 7/29)	Coach our executives on cultural and business protocols prior to each exchange with client/prospect executives. Focus on GGTG values and operating principles and how to align with them.	Acct Mgr with HR support	Ongoing	Research latest innovations in proposal and presentations.	Jan Ord	8/25
Develop executive summary brochures to replace current generic brochures. Focus on key issues the pipeline market faces in moving gas today.	Acct Mgrs (all) with Marketing	9/1	Determine account team members behavioral selling skills competencies and develop training plan for skill building where needed.	Acct Mgr with HR support	8/15	Create new design protocols for proposals and presentations to GGTG.	Acct Mgr Don Hicks Jan Ord	9/30
Work with marketing on collateral to communicate our reputation for integrity and quality. Implement through display ads, publications, and focused-customer marketing campaigns in targeted markets.	Acct Mgrs (all) with Marketing	10/10	Develop contact plan and implement to increase average total account team face time with GGTG from current one day (8 hours) per week to two days per week (16 hours) ASAP. Develop value planner to be used for every contact with customer counterparts.	Acct Team (all)	9/1 launch & ongoing	Contract for training in tools and processes for producing proposals and presentations to satisfy new protocols.	Acct Mgr HR Mgr	10/20
In target markets, strengthen connections with community and political leaders. Launch a contact plan with local and regional managers. Also, identify the right local charities for philanthropic contributions and community outreach.	Regional Marketing Mgrs	11/15	Sponsor on-site client workshop re pipeline integrity QA/QC hosted by our executives.	Acct Mgr	10/1	Train account team and support staff in proposal and presentations.	Acct Team Support Staff	11/25
			Conduct supply chain analysis on GGTG to determine if, where, and how they can reduce costs in partnership with us and our proprietary inventory control process (ICT).	Jody Feline	11/1	Develop tool for creating differentiation strategies as part of win strategies for the design of every proposal and presentation for this account; incorporate into training above.	Acct Mgr	11/25
			Deliver findings of supply chain analysis to their VP of Procurement and any other execs we can gather.	VP of Ops & Acct Mgr	11/15	Create and implement post-delivery protocols for debriefing every proposal and presentation, win or lose, with GGTG; incorporate into training above.	Bill Dukes	11/25
						Establish and implement policy of always getting an appointment with the designated GGTG point of contact and hand deliver each proposal, never mailing it; create behavioral model for how to do this and what to do during the meeting.	Acct Mgr	11/25

FIGURE 10-3. Part 3—Differentiation needs analysis (Behavior). In this part of the DNA tool, identify your action plans for improving your differentiation in each of the relevant domains. This example shows only the behavior strategy. A complete DNA tool would include strategies for all relevant domains.

Opening Game		

Objective:

By the end of this calendar year, reassure all existing and potential pipeline integrity customers that we are in the game and intend to win.

Actions	Who	When
Deliver information packages to integrity customers in person wherever humanly possible.	Account Mgrs (all)	8/19 (GGTG by 7/22)
Collaboratively develop value plans for all key customers.	Acct Mgrs (all)	8/26 (GGTG by 7/29)
Develop executive summary brochures to replace current generic brochures. Focus on key issues the pipeline market faces in moving gas today.	Acct Mgrs (all) with Marketing	9/1
Work with marketing on collateral to communicate our reputation for integrity and quality. Implement through display ads, publications, and focused-customer marketing campaigns in targeted markets.	Acct Mgrs (all) with Marketing	10/15
In target markets, strengthen connections with community and political leaders. Launch a contact plan with local and regional managers. Also, identify the right local charities for philanthropic contributions and community outreach.	Regional Marketing Mgrs	11/15

FIGURE 10-3.1. Opening game behavior strategy. This strategy includes an objective plus action plans for opening game. The *Who* and *When* columns help make this a manageable and measurable process.

presumption is that if the actions identified are completed successfully, you will have improved your differentiation and resolved any problems cited in Part 2 of the DNA tool. These actions should become an integral part of your pursuit strategy for the opportunity. You may do more than is shown here to try to position yourself for the win, but the actions listed here should be central to your pursuit strategy. Figures 10-3.2 and 10-3.3 show the middle and endgame action plans for improving behavioral differentiation in pursuit of this opportunity.

We have devoted much of this book to showing how you can behaviorally differentiate yourself throughout the B2B business development process. In this chapter, we've discussed how to create a BD

Middle Game

Objective:
By the end of this year, demonstrate top-down support for commitments made to GGTG as part of our product-service uniqueness and people differentiation objectives.

Actions	Who	When
Arrange for executive sponsors to visit GGTG COO and Regional VPs worldwide to review our product development/roll-out and GGTG implementation plans, discuss their concerns, and establish a regular calendar of meetings.	Acct Mgr	7/29
Coach our executives on cultural and business protocols prior to each exchange with client/ prospect executives. Focus on GGTG values and operating principles and how to align with them.	Acct Mgr with HR support	Ongoing
Determine account team members, behavioral selling skills competencies and develop training plan for skill building where needed.	Acct Mgr with HR support	8/15
Develop contact plan and implement to increase average total account team face time with GGTG from current one day (8 hours) per week to two days per week (16 hours) ASAP. Develop value planner to be used for every contact with customer counterparts.	Acct Team (all)	9/1 launch & ongoing
Sponsor on-site client workshop re pipeline integrity QA/QC hosted by our executives.	Acct Mgr	10/1
Conduct supply chain analysis on GGTG to determine if, where, and how they can reduce costs in partnership with us and our proprietary inventory control process (ICT).	Jody Felind	11/1
Deliver findings of supply chain analysis to their VP of Procurement and any other execs we can gather.	VP of Ops & Acct Mgr	11/15

FIGURE 10-3.2. Middle game behavior strategy. Middle game includes the opportunity itself, so this part of the strategy should become a critical part of your pursuit strategy for winning the opportunity. Each of the behaviors identified here should improve your position in the customer's mind and give you a behavioral advantage over your competitors, who may not be doing the same things.

strategy—both to improve your company's overall behavioral differentiation and, in the final part of the chapter, to improve your BD as part of an opportunity pursuit. Earlier in this chapter, we said that we begin with two premises: (1) that you *can* gain a behavioral advantage if you think strategically about your behavior toward customers but (2) that you are unlikely to do so *unless* you actively manage how you and others in your company behave.

In our work with clients, we have seen an amazing number who pursue new business opportunities with only the vaguest notion of how they are going to win them. The smarter businesspeople we've known

Endgame

Objective:

Raise GGTG's expectations by breaking from the industry standards for endgame communications with the account, particularly all future proposals and presentations.

Actions	Who	When
Gain meeting with GGTG's Dir. of Sales Support to benchmark their best practices for proposals and presentations with their customers.	Don Hicks	8/15
Research latest innovations in proposal and presentations.	Jan Ord	8/25
Create new design protocols for proposals and presentations to GGTG.	Acct Mgr Don Hicks Jan Ord	9/30
Contract for training in tools and processes for producing proposals and presentations to satisfy new protocols.	Acct Mgr HR Mgr	10/20
Train account team and support staff in proposal and presentations.	Acct Team Support Staff	11/25
Develop tool for creating differentiation strategies as part of win strategies for the design of every proposal and presentation for this account; incorporate into training above.	Acct Mgr	11/25
Create and implement post-delivery protocols for debriefing every proposal and presentation, win or lose, with GGTG; incorporate into training above.	Bill Dukes	11/25
Establish and implement policy of always getting an appointment with the designated GGTG point of contact and hand deliver each proposal, never mailing it; create behavioral model for how to do this and what to do during the meeting.	Acct Mgr	11/25

FIGURE 10-3.3. Endgame behavior strategy. The DNA tool is typically used during mid-middle game, but this part of it is forward-looking. You should anticipate what you can do behaviorally during endgame to improve your position.

always take the time to develop a win strategy when they pursue opportunities. They analyze the situation; reflect on their competitive strengths and weaknesses; consider where their competitors are strong and weak and what they are likely to do; and then develop a strategy (including a plan of action) for starting early, strengthening their position with the customer, building preference in the customer's eyes, and preselling their solution and people before the matter reaches endgame. The smartest businesspeople we've seen understand the extraordinary power behavior has in shaping the customer's perceptions; they use behavior strategically throughout the business development process to compete more successfully than their rivals and, consequently, to win more than their fair share of the business.

CHALLENGES FOR READERS

1. Centex Construction Company in Dallas created a new position called chief relationship officer (CRO), who is responsible for building customer relationships and improving the company's behavioral differentiation. Do you have a CRO in your company? If not, should you create such a position? Who in your company is currently responsible for developing greater behavioral differentiation? How much executive emphasis are you giving to BD?

2. Do you have an overall strategy for improving your BD? Do you know what your customers normally expect from suppliers like you? Do you know what behaviors they would consider remarkably bad or good? How self-aware are you as an organization about the impact of your behavior on customers and the potential you have for developing a behavioral advantage?

3. As we discussed behavioral benchmarking, we suggested that you look outside your own company and industry for creative ideas on BD. If you have never done this, take some time to do so. Look at businesses and organizations that are very different from your own. How do the best of them differentiate themselves behaviorally, and what can you learn from what they do? Go way outside the box as you do this exercise and look for some breakthrough ideas.

4. Earlier in this chapter, we cited a number of potential positive differentiating behaviors. How many of these behaviors do you and your people currently exhibit? Which ones could you adopt if you are not already doing them?

5. In the final part of the chapter, we described the DNA tool, which we developed to help clients create opportunity-specific differentiation strategies. Try using this tool on your next major opportunity pursuit. Be diligent about using the tool and enhanc-

ing your differentiation in all the relevant domains. Afterward, think about this process. What did you learn from it? How did it help you? What decisions did you make that you may not have thought of had you not used the DNA tool? What could you do to use the tool more effectively next time?

CHAPTER 11

When the Going Gets Tough . . .

> *There are a number of studies within single industries demonstrating that there are superior ways of managing people and organizing their work. Yet although these superior management practices are reasonably well known, diffusion proceeds slowly and fitfully, and backsliding is common.—Jeffrey Pfeffer and Robert I. Sutton,* The Knowing-Doing Gap
>
> ■
>
> *Our traditional markets are rapidly maturing, resulting in a growing number of companies around the world that can provide the same services we do. Our behaviors, and the resulting trust and respect, are proving to be our real differentiators.—Marketing director for a multinational corporation*

A remarkable number of managers today are like Wile E. Coyote, the Roadrunner's cartoon foe who keeps getting hit in the face with a frying pan but never seems to learn from it. Although evidence abounds that superior behavior toward employees and customers can make an enormous difference,* they instead focus on operational efficiency, cycle times, throughput, total quality management (TQM), customer relationship management (CRM), and other such matters that are unquestionably important in running a business but will not distinguish them from their rivals unless those rivals are inept business managers. It is certainly true that you will not create a stellar business enterprise unless you have mastered the basics of business management and have created outstanding teams to run the various parts of your company. However, the managers who fail to grasp the

---

*Look, for instance, at *Fortune* magazine's annual lists of Best Companies to Work For and Most Admired Companies. The organizations at the top of these lists typically excel at behavioral differentiation, especially those appearing on both lists.

benefits and opportunity of BD will find their growth and profit lines to be about as flat as their faces after being hit yet again by that frying pan.

Some B2C companies have learned this lesson and become exemplars of both customer service and behavioral differentiation, internally and externally. But for reasons that defy comprehension, many B2B companies act as though their markets and customers will be there for them no matter how they behave. Perhaps they were seduced by the roaring 1990s, an era of triple-digit growth, overnight e-billionaires, and customers so hungry for products that you could produce almost anything and sell it overnight. Before the dot-com collapse and a staggering economic reality check, the theme of the 1990s might have been "How to succeed in business without really trying." Things have definitely changed.

In Chapter 2, we reported the results of research we have done with purchasing executives in customer organizations. In this chapter, we report the results of a supplier survey on current market challenges, using behavior for competitive advantage, and self-perceptions of how suppliers are viewed and what they value most in their company. The results are illuminating because they help us understand why some B2B companies are struggling in today's markets and why differentiating themselves behaviorally is challenging for them.

Lore Behavioral Differentiation Study

In 2002 and 2003, our firm, Lore International Institute, surveyed hundreds of managers in the telecommunications, manufacturing, defense, chemicals, energy, and engineering and construction industries—all B2B companies—regarding market conditions, their image of themselves and their values, and their use of behavior to differentiate themselves from their competitors. In Part 1 of this study, we asked them to give themselves a rating from 1 (strongly disagree) to 5 (strongly agree) for the fifteen statements shown in Table 11-1. In this table, their responses are shown in descending order based on the average response.

As you can see, the pattern of responses supports our hypothesis that companies today cannot rely on traditional methods of differentiation to create a sustainable competitive advantage in their markets. The two highest average responses were *"Increasingly, we are being*

Rank	Statement	Average
1	Increasingly, we are being forced to compete on price as the single major driver of buying decisions.	3.84
2	We are finding it increasingly difficult to differentiate ourselves from our competitors based on product or service uniqueness.	3.81
3	We don't do enough to use our behavior toward customers as a tool and a strategy for differentiating ourselves from our competitors.	3.76
4	We go to extraordinary lengths to ensure that our customers get what they need and are delighted to be working with us.	3.72
5	Our products and services are more of a commodity now than they ever have been.	3.54
6	Our executives and employees walk the talk; they behave in ways that are consistent with what they say.	3.49
7	We routinely treat customers in ways that positively differentiate us from our competitors.	3.45
8	Our competitors copy any innovative product or service features we introduce.	3.38
9	Our customers would agree that our employees are friendlier and more helpful to them than our competitors' employees are.	3.34
10	Candidly, beyond customer service, we have not examined ways in which our behavior toward customers could give us a competitive advantage.	3.26
11	Our company policies and procedures encourage and support employees who go the extra mile for customers or otherwise treat them in exceptional ways.	3.24
12	We know how our customers perceive the way we treat them. We know which behaviors they really like and which ones they don't like.	3.23
13	Our company's products and services are highly differentiated from our competitors' products and services. We can easily differentiate ourselves from our competition.	3.11
14	Our standard procedures for serving customers result in exceptional customer treatment that differentiates us from the treatment they usually get from our competitors.	2.85
15	We have good intelligence on how our competitors treat their customers. We know which behaviors those customers really like and which ones they don't like.	2.80

TABLE 11-1. Market and behavior impressions. Respondents indicated that traditional forms of differentiation are fading, but they are not yet doing what it takes to improve their BD.

forced to compete on price as the single major driver of buying decisions" and *"We are finding it increasingly difficult to differentiate ourselves from our competitors based on product or service uniqueness."* The fifth highest response was *"Our products and services are more of a commodity now than they ever have been,"* and one of the statements they most strongly disagreed with was *"Our company's products and services are highly differentiated from our competitors' products and services. We can easily differentiate ourselves from our competition."* Respondents moderately agreed with the statement *"Our competitors copy any innovative product or service features we introduce."* Collectively, these responses indicate that the business environment is becoming tougher and that relying on traditional means of differentiation will quickly condemn you to the purgatory of price competition.

Respondents did agree with the statement *"We go to extraordinary lengths to ensure that our customers get what they want and are delighted to be working with us."* However, they also agreed *"We don't do enough to use our behavior toward customers as a tool and a strategy for differentiating ourselves from our competitors."* So, while they strive to satisfy customer needs and create customer delight, they nonetheless see more opportunity to use behavior as a differentiator. As we scan the bottom of the list—the items they disagreed with most strongly—we can begin to understand why they haven't used behavior more effectively to create a competitive advantage. Note these two statements:

1. *Our company policies and procedures encourage and support employees who go the extra mile for customers or otherwise treat them in exceptional ways.*

2. *Our standard procedures for serving customers result in exceptional customer treatment that differentiates the treatment they get from us from the treatment they usually get from our competitors.*

The first of these relates to exceptional BD and the second to operational BD (see Chapter 3). The very low scores here suggest that the respondents' companies do not do enough to establish normal ways of behaving that are significantly better than the ways their competitors behave toward customers. In other words, they haven't found ways to operationalize BD so that it occurs routinely in their customer interactions. The three drivers of behavioral differentiation are leadership, culture, and process.* Without the process driver, it is difficult to make BD consistent and sustainable. So one of the insights we glean from this study is that the B2B companies studied are not doing enough to convert best practice behaviors into their normal processes.

Respondents also strongly disagreed with these two statements:

1. *We know how our customers perceive the way we treat them. We know which behaviors they really like and which ones they don't like.*

2. *We have good intelligence on how our competitors treat their customers. We know which behaviors those customers really like and which ones they don't like.*

These outcomes indicate a general lack of awareness about the impacts of behavior. The respondents don't know how their customers perceive them or how their competitors treat customers—and how customers respond to that treatment. In our discussion of developing an overall BD strategy in Chapter 10, we said that the first step is behavioral benchmarking. These outcomes suggest that companies either are not benchmarking behavior in their industry and among their customers or are not terribly good at it. In either case, it's not surprising that they aren't doing more to create a behavioral advantage. This is no different than trying to produce a high-quality product in your manufacturing without knowing what exceptional quality is.

In Part 2 of our study, we asked respondents to identify the single highest value in their company from among this list of possible values: beating the competition, being collaborative (working well in teams), being state-of-the-art or cutting edge, delighting customers, following policies and procedures, making money, or providing high-quality products or services. The percentage of respondent choices is shown in Table 11-2.

Without question, making money is important in business; however, it was surprising to us that nearly half of the respondents said it

---

*For a lengthy discussion of these drivers, see chapter 9 of Terry R. Bacon and David G. Pugh, *Winning Behavior: What the Smartest, Most Successful Companies Do Differently* (New York: AMACOM, 2003).

Rank	Value	%
1	Making money	43.3
2	Providing high-quality products or services	27.9
3	Delighting customers	15.4
4	Being state-of-the-art or cutting edge	4.8
5	Following policies and procedures	3.85
6	Being collaborative; working well in teams	3.85
7	Beating the competition	0.96

TABLE 11-2. Supplier company values. Just over 70 percent of respondents said the highest value in their company is making money or producing high-quality products or services.

was the highest value in their company. More than a quarter of the other respondents cited "providing high-quality products or services." Fewer than one person in six identified "delighting customers" as the highest value. Values drive decisions, create attitudes, and shape behavior, so it's not surprising that a number of B2B companies have difficulty managing BD when over 70 percent of them place higher value on money and quality than they do on delighting customers. We don't wish to overstate the point, because most people in business probably do care a great deal about satisfying or delighting customers—you'd be a fool not to—but if money is more important to you than customers, you will be driven to make decisions that maximize your return at customers' expense. It's inevitable.

Finally, Table 11-3 shows the results of Part 3 of our survey, in which we asked respondents to indicate how they believed their customers perceived them. This was a bit of a tricky question because we were asking for a self-perception of their customers' perceptions of them, so the results reflect what customers have told the respondents, what the respondents surmise about their customers' perceptions, and how they would like to be thought of.

It's not surprising that "routine" and "aggressive" were ranked last. Few people would want to be characterized by those words. It's fascinating, however, that "professional" and "smart" were ranked highest. Furthermore, the two items were significantly higher (4.36 and 4.16, respectively) than the third-rated item, "responsive" (3.79). Whether or not this reflects how customers would describe them, it is remarkable that managers in B2B selling organizations are most likely to view themselves (and perceive that customers perceive them)

Rank	Characteristic	Average
1	Professional	4.36
2	Smart	4.16
3	Responsive	3.79
4	Nice	3.63
5	Easy to work with	3.57
6	Creative	3.57
7	Personable and caring	3.53
8	Efficient	3.41
9	Outgoing	3.39
10	Flexible	3.21
11	Aggressive	3.16
12	Routine	2.91

TABLE 11-3. Self-perceptions of suppliers' images. Suppliers believed that customers mostly perceived them as smart professionals.

as smart professionals. Smart professionals may add a lot of intellectual value, which is gratifying for them, no doubt, but they are not necessarily responsive, nice, easy to work with, creative, personable and caring, outgoing, or flexible—items that were ranked much lower on this part of the survey.

> Behavioral differentiation has played an increasingly larger role in several of our markets over the past ten years. As our customers narrow their focus to their core competencies, they have eliminated internal support functions, choosing to buy services rather than maintain their own capability. They have learned that alliances with customer-oriented service providers allow them to exercise greater control over the services they buy than purchasing from technically differentiated vendors.—*James B. Hamlin*

So, what do we make of this? First, their internal values and the image they wish to project are not consistent with superior behavior internally or externally. Of course, smart professionals who want to make a lot of money can conceivably still behave in ways that positively differentiate them from their rivals. However, the Arthur Andersens and Enrons of the world suggest that although this may be conceivable, it is unlikely. The organizations more likely to differentiate themselves behaviorally put customers and employees first, care about how they treat all stakeholders, understand and value the importance of behavior as a competitive advantage, and have inspired leaders who are in it for more than just themselves.

Second, you need to be conscious about the behavioral benchmarks in your industry. Awareness is the first step toward knowledge and is a prerequisite for action. If you do not know how your customers perceive your behavior—and what they like and don't like—and if you are unaware of how they view your competitors' behaviors, then you will not know what to do differently in order to differentiate yourself. Of course, you can ignore all this. However, with the vicious cycle of innovation and imitation that characterizes today's markets, if you try to rely on traditional sources of differentiation alone, you will find yourself increasingly subject to the brutal effects of price competition.

Walking the Talk

In Chapter 3, we told the story of a competition that Anontus Engineering Group won because it had a sound technical solution and because it outbehaved its competitors. As this book draws to a conclusion, we are returning to Anontus because, in many ways, this company represents a solid B2B company that understands and values behavioral differentiation. We asked Erich E., a program manager for Anontus, what enabled Anontus to sustain BD. Here is what he told us:

> Being a relationship-based company (and not a transactional one) shines a bright light on our behavior toward our customers as a key to success. Along with following our internal standards, guidance, and procedures for successfully executing a project (essential to customer delight, to be sure), building and advancing that customer relationship receives at least equal emphasis. And what generates and sustains a relationship but communication and behavior?
>
> Successful people in Anontus walk the talk of these customer relationships. We firmly believe that our relationship-based business

model is a strong differentiator for us in the marketplace, especially as we see the technical capabilities of competitors rise—in part through advances in and deployment of technology and in part through industry consolidation and the aggregation of disparate specialty firms into more formidable integrated ones. We find that our behavior toward customers more and more sets us apart from our competitors. That behavior includes such things as active listening; getting in the customer's head and understanding his drivers and fears; and then putting that understanding into action—demonstrating the flexibility to accommodate change or adapt to a client's idiosyncrasies, solving problems in a balanced and responsible fashion (not caving in to the client when it doesn't make sense for the project or the business relationship), and going beyond stated requirements and creating outcomes that meet the real needs.

It includes the highest standards of business conduct. Anontus is an extremely ethical firm. We also take particular delight in making our customer a hero in his world: earning through our performance an award, bonus, or other recognition for him, not us; and getting him promoted by his employer. Relationship-based business behavior starts long before a contract is signed, of course. Anontus' sales people are some of the most ardent practitioners of building and advancing relationships with clients. A big part of our job is to get to know the customer and his business well before any particular business opportunity is known; to create a relationship in the work context; and to advance the relationship by adding value for the customer in each interaction. What a customer observes in his relationship with the Anontus sales representative creates in him an expectation of the behavior he will enjoy with us on a project.[1]

Companies that distinguish themselves through behavioral differentiation are self-conscious about their behavior. Moreover, there is never a point where they have arrived at the mountaintop and have no farther to go. Their smarter competitors are watching and learning and doing what they can to raise the behavioral standard—or smarter companies in other industries are raising the standard, and customers keep learning what else is possible. The smarter companies never rely on their technology alone because in today's markets it won't make a lasting difference, as Erich E. explains:

> Technology is rarely a differentiator in our markets. Many firms can deliver a highly satisfactory technical service. The difference is

people and that difference is manifested in behavior. Our experience tells us that long after a client forgets the details of a particular project, he remembers the positive experience he had in working with Anontus. Calling it by another name, Anontus has successfully practiced behavioral differentiation for years. Have we perfected it? Of course not. Have we fully capitalized on it? No, we have not. We have much to learn, and we have the happy circumstance of needing to spread the gospel to new parts of the company that have joined us through carefully chosen acquisitions in recent years.[2]

Throughout *Winning Behavior*, we observed that behavioral differentiation cannot take the place of outstanding products or services and excellence in execution. It's not a panacea for poor business performance in other areas. However, if you have a well-oiled machine in other respects, then BD can lift you above your competitors who also have well-oiled machines but are not insightful about the use of behavior as a competitive tool. Ken Bailey, a smart and successful businessman until his retirement a few years ago, made this observation about BD:

Positive behavioral differentiation will certainly extend the lifespan of a relationship but only if the technical side delivers—every time. BD with outstanding service will live long. BD with average or poor service will be short lived. Having good relationships through good BD will probably help you survive a short period of poor performance and may give you a second chance where it would not be otherwise. In summary, good, positive BD is always a very good asset. It is never a negative.[3]

Behavioral differentiation offers you an extraordinary opportunity to improve not only your business development—from opening game through next game—but to create an enterprise that attracts and retains loyal and talented employees. Why? Because people want to feel that their life and work have meaning, that the organizations they are part of care for them, and that the work they are doing is valued by the people receiving and using the products and services they create. People also like working for winners, and when you can sustain behavioral differentiation over the long term, you create the kind of strong cultures that have sustained winners like Southwest Airlines, Men's Wearhouse, Ritz-Carlton, Nordstrom, Anontus Engineering

Group, EMC, Hall Kinion, Centex Construction Company, Marshall Field's, and Harley-Davidson. To join that elite group, you just need to create a behavioral advantage.

CHALLENGES FOR READERS

1. Are you more like Wile E. Coyote or the Roadrunner? Are you wielding the frying pan or being smacked in the face with it? In other words, are you aware of the competitive advantages inherent in behavior toward employees and customers? Assuming that this is true, what are you doing about it?

2. Take the BD survey yourself. Look at Tables 11-1, 11-2, and 11-3. How would you have ranked these items or answered the questions? What would your results indicate about your company?

3. What values truly drive your business? Are those values consistent with behavioral differentiation? Or do they block you from behaving in ways that might differentiate you positively from your competitors?

4. It's time for action. What *can* you do to establish or improve your BD? What *will* you do?

Notes

INTRODUCTION

1. Jim Collins, *Good to Great* (New York: HarperCollins, 2001), p. 39.
2. Nitin Nohria, William Joyce, and Bruce Roberson, "What Really Works," *Harvard Business Review* 81, no. 7 (July 2003): 43.
3. Ibid., pp. 48–49.

CHAPTER 1

1. William Miller, *The Art of Canvassing: How to Sell Insurance,* 5th ed. (New York: The Spectator Company, 1901), p. 41. [The original copyright on this book is 1894.] NOTE: Throughout this chapter, when quoting from historical sources, we will follow their language conventions, although the sexism in this language is inconsistent with modern sensibilities. Throughout the rest of this book, we will either use the plural forms of pronouns or alternative *he* and *she* to indicate that buyers and sellers can be male or female.
2. Ibid., p. 2.
3. Ibid., p. 49.
4. Ibid., pp. 48–49.
5. Ibid., p. 35.
6. Ibid., pp. 76–77.
7. Walter D. Moody, *Men Who Sell Things* (Chicago: A.C. McClurg & Co., 1907), p. 26.
8. Ibid., p. 22.
9. W. F. Hypes, "The Salesman as the Customer's Partner," in *How to Increase Your Sales: 126 Selling Plans Used & Proven by 54 Salesmen & Salesmanagers* (Chicago: The System Company, 1908), p. 100.
10. System: The Magazine of Business, "First—Mapping Out the Canvass," *The Knack of Selling* (Chicago: A.W. Shaw Company, 1913), p. 3.
11. Ibid., p. 5.
12. Ibid., p. 8.
13. Ibid., p. 5.
14. Ibid., p. 4.
15. Frederick Winslow Taylor, *The Principles of Scientific Management* (New York: Harper & Brothers Publishers, 1919), p. 7. See also Ed Michaels, Helen Handfield-Jones, and Beth Alexrod, *The War for Talent* (Boston: Harvard Business School Press, 2001).
16. Ibid.
17. Edward K. Strong, *The Psychology of Selling Life Insurance* (New York: Harper & Brothers Publishers, 1922), p. 14.

18. Ibid.

19. Ibid., p. 133.

20. Ibid., pp. 260–261.

21. Cooper Underwear Company, *Tips and Pointers for Underwear Dealers and Their Salesmen* (Kenosha, Wisc.: Cooper Underwear Company, 1923), p. 84.

22. Strong, p. 181.

23. *Women and Diversity Wow! Facts 2001* (Washington, D.C.: The Business Women's Network, 2001), p. xxxi.

24. Theodore Levitt, "Marketing Myopia," reprinted in *The Marketing Imagination,* new, expanded ed. (New York: The Free Press, 1983), p. 166.

25. Mack Hanan, James Cribbin, and Herman Heiser, *Consultative Selling* (New York: American Management Association, 1970), p. 11.

26. Mack Hanan, *Consultative Selling,* 5th ed. (New York: AMACOM Books, 1995), p. 1.

27. Ibid.

28. Ibid., p. 3.

29. Robert B. Miller and Stephen E. Heiman, with Tad Tuleja, *Strategic Selling* (New York: William Morrow and Company, 1985), p. 22.

30. Ibid., p. 55.

31. Neil Rackham, *SPIN Selling* (New York: McGraw-Hill, 1988), p. ix.

32. Ibid., p. 141.

33. David H. Maister, *Managing the Professional Service Firm* (New York: The Free Press, 1993), p. 112.

34. Ibid., p. 119.

CHAPTER 2

1. Anonymous source.

2. Lisa Ellram, conversation with Terry Bacon, March 2003. Used with permission.

3. Interview with Bob Douglass, January 23, 2003. Used with permission.

4. Lisa Ellram.

5. Lisa M. Ellram, *Strategic Cost Management in the Supply Chain: A Purchasing and Supply Management Perspective* (Tempe, Ariz.: CAPS RESEARCH, 2002), p. 13.

6. Ibid., pp. 13–14.

7. Ibid., p. 13.

8. Interview with Paul Seibold, January 2003. Used with permission.

9. Ibid., p. 18.

10. Interview with Tony Millikin, January 2003. Used with permission.

11. Ibid.

12. Interview with Art Schick, January 2003. Used with permission.

13. Interview with Greg Schwartz, January 2003. Used with permission.

14. Interview with Bonnie Keith, January 2003. Used with permission.

15. Anonymous source.

16. Paul Seibold.

17. Interview with Joan Selleck, January 2003. Used with permission.

18. Interview with Dave Gabriel, January 2003. Used with permission.

19. Bonnie Keith.

20. Ibid.

21. Greg Schwartz.

22. Paul Seibold.

23. Joan Selleck.

24. Interview with Frank Muschetto, January 2003. Used with permission.

25. Anonymous source.

26. Interview with Francois Gauthier, January 2003. Used with permission.

27. Ibid.

28. Interview with Jim Kozlowski, January 2003. Used with permission.

29. Interview with Lance Kaye, January 2003. Used with permission.

30. Greg Schwartz.

31. Lance Kaye.

32. Francois Gauthier.

33. Bonnie Keith.

34. Bob Douglass.

35. Interview with Doug Beebe, January 2003. Used with permission.

36. Dave Gabriel.

37. Francois Gauthier.

38. Art Schick.

39. Anonymous source.

40. Lore Purchasing Manager Survey, 2003. Comments received from various respondents. Used with permission.

41. Dave Gabriel.

42. Anonymous source.

CHAPTER 3

1. Danny Hicks and other anonymous sources inside Global Oil. E-mail communications and telephone discussions with David G. Pugh, May–July 2003. Story used with permission.

2. *Merriam-Webster's Collegiate Dictionary, Tenth Edition* (Springfield, Mass., 1999), p. 103.

3. Disney "cast members" whose behavior resulted in an exceptional experience for guests are recognized on a Web site called "What Would Walt Do?" (www.whatwouldwaltdo.com). This site is a virtual catalog of exceptional customer service behaviors. It's worth reading, if for nothing else to learn what behaviors are so remarkable to customers that they will write about it. Companies can build sustainable behavioral differentiation when these kinds of memorable behaviors occur regularly.

4. For many other examples of these four types of behavioral differentiation, see Terry R. Bacon and David G. Pugh, *Winning Behavior: What the Smartest, Most Successful Companies Do Differently* (New York: AMACOM, 2003).

5. Edward K. Strong, *The Psychology of Selling Life Insurance* (New York: Harper & Brothers Publishers, 1922), p. 277.

6. Ibid.

CHAPTER 4

1. Donald G. Krause, *The Art of War for Executives* (New York: The Berkley Publishing Group, 1995), pp. 1–2.

2. Eugene A. Znosko-Borovsky, *The Middle Game in Chess.* (New York: Dover Publications, 1980), pp. 9–10.

3. Ron Curry, *Win at Chess!* (Davenport, Iowa: Thinkers' Press, 1997), p. 12.

4. Ibid., p. 32.

5. Jeremy Silman, *The Complete Book of Chess Strategy* (Los Angeles: Siles Press, 1998), p. 109.

6. James Eade, *Chess for Dummies* (New York: IDG Books, 1996), p. 191.

CHAPTER 5

1. Jeremy Silman, *The Complete Book of Chess Strategy* (Los Angeles: Siles Press, 1998), p. 1.

2. Jeremy Silman, *How to Reassess Your Chess,* 3rd ed. (Los Angeles: Siles Press, 1993), p. 313.

3. Eric Ransdell, "They Sell Suits with Soul," *Fast Company*, October 1998, p. 66.

4. Chris Argyris, *Flawed Advice and the Management Trap* (Oxford: Oxford University Press, 2000).

5. Ron Curry, *Win at Chess!* (Davenport, Iowa: Thinkers' Press, 1997), p. 12.

6. Don Peppers and Martha Rogers, *The One to One Future: Building Relationships One Customer at a Time* (New York: Doubleday, 1996), p. 137.

7. Ibid.

8. James Eade, *Chess for Dummies* (New York: IDG Books, 1996), p. 156.

9. Eugene A. Znosko-Borovsky, *The Middle Game in Chess* (New York: Dover Publications, 1980), p. 10.

CHAPTER 6

1. Ron Curry, *Win at Chess!* (Davenport, Iowa: Thinkers' Press, 1997), p. 32.

2. Eugene A. Znosko-Borovsky, *The Middle Game in Chess* (New York: Dover Publications, 1980), p. 29.

3. Lev Alburt and Larry Parr, *Secrets of the Russian Chess Masters, Volume 1* (New York: W.W. Norton & Company, 1997), p. 144.

4. www.quotationreference.com/quotefinder.php.

5. David H. Maister, *Managing the Professional Service Firm* (New York: The Free Press, 1993), pp. 114–115.

6. For more information on tactical account management, see Terry R. Bacon, *Selling to Major Accounts* (New York: AMACOM Books, 1999).

7. Michael Flagg, interview with Meredith Ashby and Stephen Miles, April 2002. Used with permission.

8. Joanne Kincer, communication with Terry Bacon, January 2002. Used with permission.

9. Jeffrey Neal, interview with Laurie Voss, November 2001. Used with permission.

10. John Gardner, interview with Meredith Ashby and Stephen Miles, April 2002. Used with permission.

11. Kyung Yoon, interview with Meredith Ashby and Stephen Miles, April 2002. Used with permission.

12. Emeric Lepoutre, interview with Meredith Ashby and Stephen Miles, April 2002. Used with permission.

13. Robert B. Cialdini, *Influence: The Psychology of Persuasion* (New York: William Morrow, 1993), p. 173.

14. David H. Maister, Charles H. Green, and Robert M. Galford, *The Trusted Advisor* (New York: The Free Press, 2000), pp. 17–18.

15. Theodore Levitt, *The Marketing Imagination, New, Expanded Edition* (New York: The Free Press, 1986), p. 77.

CHAPTER 7

1. Don Traywick, personal communication with David Pugh, December 2001. Used with permission.
2. Jeremy Silman, *The Complete Book of Chess Strategy* (Los Angeles: Siles Press, 1998), p. 197.
3. Ron Curry, *Win at Chess!* (Davenport, Iowa: Thinkers' Press, 1997), p. 39.
4. Ibid., p. 51.

CHAPTER 8

1. Jeremy Silman, *The Complete Book of Chess Strategy* (Los Angeles: Siles Press, 1998), p. 335.
2. Ibid.
3. Eugene A. Znosko-Borovsky, *The Middle Game in Chess* (New York: Dover Publications, 1980), p. 147.

CHAPTER 9

1. Jeremy Silman, *The Complete Book of Chess Strategy* (Los Angeles: Siles Press, 1998), p. 283.
2. DeNeil Hogan Petersen, story told to Terry Bacon, March 2001. Used with permission.
3. Anonymous, story told to David Pugh, January 1999. Names have been changed to protect confidences.
4. Anonymous, story told to David Pugh, October 2000. Names have been changed to protect confidences.
5. Paul Krauss, story told to Terry Bacon, February 2002. Used with permission.
6. Dennis Fukai, "Don't Be Snowed by High-Tech," *Engineering News Record* 245, no. 22 (December 4, 2000): 79.
7. John Tarpey, story told to David Pugh, July 2001. Used with permission.
8. Deke Lincoln, story told to David Pugh, August 2001. Used with permission. This story has another interesting element. When they learned of the initial opportunity with Global, Deke Lincoln said that not only was Global a new customer but oil refining was a new industry for them. "We had not done any refinery work out of this office before. In fact, I had never stepped foot in an oil refinery. I thought 'crackers' and 'cokers' referred to people with a serious case of the munchies. Lack of experience can be quite difficult to overcome, if you let people's objections drag you down. We overcame our lack of experience by simply listening and asking questions, rather than speaking first, which is another example of behavioral differentiation. Writing this down really blows me away. It's hard to believe these simple things can differentiate you from others. But it's really true."

CHAPTER 10

1. Eric Krueger, interview with David Pugh, April 2003. Used with permission.
2. Jan Carlzon, *Moments of Truth* (New York: HarperCollins, 1987), p. 3.

CHAPTER 11

1. Erich E., comments on Lore Behavioral Differentiation Survey, 2003. Used with permission.
2. Ibid.
3. Ken Bailey, comments on Lore Behavioral Differentiation Survey, 2003. Used with permission.

Index

77340482R00180

Made in the USA
San Bernardino, CA
22 May 2018